Children's Literature

Volume 17

Children's Literature

Volume 17

Annual of
The Modern Language Association
Division on Children's Literature
and The Children's Literature
Association

Yale University Press

New Haven and London

1989

The editors gratefully acknowledge support from the University of Connecticut.

Editorial correspondence should be addressed to:
The Editors, *Children's Literature*
University of Connecticut
Department of English, U-25
337 Mansfield Road, Room 332
Storrs, Connecticut 06268

Manuscripts submitted should conform to the new *MLA* style. An original on non-erasable bond with two copies, a self-addressed envelope, and return postage are requested. Yale University Press does not accept dot-matrix printouts, and it requires double-spacing throughout text and notes. Unjustified margins are preferred.

Volumes 1–7 of *Children's Literature* can be obtained directly from John C. Wandell, The Children's Literature Foundation, Box 370, Windham Center, Connecticut 06280. Volumes 8–17 can be obtained from Yale University Press, 92A Yale Station, New Haven, Connecticut 06520, or from Yale University Press, 13 Bedford Square, London WC1B 3JF, England.

Library of Congress catalog card number: 79–66588
ISBN: 0–300–04421–6 (cloth); 0–300–04422–4 (paper)

Set in Baskerville type by Tseng Information Systems, Inc., Durham, N.C. Printed in the United States of America by Vail-Ballou Press, Binghamton, N.Y.

Published with assistance from the foundation established in memory of Calvin Chapin of the class of 1788, Yale College.

10 9 8 7 6 5 4 3 2 1

Contents

Articles

The Victorian Auntly Narrative Voice and Mrs. Molesworth's *Cuckoo Clock* — *Sanjay Sircar* — 1

Instructing the Children: Advice from the Twelfth-Century *Fables* of Marie de France — *Harriet Spiegel* — 25

Shakespeare for Girls: Mary Lamb and *Tales from Shakespeare* — *Jean I. Marsden* — 47

Cleanliness and Class in the Countess de Ségur's Novels — *Marie-France Doray* — 64

A Portrait of the Artist as a Little Woman — *Beverly Lyon Clark* — 81

Dismembering the Text: The Horror of Louisa May Alcott's *Little Women* — *Angela M. Estes and Kathleen M. Lant* — 98

"If We Have Any Little Girls among Our Readers": Gender and Education in Hawthorne's "Queen Christina" — *Laura Laffrado* — 124

Varia

The Story of the Unhappy Willow — *Claribel Alegría* — 135

Reviews

Critical Apertures — *Margaret R. Higonnet* — 143

Adults and Children — *Hugh T. Keenan* — 151

Feminist Revisions: Frauds on the Fairies? — *Elizabeth Keyser* — 156

Child Readers and Renaissance Writers — *Juliet Dusinberre* — 171

German Children's Literature — *Ruth B. Bottigheimer* — 176

Grimm Translation and Scholarship — *J. D. Stahl* — 182

Traditions and Modernity: A Rediscovery of India — *Meena Khorana* — 193

Bloomsbury and Wonderland — *Regina Barreca* — 202

Writing for Children about the Unthinkable
Hamida Bosmajian 206

Dissertations of Note *Rachel Fordyce* 212
Contributors and Editors 226

The Victorian Auntly Narrative Voice and Mrs. Molesworth's Cuckoo Clock

Sanjay Sircar

Much Victorian work for children addresses its audience in a special way, "talking down" to it. Paradoxically, what strikes the modern reader as a dated rhetoric may explain the power of works that for more than half a century were ranked as classics. The intricately interwoven features of what I term the "auntly" (or avuncular) voice establish a special relationship to the audience in works that were once widely read, ranging from Mrs. Molesworth's *Cuckoo Clock* (1877) to Charles Kingsley's *Water Babies* (1863) and W. M. Thackeray's *Rose and the Ring* (1855). As any one of these texts can show, children's literature employs a broad array of rhetorical strategies to ensure the readers' or listeners' sense of relaxation, equality, and creative—even conspiratorial—involvement.

Mrs. Molesworth (1839–1921), "the last great writer of fantasy in the nineteenth century" (Ellis 121), was a prodigiously prolific author whose name "dominated children's books for some thirty years, at the end of the last century and the beginning of this" (Avery, "Introduction" 9). As late as 1938 a popular novel could assume that its audience would agree that her first work of juvenile fantasy, *The Cuckoo Clock* (1877), was "a classic" (Spring 147). It tells the tale of a lonely little girl called Griselda, who lives with her two great-aunts in an old house and is taken on a series of four dream-adventures by one of the "household gods," a wooden cuckoo out of a European clock. The cuckoo becomes her mentor, teaching her such virtues as obedience and good temper. At the end, Griselda acquires new friends: a little boy, Phil, and his understanding mother.

Today, despite Roger Lancelyn Green's chapters in *Tellers of Tales* and *Mrs. Molesworth* and her secure place in literary histories, Mrs. Molesworth is not much discussed. My aim here, besides drawing attention to an author whose "books and reputation have suffered an unjust eclipse" (Salway 520), is to explore the variety and in-

Children's Literature 17, ed. Francelia Butler, Margaret Higonnet, and Barbara Rosen

tricacy of Victorian narrative strategy, using *The Cuckoo Clock* as my prime example. It remains in print in a number of editions (the most recent, a 1987 Dell reprint), at least nine artists have illustrated it, and all the standard histories of English children's literature mention it.[1] In short, it is still alive. Even more to the point, *The Cuckoo Clock* offers rich examples of the rhetorical innovations that characterize Victorian fiction for children.

The Theory of Narrative Voice

In my analysis of this juvenile novel, I shall draw on theories of narrative that describe the way the voice of a text shapes its relationship to the audience. In doing so, I follow up a hint by G. W. Turner, one of the few stylisticians who has taken children's literature seriously: "Such special forms of writing as technical books or children's literature remind us that an author may choose an audience. He may also create one" (173). I also hope to counteract Frederick C. Crews's *Pooh Perplex*, whose joking about "Milnean voices" and "Christophorean ears" seems to suggest that children's literature is not susceptible to literary analysis of the kind applied to mainstream adult work.

One of the first to attempt to classify the structures of narrative relationships was Wayne Booth, whose discussion of the "implied author" and "implied reader" in *The Rhetoric of Fiction* has influenced all subsequent theorists. As Booth pointed out, the implied author whom we deduce from all the components of the text (and whose moral norms may differ from those of the real author) should be distinguished from the "speaker" of the text, who is part of the fiction itself (71–77). This is easy to do when the speaker is a developed character with a name, the kind of explicit "narrative persona" to whom Robert Elliott devoted his book. An anonymous narrator may be more difficult to define, but every text, however minimally narrated, implies one person who speaks or writes the text and another (the "narratee") who receives it (Rimmon-Kenan, 103–05). Where the anonymous narrator has a relatively obtrusive style, as in *The Cuckoo Clock*, we get a strong sense of an unseen personality, stance, and set of attitudes—a personality that may even be sustained through a number of texts by the same author.

Narrative voice describes our sense of a textual speaker who has verbal specificity and yet does not acquire the full-bodied presence of a narrative persona. Recognizably similar narrative voices may recur not only in an oeuvre but in texts by various authors and help define period style. Narrative voice is created by the selection of words, syntax, register, tone, and attitude toward the story and the audience. The metaphor of a voice is particularly apt for texts that simulate orality. In this regard, my use of narrative voice differs from Gérard Genette's voice, a metaphor taken from grammar rather than real-life oral communication. *Voice* in this essay is close to what linguists call register, the adaptation of words and phrases in accordance with the constraints of the circumstances of communication, such as a particular sort of hearer (Turner 165–202). When discussing the fictive speaker as agent rather than the quality of the voice, I shall continue to use the term *narrator*.

A hallmark of much children's literature, simulated orality figures prominently in Victorian literature, since adults still read aloud then even to older children, and readings within a family circle continued. This ostensibly oral voice can have a theatrical quality, not only because such readings were performative occasions but because reading aloud assimilates a disjunction between reading as an adult and telling a story to a child or children.

Booth has attuned us not only to the layers of narrative production but to questions of audience. Aside from the historical audience, whether contemporaneous with the original publication or subsequent, every text by its deployment of norms and conventions implies its own audience, which may or may not correspond to the real one. Gerald Prince has proposed that we distinguish the "virtual" reader, who an author hopes will respond adequately to the moral norms of the work, from the "ideal" reader, who can grasp completely nuances of which even the real author was unaware. Such readers must also be distinguished from the "narratee," the fictive reader or listener implied more or less overtly in the text (Tompkins 9).

In a text for children, the *narratee* may be a listener or a reader, single or in a group, child or adult, and often a text wavers among these possibilities. The more oral the text seems, the more likely it is that some narratee will be directly addressed. The complexities of the actual reception of children's literature lead to a complex representation or inscription of the text's narratee or audience. Often, of course, there will be a gap in age between the narrator and narratee in a children's book; if the narratee mediates between author and reader, as Prince reminds us, further rhetorical strategies may be in order to mediate between adult and child. The intricate situation of reception, then, demands complex strategies from the narrator and may explain what appear to be tensions among the "rhetorics" we shall observe in *The Cuckoo Clock*.

Rhetoric is the term I use for a particular group of verbal devices by which the narrative voice establishes a particular relation with its narratee. My use of rhetoric is thus more classical, more explicitly verbal, than that of Booth, who sets aside "the merely verbal" level of style (74). Within the text, these rhetorics seek to persuade and seduce a fictive audience; at the same time, of course, they work upon the real audience in ways that have clearly changed over the last century. *Topos* is a term I have reserved to describe the concerns that characterize a narrative voice.

Mrs. Molesworth's Auntly Narrative Voice

Mrs. Molesworth was "in opposition to the modern theory that it is inartistic to write down to a child's level."[2] Her narrators are adults who are not always specifically embodied but whose imposing voices consciously "talk down" to children. She created this tone of voice through a set of verbal mannerisms or characteristics that, to begin with, were the mannerisms of a particular narrative persona. In her first book for children, *Tell Me a Story* (1875), a woman with a daughter named Sybil announces that she will tell the short stories that follow to her nieces and nephews. In Mrs. Molesworth's second book, the full-length novel *Carrots* (1876), there is no explicit narrative persona until Carrots and his sister go to visit their aunt, who tells them a story interpolated into the main narrative. This aunt also has a daughter called Sybil. (Although Marghanita Laski assumes that "Auntie" is Mrs. Molesworth herself (63),[3] it is more accurate to see "Auntie" as an explicit narrative persona within a fiction narrated by a voice.)

By the time of her third book for children, *The Cuckoo Clock*, "Auntie" has dissolved into the narrative itself, leaving only the voice of a disembodied "I" without name, gender, or other personal traits. Yet the tone and mannerisms, so similar to those of "Auntie," justify calling this voice "auntly." After *The Cuckoo Clock* Mrs. Molesworth never again attached the auntly narrative voice to a specific narrative persona within a book, though aunts or auntly figures (fairy godmothers or ordinary godmothers) often tell interpolated stories.[4] She created a number of other narrative personae at varying degrees of distance from the events they recount, but these all differ in tone and mannerisms from the auntly voice itself.[5]

In *The Cuckoo Clock*, Mrs. Molesworth's auntly narrative voice directly addresses its narratees as "children" (45, 92, 110), thus establishing a group undifferentiated as to gender. The address also betrays the older age and attitude of the narrative voice, which claims superior wisdom; indeed, only an adult would address children as "children." Mrs. Molesworth hardly ever uses the vocative "readers" in her writing for children and never alludes directly to writing. Instead, she uses such words as "speak" or "say" that imply not readers but a group of listeners whose responses she seeks to control. As the auntly voice of Mrs. Molesworth's *Enchanted Garden* (1892) remarks, "I have noticed that children rather enjoy a book story retold by voice" (4).[6]

The auntly narrative voice of *The Cuckoo Clock*, the speaking voice, may well stem from Mrs. Molesworth's own experiences of storytelling. As a child she told stories to her siblings ("How I Write" 16–17, "Story Writing" 160). When she became a writer she tried out her stories on her children by concealing the manuscripts in a book and reading them aloud (Bella Woolf 675). She advised aspiring writers for children to read their stories to real children ("On the Art" 344, "Story-Reading" 775) or to read aloud to family or friends (Bainton 94). To be sure, many people who have told stories to children have not become popular children's writers, but there is probably a direct correlation between the auntly and avuncular voices in such classic Victorian texts as those of Carroll, Kingsley, and MacDonald (and later Kenneth Grahame and A. A. Milne) and the oral storytelling relationships between adult and child in which these texts originated. Likewise, the auntly narrative voices of texts by Beatrix Potter and later Hugh Lofting stemmed from real, informal epistolary storytelling. What is noteworthy is the art by which Mrs. Molesworth and these other writers could re-create the illusion of an informal speaking voice in print.

Rhetorical Devices

In her 1886 essay on Mrs. Ewing, Mrs. Molesworth remarked that children's books "should be written in such a style and in such language that the full attention and interest of the young readers should be at once enlisted and maintained to the end without any demand for mental straining or undue intellectual effort" ("Ewing" 505). Later she was to stress that an author should not refrain from using long words because they would be explained by the context (Bainton 93–94; "On the Art" 343; "Story-Writing" 164; Bella Woolf 675–76). But the early *Cuckoo Clock* avoids long words or brackets them, inviting an audience response. "Gingerly" is put in quotation marks (120), and the narrative voice draws out the listeners: "'flabbergasted,' if you know what that means" (150). Not only are "hard" words signaled by quotation marks, but "easy" and childish nonce words bridge the gap between narrator and fictive listeners. The auntly voice establishes an "equal" or familiar relationship with the listeners by using colloquial mannerisms and locutions in what may be called the *rhetoric of equality*.

This rhetoric imitates the verbal innovations of a constructed, "childish" conversation or perspective. The narrative voice plays with suffixes to make up nouns, like "old-fashionedness" (11), but more often adjectives and adverbs: "cuckoo-y" (35), "chilblainy" (52), "fruzzley" (62), "mandariny-looking" (65), "lazy-easy" (95), "mixty-maxty," a Scots dialect word (112), "charminger" (150), "rushy" (162, 164). The narrative voice also affects "nursery" adjectives which reflect a childish viewpoint: a lamp is thus described as "dear" (52). With the emphasis on food typical of children's fiction, it is not surprising that a palace, a garden, and a flight can all be described as "delicious" (12, 109, 162). In so far as this childish vocabulary is an adult invention, the narrative voice seems not only to talk in the hypothetical manner of the fictive listeners but to talk down to them. "Dear" or "delicious" are never found in communication between adults.

At the same time the narrative voice takes up and mirrors the child-protagonist's manner of speech. Griselda too uses made-up words: "'I hate *must*-ing to do anything,'" she says (97). Such special words, when used by the narrative voice, remind us of the way in which a certain kind of adult responds to a child by imitating a child's speech. These special words have nothing in common with the sophisticated, puzzling nonsense words of Lewis Carroll and Edward Lear, although they may superficially resemble them. Mrs. Molesworth's neologisms serve only to guarantee a sympathetic alignment of the narrative voice, the child protagonist, and the narratees.

Just as the narrative voice echoes the kind of childish words Griselda uses, it imitates her childish intensity and zest. Griselda tends to talk with great emphasis, indicated by italics: "'I'd *far* rather have the fairy carpet'" (41) or "'What a *lovely* cloak!'" (52). Similarly, the narratorial italics echo the rhythm of oral emphasis: Griselda's shoes are beautiful, "*only* they were rather a stumpy shape" (66); Sybilla's grandfather "did not look *poor*" (81); Griselda and Phil were "very hot and very tired and *rather* dirty" (189). Between Griselda and the narrative voice, almost every page of the book has at least one italicized word. These italics reproduce the cadences of conversation as well as creating an intimacy that binds the narratees with the narrative voice and protagonist.

Griselda's enthusiasms are further mirrored in the narratorial penchant for hyperbole. Griselda wears "the most magnificent dress you ever saw" (65), her shoes are "the dearest, sweetest little pair" (66), Sybilla is the "dearest little girl you ever saw, and so funnily dressed!" (81). Many of these superabundant superlatives are tautologous: to feel slightly ill is "very extremely" nasty (193), the butterfly garden is "the loveliest, loveliest garden" (109), Griselda's head is "crammed full, perfectly full, of fairy lore" (133).

Sometimes the narrative voice, growing almost incoherent, resorts to the rhetorical figure of *occupatio*; it protests that words are insufficient to describe the food in Mandarin Land, Sybilla's grandfather's workshop, the butterfly garden, the butterfly dress, Griselda's enjoyment of the spring, Griselda's flight on the cuckoo's back. When Griselda sees the sea on the moon, the voice remarks that it "is something that I can only give you a faint idea of, children . . . if I could [describe it adequately] my words would be as good as pictures, which I know they are not" (173).

The speaking voice re-creates with specific childish words, locutions, and heavy emphases a conversational dynamic and establishes intimacy with the fictive listeners. This is not the voice of one child speaking to another but of an adult indicating sympathy for children by addressing them in what is ostensibly their own manner. The adult comes down to the level of the child as part of the compact between teller and listener. In turn, by echoing the voice of the protagonist, the narrative voice invites the child narratees' sympathy with the child protagonist.

The rhetoric of equality establishes familiarity with the fictive audience, a familiarity enhanced by a group of devices that together make up the *rhetoric of participation*. To a certain extent, the narrative voice already invites the implied listeners to participate in the story by addressing them directly as "you." A common temporal ground with the listeners is implied by such phrases as "you will see" (133), "you must have seen" (93), "the dearest . . . you ever saw" (81), and "I can assure you" (189). These phrases create an illusion of shared knowledge and of direct interplay between the narrative voice and the fictive listener, as in an oral storytelling situation.

This interplay is furthered by rhetorical questions ("Had ever a little girl such a flight before?" [167]). When Griselda feels like crying out before her aunts and Lady Lavander, the narrative voice asks, "What *would* the three old ladies have thought if she had called it out?" (23). Here the narrative voice invites the listeners to acknowledge the horrified reactions of the ladies, assuming the listeners share its own experiences and attitudes. More important, when the narrative voice interrupts itself with such questions as "What did she see?" (109), "And how do you think they dressed her?" (118), or "Where was she?" (173), it evokes and directs the response of the narratees, thus asking for their participation in the story.

Most striking are moments when the narrative voice suggests that the narratees can collaborate in making the story. Using *author's metalepsis* the narrator transgresses the boundary between the world of telling and that about which is told.[7] The first such passage is one of the opening flourishes of *The Cuckoo Clock*. Like the familiar opening of George Eliot's *Adam Bede* (1859), it serves to assert both the fictionality of the text and the power of the fiction-maker. George Eliot's voice calls attention to the written aspect of her text and to the magical power of the written word to evoke pictures and images in order to draw the reader into the fictional world. Mrs. Molesworth's narrative voice instead provides an almost cinematic descriptive movement from a broad view outside the house to a narrower view inside while asking the narratees' permission. It is here that the characteristic feature of the auntly narrative voice is seen: Whereas George Eliot's narrative voice *tells* the narratee what it will attempt ("This is what I undertake to do for you, reader. With this drop of ink at the end of my pen I will show you the roomy workshop . . ." [*Bede* 49]), Mrs. Molesworth's narrative voice, much less overtly authoritarian, more playfully collaborative, seeks the narratees' consent. "A gentleman lifted [Griselda] out of the carriage and disappeared with her into the house. . . . That was all that the rooks saw. . . . Shall we go inside to see more?" (3). Here is another passage calling for collaboration or assent in making the story: "And Mr.—I can't remember the little old gentleman's name. Suppose we call him Mr. Kneebreeches—Mr. Kneebreeches . . . conscientiously put her back to the very beginning" (18).

The playful atmosphere of the rhetoric of participation reinforces the group of devices which together make up the *rhetoric of relaxed narration*. These indicate that storytelling is an informal activity that does not demand a rigorously attentive response. The narrative voice conveys this impression by using emphatic dilation and by reproducing childish babble, a vocabulary that by definition is not "serious." Here the patterns of conversation become important: the digression, which disrupts the ordered sequence of events, the dislocated sentence, and interjected comments on the story from a distance.

Without compunction, the narrative voice rambles about, interrupting regularly to comment on a word or image. For example, after Miss Grizzel hopes that Griselda's cold will get better, the narrator comments:

> Griselda's cold *was* much better by "to-morrow morning." In fact, I might almost say it was quite well.
>
> But Griselda herself did not feel quite well, and saying this reminds me that it is hardly sense to speak of a *cold* being better or well—for a cold's being "well" means that it is not there at all, out of existence, in short, and if a thing is out of existence how can we say anything about it? Children . . . give me your opinion. In the meantime, I will go on about Griselda. [92–93]

This passage is obviously derived from a portion of *Alice* which runs: "And she tried to fancy what the flame of a candle looks like after the candle is blown out, for she could not remember ever having seen such a thing." This is glossed by one annotator, referring to Goethe, Freud, and Descartes, as "a puzzle about existence" (Heath 19). Similarly digressive is the narrative description of spring's arrival (*Cuckoo Clock* 149).

Invariably humorous, the digressions may amplify the narrative with myths and folklore that are obviously intended to create a bond between teller and listener. The sea on the moon evokes a topsy-turvey comparison to a familiar earthly sea: "King Canute might have sat 'from then till now' by this still, lifeless ocean with the chance of reading his silly attendants a lesson—if indeed, there were such silly people, which I very much doubt" (174). In one instance, the narrative voice digresses in mid-sentence, in the guise of simile that swells into an anecdote: "'If it was summer now, or spring,' [Griselda] repeated to herself, just as if she had not been asleep at all—like the man who fell into a trance of a hundred years just as he was saying 'it is bitt—,' and when he woke up again he finished the sentence as if nothing had happened '—erly cold.' 'If only it was spring,' thought Griselda" (6). These digressions are in keeping with the simulation of oral narrative as well as with the affected naiveté of the narrative voice. Both examples refer to other stories as if teller and listener alike would recognize them, so that narrative voice and narratees are drawn into a community of equals who respond to shared cultural artifacts. But the examples here serve primarily to indicate the playfulness of the narrative voice and to foster the relaxed enjoyment of the listeners.

The process of narration and of finding the right words comes to the fore through these humorous digressions and interruptions. To describe Griselda's trials at the hands of her tutor requires a halt and turn as the voice searches for the most expressive term: "It was dreadful, really. He came twice a week, and the days he didn't come were as bad as those he did, for he left her a whole *row* I was going to say, but you couldn't call Mr. Kneebreeches' addition sums 'rows,' they were far too fat and wide across to be so spoken of!—whole slatefuls of these terrible mountains of figures to climb wearily to the top of" (18–19). A conversational effect of immediacy, of thought in process is achieved by such dislocations. In addition, the voice slips toward Griselda's view of the sums by the affected naiveté, the emphases, the humor, and the breathlessness of the sentence with its subordinate clauses and parenthetical remarks.

This broken, interruptive style has been criticized as typical of Mrs. Molesworth's faults. Marghanita Laski, who believes the long passage in which the butterflies dress Griselda is "probably the most dearly remembered passage in any children's book," nonetheless complains: "Read this passage as a critical adult and a multitude of faults glare out at you. The syntax is shaky, the sentence structure clumsy—both very usual faults in Mrs. Molesworth's children's books. The choice of words is limited and unimaginative. . . ." Yet Laski would create a separate set of critical voices for children's literature, arguing that "her whole passage was written for a child and is properly susceptible only to children's criticism" (66–67).

In fact, these stylistic "faults" are absent from Mrs. Molesworth's "stories for girls," which move at a conventional, sedate pace without childish mannerisms. Mrs. Molesworth could write "correctly" when she chose. What Laski calls faults, I call narrative art. Without resorting to the ambiguities of "children's criticism," we may suggest that Mrs. Molesworth deliberately resorts to clumsy syntax to reproduce the warm and chatty voice of a storytelling adult and to create intimacy with young narratees.

There are suggestive similarities between the digressions of the auntly narrative voice and the associative monologues of Miss Bates in Austen's *Emma* or Mrs. Lirriper in Dickens's "Mrs. Lirriper's Lodgings" (1863). Even more than these characters, the digressive narrator in humorous fiction in the wake of Sterne foreshadows the stream-of-consciousness techniques of the new century. The rhetorical devices of the rambling auntly voice combine features we normally separate as conscious and unconscious, outer and inner voice, disturbing our sense of linear order to reduce the reader's distance from the character who speaks.[8]

Occasionally, the auntly voice does appear to be distanced temporally or otherwise. For instance, the narrator may deny knowing a particular fact, paradoxically enhancing the verisimilitude of the story by insisting on the putative previous transmission of the story. How did the rooks react to Griselda's arrival? "I never heard if *they* slept well that night; after such unusual excitement it was hardly to be expected they would" (5). In a strategy of collaboration, the narrator conjectures about causes indispensable to understanding the plot. The verbs "suppose" and "think" (2, 45, 130) avow ignorance. Indeed, pretended ignorance may even convey needed facts: "For some reason that I do not know enough about the habits of 'flesh-and-blood' cuckoos to explain, that bird was not known in the neighbourhood" (133). She thus ensures that young listeners will understand how unusual it was for Griselda to hear the live cuckoo in that garden in spring. At other times, the narrative voice catches itself in an omission and loquaciously explains in retrospect: "'What a *lovely* cloak!' said Griselda, wrapping it round her . . . as she watched the little lamp in the roof—I think I was forgetting to tell you that the cuckoo's boudoir was lighted by a dear little lamp set into the red velvet roof like a pearl on a ring—playing softly on the brilliant colors of the feather mantle" (52–53).[9] Inconsistencies seem almost deliberate occasions for self-interruption or tokens of enthusiastic haste: "The bowling green was certainly very delightful . . . but lovely as the roses were (I am speaking just now, of course, of later on in the summer, when they were all in bloom), Griselda could not enjoy them" (130). The narrative voice can even comment on itself: "The cuckoo smiled, I was going to say, but that would be a figure of speech only, would it not?" (110).

All these interventions testify to the spontaneous *invention* of Griselda's story. While the narrator claims to have heard the story, her rhetoric implies that she is making the story up as she goes along and must cover the tracks of her art. These signs that the storytelling is a relaxed occupation for which the narrator has not prepared rigorously invite the narratees to respond in a corresponding manner.

The jocularity goes even further with the *rhetoric of nonsubversive irony*, an additional bond between adult and child since irony always depends on some shared understanding between two parties from which somebody else is at least potentially excluded. The irony may be directed against Griselda, as when her "weighty cares" are nothing more than brushing her hair (8), or when she talks "sagely" to Phil (144). Two passages illustrate this irony:

> [Miss Grizzel:] "Respect to your elders, my dear, always remember that. The mandarins are *many* years older than you—older than I myself, in fact."
>
> Griselda wondered, if this were so, how it was that Miss Grizzel took such liberties with them herself, but she said nothing. [12]

> [The cuckoo:] "Don't you know that if all the world and everything in it, counting yourself of course, was all made little enough to go into a walnut, you'd never find out the difference?"
>
> "*Wouldn't* I?" said Griselda, feeling rather muddled; "but *not* counting myself, cuckoo, I would then, wouldn't I?"
>
> "Nonsense," said the cuckoo hastily; "you've a great deal to learn, and one thing is, not to *argue*." [49]

In both cases Griselda only half perceives what is perfectly obvious to the narrative voice and to the narratees: that adults are often not logically consistent. There is a great difference between subversive writing and subversive reading, and it would be advisable to resist salting these passages with our own dislike of authority. Here, because the narrative voice is an adult one, the irony is divested of any subversive intent: it becomes merely another instance of attempted sympathy between adult auntly narrator and a group of fictive child listeners. In the same way, after Griselda's final declaration of her good intentions, the maid Dorcas wonderingly hopes that " 'the child's not going to be ill' " (185). Here, the narrator invites the narratees to laugh at the stereotype of the ideal, perfect pious child not long for this world, thereby indicating that Griselda, who knows nothing of this, does not fit that stereotype.

The narrative voice also creates intimacy with the narratees in an act of self-mockery by affecting naiveté; for example, when describing Griselda's sums the voice asserts "I can't explain it—it is far beyond my poor powers" (19). Or again, a direct address to the narratees may be part of a shared jest: "Children, I feel quite in a hobble—I cannot get my mind straight about it—please think it over and give me your opinion" (92–93). The exaggerated, self-deprecating pose (as also in forgetting Mr. Kneebreeches' name) is an ironic rhetorical device. In making fun of itself, the narrative voice requests the tolerance of the listeners.

Topoi

With the groups of devices used to establish equality, participation, relaxation, and shared irony, I have so far been dealing mainly with the relation set up between the auntly voice and its *audience*. I now turn to two aspects of the relation between the narrative voice and its *content,* that is, to why and how the kinds of rhetoric are applied. Primarily, Mrs. Molesworth establishes a relation between her auntly narrative voice and its narratees for a didactic purpose. The narrator conveys an impression of casualness, relaxation, even disorder only to conceal the seriousness of purpose and commitment to moral order which are the raison d'être of the work. Here is a case in which *ars est celare artem*: the art consists in concealing the art. Since the narrator is so obtrusive, commenting about so many things, the didactic comments it makes are passed along with the others. These didactic comments constitute what might be called the *topoi of instruction*.

The narrative voice makes its point about courage through one of its many rhetorical questions: Griselda "was afraid of nothing. Or rather perhaps I should say she had never learnt that there was anything to be afraid of! And is there?" (31). It condemns Griselda's ill-tempered and lazy self-pity with a similar ironical rhetorical question: "Upstairs Griselda was hurry-scurrying into bed. There was a lovely fire in the room—fancy that! Was she not a poor neglected little creature?" (99).

Protected by the sympathy and intimacy it projects, the narrator can even make flatly didactic generalizations. For instance, when Griselda sulks after she is told that her lessons will resume with her tutor, the narrator combines description with comment: "She was 'so tired,' she said; and she certainly looked so, for ill-humor and idleness are excellent 'tirers,' and will soon take the roses out of a child's cheeks, and the brightness out of her eyes" (99). Again, after describing Griselda's anxiety in asking permission to play with Phil, an anxiety that makes her take "a sort of spiteful pleasure in injuring her own cause," the narrator comments, "How *foolish* ill-temper makes us!" (149). In both these cases the narrative voice shifts from the particular to the universal, making general points about conduct and human nature.

Moral prescription wears the mask of a novel of education: "And Griselda became gradually more and more convinced that the only way as yet discovered of getting through hard tasks is to set to work and do them; also, that grumbling, as things are at present arranged in this world, does not *always,* nor may I say *often,* do good; furthermore, that an ill-tempered child is not, on the whole, likely to be as much loved as a good-tempered one; lastly, that if you wait long enough, winter will go and spring will come" (129). Here, Mrs. Molesworth blurs the focus and preaches rather than displays the moral. Yet her art remains much the same. Though the rhythm is slower, she uses those long, rambling, interrupted sentences that elsewhere contribute to the impression of childish zest; the italics imply a spoken stress. The meiosis in "not *always,* nor . . . *often*" appeals to a compact between narrator and narratees; both understand that the words mean "never." With the obtrusive "may I say" the narrator turns from Griselda's learning her lesson about grumbling toward the narratees who must learn the lesson, too. Whereas the voice and plot show Griselda's awareness of the inevitability of hard work and the use of patience, nowhere in the book does she really learn that "an ill-tempered child is not . . . likely to be as much loved as a good-tempered one," a point addressed instead to the narratees. Suggestively, Griselda learns not that "if *she* waited long enough, winter would go," but that "if *you* waited long enough" —Griselda's personal education has been transformed into a set of universally valid moral generalizations. This passage is immediately followed by the light digression on winter and spring. Hence, the narrative manner—egalitarian, interactive, relaxed, and gently ironic—works to a didactic end. Like the fantasy adventures themselves, the warmly inviting auntly voice provides the sugarcoating for the moral pill.

The very situation of the voice's audience, a group of children, conveys a potential lesson. Their condition does not mirror that of the child protagonist, who is not surrounded by other children, has few books to read (77), and has no one to tell her stories to. Perhaps this difference is created in order to indicate subliminally that the children who read the book or have it read to them should be grateful for the advantages that they enjoy in contrast to Griselda. (The name itself suggests long-suffering and patience.) Here Mrs. Molesworth refines the Evangelical attitude of "there but for the grace of God go you," which is obvious in many nineteenth-century stories of "street arabs."

While overt didacticism today seems out of fashion, far more serious stumbling blocks for modern readers are the *topoi of prettification and pathos*. These appeals to emotion constitute one of the temptations of works which deploy the auntly narrative voice, temptations to which Mrs. Molesworth succumbs at certain points in the work.

Legitimate pathos in the novel centers on Griselda's loneliness, as when she stands in the dark room apologizing to the unresponsive clock (34) or when she weeps to Dorcas because she has been forbidden to meet Phil the next day and fears he will think she has deserted him (155). Pathos is inherent in the figure of the deprived, lonely child. The moments of pathos centering on Griselda are conveyed through dialogue and description, not comment. In the presentation of Phil, however, "loaded" descriptions turn pathos into unwarranted sentimentality. In a hyperbolic and stereotyped contrast we are told Phil is "a very sturdy, very merry, very ragged little boy" (135). When Griselda attempts to send him away, the description stresses emotions perceived and felt. "His voice sounded almost as if he were going to cry, and his pretty, hot, flushed face puckered up. Griselda's heart smote her . . ." (137). Evidently the hearts not only of fictive listeners but of real readers should be smitten, too. Again, on the night when Griselda visits Phil with the cuckoo, the narrator waxes eloquent, using such emotive adjectival phrases as "lovely sleeping child," "shaggy curls," "rosy mouth," and the marker word "little"—"little hand," "little basket," "like a baby almost" (163–64). This appeal to the sentimentality about babies that lurks in the heart of the most hardened person seems to us tear-jerking self-indulgence, since it is unrelated to Phil's lonely condition. The epithets are there seemingly for their own sake.[10]

Promises and Pitfalls of the Victorian Auntly Voice

The auntly voice in its strengths and weaknesses was common to other Victorian writers for children. It cuts across considerations of genre—it is used in fantasy novels or short stories, *Kunstmärchen,* and nonfantasy works alike. The most striking instance of an explicitly auntly narrative voice among other Victorian writers for children is in Christina Rossetti's *Speaking Likenesses* (1874). This long dramatic monologue gradually reveals that the speaker is indeed an aunt; the text inscribes the nature, number, and responses of her listeners, as well as her own character and relationships with them. Of course, not only in children's books but in works for adults, such as Mrs. Gaskell's *Ruth* (1853), Victorian narrative voices convey similar qualities of responsibility, sympathy, intimacy, relaxation, wisdom, and playfulness.

Most novels do not betray the gender of the narrative voice. If we project our knowledge about the author, we may call the intimate narrative voice in children's books either auntly or avuncular. The latter might be more appropriate for a male author such as Charles Kingsley in *The Water Babies* (1863), or Lewis Carroll in *Alice* (1865). When Virginia Woolf comments on the "perpetual admonitions" of the "eternal pedagogue" and the "too conscientious governess," she describes "that persistent voice, now grumbling, now patronising, now domineering, now grieved, now shocked, now angry, now avuncular, that voice which cannot let women alone, but must be at them" (75). In this negative context the avuncular voice speaks down to women and children, teaching, moralizing, admonishing, with less than kindly condescension. The situation, tone, and verbal mannerisms of this kind of voice, whatever the gender, remain remarkably similar from author to author.

The adjective "auntly" is a metaphor intended to convey the relation between the narrative voice and narratee in a given Victorian children's book: to evoke the adult, superior in authority, but potentially receptive and willing to entertain and play with children—like the quintessential storytelling aunt evoked in *Tell Me a Story* and *Carrots*. By contrast, the metaphor "uncle" should evoke someone like the kind, eccentric uncle in Hugh Walpole's later *Jeremy* books. And kinship words like "maternal" or "paternal" evoke yet a different set of nineteenth-century images or notions. The mother stereotype, as exemplified in Miss Yonge's work, is largely that of a childbearing figure, loving but relatively effaced or absent, not primarily playful. Victorian fathers—like the father in *Carrots*—inherit a shadow from the stern Georgian father in Mrs. Sherwood's *Fairchild Family* (1818), who explicitly and proudly took the responsibility of standing in the position of a Calvinist, judgmental God in relation to his children. It may even be hazarded that the line between Georgian and Victorian children's literature is drawn by a shift from hortatory parental narrative stances and voices to playful auntly or avuncular ones.[11]

In Victorian children's fiction, the narrative voice often establishes the nature of its narratee by using vocatives. Sometimes the narratee may be an individual, even of a particular sex: Kingsley's narrator addresses "my little man" in *The Water Babies*. The narratee may in other cases be a group: Thackeray's narrator talks to "dear friends" or to "every little boy or girl" in *The Rose and the Ring* (1855). Some texts, *The Water Babies* and George MacDonald's *Princess and the Goblin* (1872), for instance, go so far as to include dialogue between the narrative voice and the narratee. Others exploit the fact that the real audience of Victorian children's books was often a simultaneous double one of children and mediating adults.[12] Thackeray's narrative voice at one point tells its boys and girls to fancy what they would like to eat but then adds a footnote, presumably addressed to an adult, to the effect that at this point in the narrative the children might play a game along the lines indicated. In Mrs. Gatty's *The Fairy Godmothers* (1851), not a page after addressing "dear little readers," the narrative voice suddenly addresses a comment to the scornful young lady who is reading the story aloud. (This shift of narratorial address from one kind of narratee to another often gives the real reader a jolt.) Finally, as the example from Mrs. Gatty shows, the narrative voice may show an awareness that it is using the medium of written communication, that its narratee is a reader or group of readers. This is even more visible in Lewis Carroll's "An Easter Greeting," which begins, "Dear Child, Please to fancy, if you can, that you are reading a real letter. . . ." There is considerable variation, then, in the degree of particularity which the auntly narrative voice can give to its narratee(s).

The auntly narrative voice is usually arch, sometimes excessively so. Mrs. Molesworth, secure in the jest shared with her implied listeners, is playfully saucy, but the archness of her contemporaries may become an exaggerated, often forced or artificial playfulness. In many the narrative voice fails to share an ironical jest or to laugh at itself or the protagonist. Moral admonitions, for instance, are not enlivened by the curious digression or odd simile. What we are left with then is no more than a collection of auntly mannerisms. Even such a master as Lewis Carroll allowed his auntly/avuncular narrative voice to degenerate into self-parody in *The Nursery "Alice,"* which is peppered with the four mannerisms (one could almost call them stylistic tics) that are easiest to adopt: the nursery adjective, the use of italics to represent exaggerated emphasis, the rhetorical question, and the rambling sentence:

> "Oh dear, oh dear!" said the Rabbit. "I shall be too late! *What would it be too late for,* I wonder? Well, you see, it had to go and visit the Duchess, (you'll see a picture of the Duchess soon, sitting in her kitchen): and the Duchess was a very cross old lady: and the Rabbit *knew* she'd be very angry indeed if he kept her waiting. So the poor thing was as frightened as frightened could be (Don't you see how he's trembling? Just shake the book a little, from side to side, and you'll soon see him tremble), because he thought the Duchess would have his head cut off, for a punishment. That was what the Queen of Hearts used to do, when *she* was angry with people (you'll see a picture of *her* soon): at least she used to *order* their heads to be cut off, and she always *thought* it was done, though they never *really* did it. . . .
>
> And so that was the beginning of Alice's curious dream. And, next time you see a White Rabbit, try and fancy *you're* going to have a curious dream, just like dear little Alice. [2–3, 4]

It is no wonder that this nursery version of *Alice* was practically stillborn.

The worst excesses of this sort of narrative voice have been accurately parodied by A. A. Milne:

> Once upon a time there was a little girl called—well, you will never guess what her name was, not if you had three hundred million guesses, and your Daddy and Mummy and your Nanny all guessed too, and you read the Englishdictionary (isn't that a long word?) right through from beginning to end, including all the twiddly-widdly bits. Because she had a special name of her very-very-very-own, which nobody had ever been called before, and it wasn't Mary, and it wasn't Jane, and it wasn't Anne, and you'll never believe it but it wasn't even Flibbertygibbet. What *could* it have been? Can't you guess? . . .
>
> It is not unfair to take this as a representative sample of the children's story manner. [128–30]

In view of Milne's own awareness of and dislike for the characteristics of the "bad" auntly narrative voice, it is somewhat ironic that his own variation of it in *The House at Pooh Corner* (1928) should have been cruelly parodied in one of the most famous book reviews of children's literature, Dorothy Parker's "Far from Well." Having quoted the "cadenced whimsy" of one of Pooh's "hums" and a bit of prose, the reviewer, Constant Reader, continues, "Oh darn—there I've gone and given away the plot. Oh, I could bite my tongue out." More quotation ends,

> "Well, you'll see, Piglet, when you listen. Because this is how it begins. *The more it snows, tiddely-pom—*"
>
> "Tiddely what?" said Piglet. (He took as you might say, the very words out of your correspondent's mouth.)
>
> "Pom," said Pooh. "I put that in to make it more hummy."
>
> And it is that word "hummy," my darlings, that marks the first place in *The House at Pooh Corner* at which Tonstant Weader Fwowed Up. [100–01][13]

This cuts close to the bone in its cunning use of pompous phrases combined with an exaggeration of auntly narrative voice features —exclamations, childish phrases, address to a putative set of child narratees, paedokakography (written baby talk), and the like—not that Milne was guilty of all these sins in his book.

Placing the analysis of Mrs. Molesworth's rhetoric beside the passage from Carroll and the sharp parodies by and of Milne, we are struck by the devices common to all these authors. It may be fairly claimed that all narrative voices which we recognize as auntly or avuncular select their rhetorical devices from a certain register, though of course not every writer uses all the devices together, in the same proportion, or to the same effect as Mrs. Molesworth. The case of Carroll's *Alice in Wonderland* and *Nursery "Alice"* would seem to indicate that the younger the intended audience, the more auntly or avuncular the voice.

"Writing down" to children is not always successful; it may convey adult condescension rather than the gracious sharing of a game. *The Nursery "Alice"* and the parodies by Milne and Parker also seem to imply that the auntly or avuncular voice has the sole purpose of padding out or otherwise trivializing and debasing content. But this is not inevitable. In *The Cuckoo Clock* the groups of devices are in control. No one device becomes predominant or annoyingly obtrusive; they are balanced and tactfully proportioned to accommodate the moral of the novel, which is conveyed both directly by the commentary and indirectly by the plot.

All auntly narrative voices create and address a fictive audience of children—and this acts as a generic marker that the work in question is children's literature. All attempt to establish a relation between a sympathetic, intimate, relaxed, wise, and above all playful adult and a child, though in some cases archness degenerates into forced playfulness. The balance is delicate. Each rhetorical cluster simulates orality of a particular kind, that of an adult "talking down" to a child; but some of the features of the rhetoric of equality and the rhetoric of participation can at the same time undo the hierarchic relationship that normally governs relationships between adult and child, and between narrator and narratee as well. One might describe this effect as controlled subversion.

In the work of Mrs. Molesworth, the rhetoric of equality establishes that the adult speaks "as" a child. The rhetoric of participation invites the child to share in the game of storytelling with the adult. The rhetoric of relaxed narration indicates that neither adult nor child need take the act of narration too seriously. The rhetoric of nonsubversive irony marks a compact between the adult and child, whereby they laugh together at child characters, adult characters, and even the adult narrative voice without seriously interrogating the values of any of them. All the previous devices are then used to make the topoi of moral instruction acceptable under cover of playfulness—concealing the powder in the jam, to use a favorite Victorian metaphor. Finally, with the topoi of prettification and pathos, the adult narrator invests a child character with features designed to appeal to the child—features which some modern sensibilities find unappealing, but in which the Victorians, both young and old, delighted.

These rhetorics are not peculiar to children's literature. Thackeray, who wrote for "great" as well as "small" children, addresses his readers in the last lines of *Vanity Fair* as "children," an extension of his puppetry metaphor. Joyce drops into a childish language at the beginning of *A Portrait of the Artist as a Young Man*: "Once upon a time moocow" assimilates the narrative voice to topos and forces adult narratees into a childlike role. Hyperbole, childish neologisms, diminutives, and the topos of prettification, by contrast, seem rare in works for adults; some of these features, like italics, have been mocked as markers of women's language. And adult literature, of course, is not likely to unleash the strange figure of nonsubversive irony.

The continued reprinting of *The Cuckoo Clock* indicates that the tone at which the auntly voice is pitched to its narratee and the use to which it is put satisfy real readers or listeners. In Mrs. Molesworth's hands, a moral vision anchors the rhetoric; the narrative voice thus rarely becomes pedestrian, irritating or portentous, badly "arch." There are of course sensibilities today to which an auntly narrative voice (or an unequivocal moral vision) automatically seems beyond the pale. I think her work answered that challenge before it was made. At its best, the auntly or avuncular voice sustains literary values that few would question today, such as the pleasurable metapoetic rupturing of narrative boundaries between story and frame. Above all this voice invites the active participation of the narratee, and therefore indirectly of all its listeners or readers.

Notes

Besides the assistance of Ruth Robertson, who is preparing a biography of Mrs. Molesworth, and who made available to me material she had collected, I wish to call attention to the thesis of Beth Humphries and an unpublished paper by Margaret Ann Paterson, "The Values and Limitations of *Carrots* as an Historical Source." See also the article by Jane Cooper, forthcoming in *Signal* (1988). A symposium volume on Mrs. Molesworth (edited by Sircar et al.) is in preparation.

1. *The Cuckoo Clock* was one of the first children's books reprinted by Puffin; it has

been translated into German. Its illustrators include Walter Crane (1877), Maria L. Kirk (1914), Florence White Williams (1927), F. Sherman Cooke (1930), C. E. Brock (1931), Edna Cooke (1939), E. H. Shepard (1954), and two anonymous American artists (1895, 1909).

2. F.H.L. (probably Frances H. Low), "A Popular Writer for Children: Mrs. Molesworth," *Westminster Budget*, 20 Oct. 1883. Typescript supplied by Ruth Robertson. The British Museum holding of this was destroyed in the war, and no other known holdings exist.

3. Ruth Robertson concludes that "Sybil" is probably drawn from Mrs. Molesworth's niece, Agnes Venetia Goring (later Hohler), daughter of Agnes and Sir Charles Goring. There is also a "Sybilla" in *The Cuckoo Clock*—the heroine's grandmother seen as a little girl.

4. See such works as *Grandmother Dear* (1878), *The Tapestry Room* (1879), *Hoodie* (1882), *An Enchanted Garden* (1892), *This and That* (1899), and *The February Boys* (1909).

5. They range from an old nurse in *Nurse Heatherdale's Story* (1891) to a boy protagonist in *The Girls and I* (1892), a young girl retelling the events of a few years before in *My New Home* (1894), and an old lady recalling her childhood in *The Carved Lions* (1895).

6. Of course, the group of narratee-listeners in *The Cuckoo Clock* is not necessarily to be identified with the actual audience, contemporaneous or contemporary, of the book. The actual audience may be an adult reader, a child reader, a child being read to, a group of children being read to, or indeed an analytical scholar. George Bainton noted in *The Art of Authorship: Personally Contributed by Leading Authors of the Day* (New York, 1891) that Mrs. Molesworth's books "have just as great a charm to older readers as to those on whose behalf they were written" (93).

7. Gérard Genette, *Narrative Discourse* 234–35. He gives many examples, and points out that the effect is always strange, whether comical or fantastic. Authorial metalepsis may appeal to the intervention of the narratee, as in Sterne, George Eliot, or Mrs. Molesworth, but need not do so.

8. See Cohn (63, 95–97) on infantile babbling.

9. Such flashbacks are called "completing analepses" by Genette (51–54).

10. Gillian Avery points out that Mrs. Molesworth tended to be more indulgent with her boy characters than her girl characters (162). Perhaps this is the reason that Phil is viewed through a rosy haze, whereas Griselda is not, though of course he is a supernumerary and she the protagonist. Though the literary ancestor of Phil and his brethren is George MacDonald's Diamond in *At the Back of the North Wind* (1871), Ruth Robertson has discovered that apparently his original in real life was Mrs. Molesworth's son Lionel, a delicate child who was consequently a little "spoilt."

A. P. Herbert in *The Water Gypsies* (1930) gives an excellent example of the continued use of "little" as a marker word. The novel is humorously describing a Communist Sunday school in England:

> Ernest said, 'Now which little Comrade will recite the text for the week?'
> A young chubby girl with long plaits stood up and said, 'If you please, Comrade, Comrade Slatter don't allow us to be called little because he says we're all Comrades same as others and there's no little about it.' And she sat down. [216]

11. A check of titles in any list of Victorian children's books, or a look at the British Library catalogue, will show more aunts than uncles, mothers, or fathers in works ranging from instruction to fairy tales.

12. The double audience of children's literature is important not only as it involves a gap in age among real readers, posing questions of economics, censorship, morals, slang, and so on; but also as the two fictive groups of narratees shape the rhetoric

of the text, one perhaps for the benefit of the inscribed, mediating adult readers (or readers-aloud), another perhaps "subversively" slipped past them. We know that Lewis Carroll's work was read by adults in real life from Rhoda Broughton's *Nancy* (1873; London, 1878, p. 362) and Anthony Trollope's *Eustace Diamonds* (1876; London, 1930, p. 251), which refer to adults reading the *Alice* books for themselves, not to children.

13. Only eight years after *The Nursery Alice* and twenty after *The Cuckoo Clock*, Max Beerbohm parodied the auntly voice in an adult work of fiction, "The Happy Hypocrite" (1897):

> None, it is said, of all who revelled with the Regent was half so wicked as Lord George Hall. I will not trouble my little readers with a long recital of his great naughtiness. But it were well they should know he was greedy, destructive and disobedient. I am afraid there is no doubt that he often sat up at Carlton House long after bed-time, playing at games, and that he generally ate and drank far more than was good for him. . . .[15]

Other parodies of the same sort include Peter Sellers's "Auntie Rotter" and Joyce Grenfell's "Writer of Children's Books" (88). Grenfell is obviously mocking Enid Blyton, whose use of the auntly narrative voice varies from book to book but is best seen in her work for a younger age group, for example, *The Enchanted Wood* (45, 165, 192).

Works Cited

Avery, Gillian. "Introduction." *My New Home*. London: Gollancz, 1968.
———. *Nineteenth-Century Children: Heroes and Heroines in English Children's Stories, 1780–1900*. London: Hodder & Stoughton, 1965.
Bainton, George, ed. *The Art of Authorship: Personally Contributed by Leading Authors of the Day*. 1890. New York: D. Appleton & Co., 1891.
Beerbohm, Max. "The Happy Hypocrite." 1897. In *The Bodley Head Beerbohm*, ed. Lord David Cecil. London: Bodley Head, 1970.
Blyton, Enid. *The Enchanted Wood*. London: George Newnes, 1939.
Booth, Wayne. *The Rhetoric of Fiction*. Chicago: Chicago U P, 1961.
Carroll, Lewis [Charles L. Dodgson]. *The Nursery 'Alice.'* London: Macmillan, 1889.
Cohn, Dorrit. *Transparent Minds: Narrative Modes for Presenting Consciousness in Fiction*. Princeton: Princeton U P, 1979.
Crews, Frederick C. *The Pooh Perplex: A Freshman Casebook*. New York: Dutton, 1963.
Eliot, George [Mary Ann Evans]. *Adam Bede*. 1859. Harmondsworth: Penguin, 1980.
Elliott, Robert C. *The Literary Persona*. Chicago: Chicago U P, 1982.
Ellis, Alec. *How to Find out about Children's Literature*. Oxford: Pergamon, 1973.
[F.H.L., probably Frances H. Low.] "A Popular Writer for Children: Mrs. Molesworth." *Westminster Budget* 20 October 1883.
Gaskell, Mrs. Elizabeth Cleghorn. *Ruth*. Leipzig: Tauchnitz, 1853.
Gatty, Mrs. *The Fairy Godmothers*. London: Bell, 1851.
Genette, Gérard. *Narrative Discourse: An Essay in Method*. Trans. Jane E. Lewin. Ithaca, N.Y.: Cornell U P, 1979.
Green, Roger Lancelyn. *Mrs. Molesworth*. London: Bodley Head, 1961.
———. *Tellers of Tales*. New York: Franklin Watts, 1975.
Grenfell, Joyce. "Writer of Children's Books," in *George, Don't Do That. . . .* London: Macmillan, 1977.
Heath, Peter, ed. *The Philosopher's Alice*. London: Academy Editions, 1974.
Herbert, A.P. *The Water Gypsies*. 1930. Harmondsworth: Penguin, 1960.
Humphries, Beth. "Fantasy and Morality in Children's Books: A Study of Mrs.

Molesworth in the Context of Nineteenth and Early Twentieth Century Writers for Children." M. A. Thesis. Sussex University, 1978.
Kingsley, Charles. *The Water Babies; A Fairytale for a Land-baby*. London: Macmillan, 1863.
Laski, Marghanita. *Mrs. Ewing, Mrs. Molesworth, and Mrs. Hodgson Burnett*. London: Arthur Barker, 1950.
MacDonald, George. *The Princess and the Goblin*. Philadelphia: Lippincott, 1872.
Milne, A. A. "Children's Books." In *By Way of Introduction*. London: Methuen, 1929.
Molesworth, Mary Louisa Stewart. *'Carrots': Just a Little Boy*. London: Macmillan, 1876.
———. *The Cuckoo Clock*. 1877. London: Macmillan, 1933.
———. *An Enchanted Garden: Fairy Stories*. London: T. Fisher Unwin, 1892.
———. "How I Write My Children's Stories." *Little Folks* (July 1894): 16–17.
———. "Juliana Horatia Ewing." 1886. In *A Peculiar Gift*, ed. Lance Salway.
———. "On the Art of Writing Fiction for Children." 1893. In *A Peculiar Gift*, ed. Lance Salway.
———. "Story-Reading and Story-Writing." *Chambers's Journal* 75 (5 November 1893): 775.
———. "Story Writing." *Monthly Packet* (4th series, August 1894): 160.
———. *Tell Me a Story*. 1875. London: Macmillan, 1891.
Morrissette, Bruce. "Narrative 'You' in Contemporary Literature." *Comparative Literary Studies* 2 (1965): 1–24.
Parker, Dorothy. *Constant Reader*. New York: Viking Press, 1970.
Prince, Gerald. *A Grammar of Stories*. The Hague: Mouton, 1973.
Rimmon-Kenan, Shlomith. *Narrative Fiction: Contemporary Poetics*. London: Methuen, 1983.
Rossetti, Christina. *Speaking Likenesses*. London: Macmillan, 1874.
Salway, Lance, ed. *A Peculiar Gift*. Harmondsworth: Penguin, 1976.
Sellers, Peter. "Auntie Rotter." *The Best of Peter Sellers*, Parlophone, n.d., side 2.
Sircar, Sanjay. "Victorian Children's Fantasy: Mrs. Molesworth." M. A. Thesis. Australian National University, Canberra, 1980.
Spring, Howard. *My Son, My Son*. New York: Viking, 1938.
Thackeray, William Makepeace. *The Rose and the Ring; or, the History of Prince Giglio and Prince Bulbo; a Fire Side Pantomime for Great and Small Children*, by M. A. Titmarsh. 1854. London: Smith, Elder, 1855.
Tompkins, Jane, ed. *Reader Response Criticism: From Formalism to Post-Structuralism*. Baltimore: Johns Hopkins U P, 1981.
Turner, G. W. *Stylistics*. Harmondsworth: Penguin, 1973.
Woolf, Bella Sydney. "Children's Classics: Mrs. Molesworth and 'Carrots.'" *The Quiver* (series 3) 41 (June 1906): 675.
Woolf, Virginia. *A Room of One's Own*. 1928. Harmondsworth: Penguin, 1974.

Instructing the Children: Advice from the Twelfth-Century Fables *of Marie de France*

Harriet Spiegel

Children's literature, in the narrowest sense, might be said to begin with the first children's books, inventions of late-eighteenth-century publishers. But historians of children's literature generally go back to the invention of printing, identifying early books that attracted a broad readership or contained inviting illustrations that might have appealed to children. Warren Wooden, for example, addresses the supportive relationship between narrative and illustration in Renaissance printed books and suggests that the effectiveness of this relationship can be a gauge for a text's appeal to children.[1] Going back even further, Gillian Adams has extended the search to Sumerian clay tablets, identifying, in addition to school texts, literature of broad appeal that would probably have included children in its audience.

The Middle Ages, of course, knew neither printed books nor inscribed tablets but vellum manuscripts, the great majority of which were in Latin—religious texts and scholarly treatises kept in monastic libraries. What medieval secular literature survives may be but a small representation of a larger body of oral tradition. One such manuscript is a work that was widely known in the Middle Ages but did not reach print until the nineteenth century, and then in editions intended primarily for a scholarly readership.[2] This work, itself perhaps a product of both oral and written tradition, is the twelfth-century Anglo-Norman *Fables* of Marie de France, the earliest extant collection of fables in the vernacular of Western Europe.

As a genre, the animal fable may well be as old as storytelling: the short, often witty narrative, the projection onto the animal world of human vices and virtues, and the combination of whimsical fantasy and moral example have appealed to people of all ages. Because the fable is at once fancifully entertaining and didactic, it has throughout history been considered appropriate for children. Surviving records indicate that ancient Middle Eastern fables were

Children's Literature 17, ed. Francelia Butler, Margaret Higonnet, and Barbara Rosen (Yale University Press, © 1989 by The Children's Literature Foundation, Inc.).

included in the school curriculum of young students for their moral instruction, teaching, as Gillian Adams has noted, "the rudiments of literary language" as well as "the importance of understanding the nature of their place in a hierarchical society mirrored by the structure of animal society" (12).

The Aesopic fable as we know it today is attributed to an elusive historical Aesop, probably a sixth-century-B.C. Greek slave and illiterate teller of tales. The texts that survive are those of Phaedrus in Latin iambic verse and of Babrius in Greek verse. Although the witty sophistication of many of these fables was probably beyond the grasp of most young children, the fables are clearly intended to be instructive. Phaedrus frequently underscores his didactic message with a direct address to a broad and attentive audience, "the citizens of Athens." Babrius, however, has a specific young audience in mind; in the introduction to these fables he addresses "Branchus my boy" with the hope that he "may learn and fully understand from wise old Aesop."[3]

In the Middle Ages and the Renaissance the classical fable was kept alive in the schools, where the Latin texts of Romulus (based on Phaedrus) and Avianus (called the *Avionnet* and based on Babrius) were included in a young student's basic education (the trivium) as part of the study of rhetoric. The fables served as models of logic and argument as well as examples of moral behavior and were evidently extremely popular; many fable manuals survive. But Latin school texts do not a children's literature make.

Caxton's version of Aesopic fables, translated from a French version of the German of Steinhöwel and published in 1483, is the first printed collection of fables in the English language; no earlier manuscript collection in English survives. Although Caxton's work is not specifically directed to a young audience, most critical historians of children's literature in England begin with it (see, for example, Darton, Thwaite, Wooden).[4] Caxton's is not the first collection of fables in a vernacular of England, though; Marie de France produced her *Fables* three centuries earlier in the contemporary Anglo-Norman dialect of medieval French. Anglo-Norman French was then not only the spoken language of the aristocracy in England, but also the language of courtly literature.

Marie has received recognition in our day for her *Lais*, or verse narratives of love and adventure; but her collection of 103 fables, virtually unknown to modern audiences, was almost certainly the more popular work in the Middle Ages. Twenty-three manuscripts from the thirteenth to fifteenth century survive (a remarkable number for a secular work), as compared to only five manuscripts of the *Lais*. These expensive handwritten volumes on luxurious vellum, often highly decorated and gilded, would have been prized possessions of monastic libraries or wealthy patrons, carefully handled and brought out only on special occasions.

The impressive number of manuscripts suggests the popularity of Marie's fables but does not tell much about their specific audience. Identification of an audience before the days of the printing press is not easy; readership cannot simply be surmised from who owned —or even had physical access to—a given text. Many people may have "known" a written text by being present as it was read aloud or recited from memory. Whether children heard Marie's fables is a matter of inference, for we have no concrete evidence.

If, however, fables are a part of a literary tradition, might it help to know how Marie received these fables? Some stem from a written Latin tradition; the first forty are derived from Romulus, a popular medieval (fourth-to sixth-century) Latin prose paraphrase of Phaedrus. But more than half of Marie's fables have no known written source; for some there may have been a source now lost, but for many others hers seems to be the earliest recorded version.[5] Furthermore, while some of her fables, like those in the Latin school texts, are clearly part of a learned tradition, others seem to be decidedly less formal and are perhaps Marie's recording of oral narratives, fabliaux, or even jokes turned into fable form for inclusion in her collection.[6] In several ways, then, Marie's fables embrace two different literary traditions: one classical, the other contemporary; one learned, the other casual; one written, the other oral.

The fables are not written in the Latin of school and church but the vernacular. As vernacular literature these fables may well be aimed at the home, an audience that would certainly have included children. Indeed, as Allen M. Barstow has commented, "it is quite plausible to say that all vernacular fiction was directed toward an audience that contained children" (41).[7]

In addition to Marie's choice of the vernacular, her verse form, octosyllabic rhymed couplets, while conventional for secular narrative verse in her day, is a particularly effective form for public delivery, and especially for children. The short snappy lines, punctuated by rhyming end words, are easy to listen to and remember; one need not hear every word to get the drift of the story. To this day its English equivalent, iambic tetrameter rhymed couplets, remains one of the most popular forms for children's verse.

The fable, by nature didactic, is traditionally presented by a narrator instructing an audience. Marie introduces her collection in the context of a father instructing his son. Following the Romulus branch of Phaedrus, she claims in a prologue that her fables come from Romulus, who

> wrote to his son, enunciating
> and through examples, demonstrating
> how it behooved him to take care
> that no one trick him unaware. (ll. 13–16)
> [A sun fiz escrit, si manda,
> E par essample li mustra,
> Cum il se deüst cuntreguater
> Que hum nel p[e]üst enginner.]

This introduction, however, is formulaic, and serves more to place Marie's fables in the Romulus tradition than to establish her own particular audience. It is tempting to say that Marie, in presenting her fables as part of this tradition, meant also to appeal not only to the courtly audience of vernacular literature but also to the audience of the classical fable. Perhaps she had in mind young females who, instead of going to school and learning their Latin fables, would have stayed home to hear hers.

Indeed Marie's audience seems to have been as broad as Caxton's "al maner of folk"; the nature of the fable makes it readily accessible to many people, perhaps each hearing something different. While a child might enjoy the life-in-miniature mouse world of "The City Mouse and the Country Mouse," for example, an adult could appreciate the comparison of rural tranquility and urban stress, of innocence and experience. Marie includes many of the familiar fables of such universal appeal: the crane that extracts a bone from the wolf's throat, the dog that sees a tempting reflection of cheese in the water, and the fox that tricks the crow into dropping his cheese. She also includes less familiar tales, ones with no classical analogues for which hers is the earliest recorded version: the hare who wanted antlers on his head and then found he could not carry them around; the peasant who, overcome by curiosity, breaks his promise to the host-dragon that he would not crack open an egg he was to guard; the badger who, trying to pass as one of the pigs, gets slaughtered with them. Then there are some fables that do not seem appropriate to children. In "The Fox and the Bear" (#70) a victimized female bear is cruelly raped and teased by a cunning fox.[8] In "The Peasant Who Saw His Wife with Her Lover" (#44) and its companion (#45), a clever woman outsmarts her husband and justifies, continues, and delights in her adultery, a fable distinctively Marie's in its emphasis on female cleverness—French fabliaux analogues are more concerned with sexual victories and transgressions—but again not appropriate (I presume) for children.

Several of Marie's fables, however, not only seem well suited to children but directly address them or their well-being. Some are of particular interest for their comments on the instruction of children, for while fables are by nature didactic, some of Marie's fables make instruction itself their subject. Some question the appropriateness of a given lesson, others are about the teaching process itself. Some present a child actually being taught by a parent; just as the audience within the fable is a child receiving instruction, so the wider audience hearing the fable becomes the child of the fable heeding (or refusing to heed) the message, or the parent coping with such a child.

While several of these fables seem to address children directly, others sympathize with issues of concern to parents—and especially to mothers. These fables directed to parents are important in establishing an audience not only of parents, but most probably of their children; one may imagine a kind of sewing circle literature. Children, as Bennett Brockman has noted, were also present at social occasions when courtly literature was read or recited (59); and, for children not present or not attentive, these fables could well have reached them later, as a parent, true to the oral tradition of these narratives, would retell them at home. Marie's fables of child rearing cover the full range of childhood, from its anticipation, the pregnant mother, to late adolescence and the struggle for independence; this sequence corresponds quite closely to the order in which Marie presents these fables.[9]

Not only are many of Marie's fables addressed to a female audience; several speak specifically to women as mothers. Here Marie begins, quite naturally, with pregnancy. In two fables, "The Pregnant Hound" (#8) and "The Wolf and the Sow" (#21), Marie demonstrates that pregnancy is a condition for which women have special feelings, and in so doing she establishes a connection with the females in her audience. In "The Pregnant Hound," a generous female dog allows a pregnant dog into her home and then, after the puppies are born and begin tearing through the house and wreaking havoc, finds that her guests refuse to leave and instead kick her out of her own house. In Marie's version we identify primarily with the hostess dog; even though we see her as a weak victim of her own goodwill, we appreciate her generosity and compassion toward the pregnant hound. Marie's sympathetic identification with the hosting dog is not found in a fourteenth-century Old French analogue from the first *Isopet de Paris,* where the hostess dog, as soon as she lets the other into her house, is called *la sotte,* the fool.[10] Classical versions of this fable are much shorter than Marie's and focus on the general truth that goodness and generosity are rarely rewarded. Marie brings to the fable sentiment—the compassion of the first dog for a pregnant stranger, as well as the latter's highly staged conniving, tearful plea for pity. She also brings in domestic and human joys, pride in the appearance of her house, delight in the romping pups, even mention of their weaning.[11] These details suggest an audience of children; one can easily imagine their being amused by the antics of the naughty pups but also learning that naughty play can be unkind and hurtful.

In another fable about a pregnant animal, "The Wolf and the Sow," Marie directly addresses the females in her audience about their responsibilities as mothers. In this fable a wolf asks a pregnant sow to give birth immediately so he can eat her baby piglets. She responds,

> I cannot bear my young outright;
> I'm so ashamed when in your sight.
> Do you not sense the implication?
> All women suffer degradation
> If male hands should dare to touch
> At such a time, or even approach! (ll. 11–16)

The wolf beats his retreat. Here, as Marie separates the experience of childbearing from the world of men, she seems to be establishing an audience not merely of women but of women united by the common and exclusive experience of childbirth. Children in the audience might hear confirmation that childbirth was a mysterious event where their presence was not welcome but might also be reassured that their mothers would do anything to protect them. In a corresponding Latin version, the wolf tries to trick the sow by telling her he is a midwife (*obstetricis*), but she is not fooled (*Romulus Nilantii* II, 4). In Marie's fable, the issue is not the wolf's unsuccessful representation of himself as midwife, but his gender—*no* male should be present at childbirth.[12] The moral to Marie's fable speaks to all mothers about their urgent and primary responsibility of protecting their young:

> All women ought to hear this tale
> And should remember it as well.
> Merely to avoid a lie,
> They should not let their children die! (ll. 21–24)[13]

Again the Latin moral, "Don't yield to your enemies, no matter how flattering their talk," lacks the specific connection to females and motherhood.

That Marie has a particular sympathy for the pride of motherhood is made clear by comparing two other fables, one involving a proud monkey father and the other a proud monkey mother. "The Monkey King" (#34) in the corresponding Romulus version (*Romulus Nilantii* III, 5) as well as the earlier Phaedrus (IV, 13) tells of two men, one virtuous and the other wicked, who find themselves in monkey (or ape) land. When the monkey king questions the two as to the nature of his royal (monkey) court, the wicked one lies, saying he sees the emperor, and is rewarded; the virtuous one, replying truthfully that he sees only monkeys, is brutally killed. To this account Marie adds a lengthy introduction (one-third of the fable) humanizing the monkey king with details of how he carefully observes and then imitates (or apes) human behavior, and of how he acquires a monkey-wife and, in due time, a son. Then the monkey king, in questioning the two men, inquires specifically about his family: "Of me and of my wife let's hear, / And of my son whom you see here" (ll. 35–36). The honest man, alas, answers,

> You're monkey and she's monkey-esse,
> Ugly, wicked, hideous.
> As for your son, all folks can see
> He's just a very small monkey. (ll. 39–42)

In Marie's fable, then, to belittle anyone's son is the ultimate insult; the honest man pays for his true words with his life.

Just as the monkey's court is a mockery of true royalty, so, in this proud monkey father, Marie shows a perversion of fatherly pride. A medieval audience would have recognized that monkeys, especially those in fable, are by nature ugly and grotesque. The monkey's pride in his son is as misplaced—and as dangerous in its consequences—as his view of his nobility. This is the only one of Marie's fables of parent and child in which there is little sympathy for the parent; it is curious that this is also the only fable in which the parent is clearly a father.[14]

When Marie demonstrates a mother's pride, however, as in "The Monkey and Her Baby" (#51), her sentiments are clearly with the mother, even though she is a monkey:

Once there was a monkey-lady
Who showed all animals her baby.
They thought this mother quite absurd
Both in her manner and her word.
But then she did to lion go.
She asked him first if it weren't so—
That it was beautiful. Said he,
An uglier beast he'd yet to see.
He ordered her to take it home
And keep in mind this axiom:
"Every fox his tail does prize,
And marvels greatly that it's his."
Sad and depressed, she went from there.
Along the way she met a bear.
Stock still the bear stood and assessed her.
Then cunningly the bear addressed her,
"Do I see here that infant small—
The talk of every animal—
The beautiful and noble one?"
"Indeed," she said, "this is my son."
"Oh let me hold and kiss the dear.
I'd like to see it closer here."
She gave it to the bear, and he
Took it and ate it hastily.

And for this reason you should not
Disclose your secret or your thought.
Some things can bring delight to one,
Which to some others prove no fun.

Disclosure brings iniquity;
This world has no integrity.

Although the mother monkey was just as foolish as the father monkey in believing the world would find her little darling adorable and admirable, Marie's sympathies are quite different here. Marie differs also from Latin analogues to this fable that merely ridicule the mother monkey for her near-sighted pride. Here the bear is not simply exposing the mother to ridicule; he is cruelly taking advantage of her maternal pride and eating her child in front of her eyes. Instead of inviting us to laugh at the bear's cleverness in exploiting a doting mother, the sudden conclusion of Marie's fable leaves us shocked and saddened. Marie's moral underscores the difference between her fable and parallel versions. Instead of confirming a well-known truism, as does the Babrius moral: "This fable makes it clear to all . . . that everyone believes his own child is handsome" (Babrius 56), Marie's moral is unsettling. Though general in its expression, it once again speaks to women, telling them that they live in a world which will not appreciate their motherly pride. While implying that she understands their pride, she warns that the swelling heart should not be worn on the sleeve. In acknowledging her understanding of a mother's private thoughts, thoughts that can be expressed publicly only at one's peril, Marie establishes a close connection with the women in her audience.

Other fables will show that beyond tempering one's pride with discretion, a good parent must balance instinct with instruction, and know what can be taught and when it can be learned. Marie's fables address the question of appropriateness on two levels: some fables focus on the nature and nurture issue, whereas other fables look at the feasibility of parental instruction for children at different ages, from young childhood through late adolescence.

An understanding of the limits of nature and nurture, and of the balance between them, is important, indeed central, to any successful attempt to educate the young. While the animal world of fables is not the human world, it may be all the better for making clear the natural limits of what can be learned. Fable animals have stereotypical characteristics corresponding to human qualities, defined conventionally and (perhaps) biologically by the kind of beast each is: wolves, mean and sly, do not make good pets; a doe will not make an aggressive hunter. It may be easier, then, to witness a parent instructing a child in the animal world, for we think we know what to expect, what is appropriate.

The typically medieval belief that each creature has a rightful position in a hierarchy and that one's nature is determined by one's birth prevails in Marie's fables. Many of her fables begin with this assumption and come to this conclusion—but not all do. In "The Two Wolves" (#88), a fable with no known source or earlier version, two wolves resolve to change their nature and do some good. In a sincere attempt to be good wolves, they go out to the fields and try to help the peasants gather wheat; the peasants, however, unable to recognize their good intentions, reject their help and chase them away. Had the peasants been better able to see the wolves' higher motives, they might have had an easier day. Indeed, Marie's fable differs from a Latin version probably based on it (LBG 65).[15] There the men "naturally hate wolves" (naturaliter lupos odiunt), nature being a condition that cannot be changed. Marie's men simply "dared not be with the wolves" (nes osot atendre). Not only is the men's hatred thus not fixed in their nature; Marie's fable seems to suggest that even the wolf, the meanest and greediest of creatures, can change his ways, though the world may not be able to accommodate him.

The belief that those who are wicked by nature could change their ways is not, however, typical of either Marie or her time. The moral to this fable is wonderfully equivocal; rather than criticizing the peasants who, the fable makes clear, lost out on offered help, Marie rebukes those who, like the wolves, give up too readily:

> (He'll) find excuse however small—
> Whatever good he starts, he'll leave,
> Should he not then and there receive
> The praises that he thinks are due. . . . (ll. 32–35)

The variety of perspectives in these fables shows that Marie understood the complexity of the relationship between inherited nature and chosen intentions. Two of Marie's fables focus specifically on the question of nature and nurture as a factor to consider when teaching the young—which force is dominant, and what are the limits of each. Here, too, Marie eschews pat solutions; the fables in fact present contrasting perspectives.

In "The Lamb and the Goat" (#32), a young lamb looking for

his true mother comes to the realization that she who nurtured him, and not she who bore him, is truly his mother. In Phaedrus (III, 15) the lamb makes this observation while talking to a dog in the field: "It is kindness, not the kinship of nature, that makes parents." Marie changes the focus of this fable, replacing the dog with the foster mother herself, a nanny goat, thus underscoring the central mother-child relationship. Here the foster mother seems to have raised and guided her young charge very successfully. Nurture seems to have been more important than nature, as the lamb says:

> My reasoning, I think, is good.
> My mother's she who gave me food.
> For that's a better one than she
> Who carried then abandoned me. (ll. 13–16)

This fable seems to address not only mothers and their mothering, but also the children; indeed, it presents mothering from a child's perspective. It is the child's words that define good mothering. The language of the young lamb's response is simple and childlike, markedly different from earlier analogues. In Phaedrus (III, 15), as in *Romulus Nilantii* (II, 6), the child gives a lengthy and bitterly ironic discourse detailing his mother's indifference:

> I suppose it was a great kindness that she did me when she bore me to a life in which I expect a visit from the butcher any hour! How did she know whether her bairn was black or white? Besides, suppose she had wanted to bear a female lamb, what good would it have done her when, as it turned out, I was born male? Why should she, who was powerless to determine what she should bear, be preferred to the one who took pity on me when I lay helpless and who now by choice shows me a kindness that makes me happy?

These words do not sound like those of a child and would presumably have lost any listening child long before the first comma.

Perhaps Marie was more critical of the biological mother's neglect than supportive of foster care, however, for another fable makes clear that nature may limit the effectiveness of raising another's young. In "The Hawk and the Owl" (#80), the mother hawk and mother owl are such good friends that they share a nest, egg-sitting and caring for each other's young, but with unhappy results:

About a hawk I'll tell you next
Who in a tree trunk made her nest.
There was an owl in that tree, too.
They got along so well, those two,
That these birds did the same nest share,
They laid their eggs and hatched them there.
And then one year it happened that
The hawk upon the owl's eggs sat
And soon she hatched the eggs of owl
Along with her own birdies small.
And then she went to look for food
Just as her nature said she should.
But when she came back to her nest,
She found it all befouled and messed:
The owls had badly dirtied it!
And as the hawk in nest did sit,
She cursed and blamed the little birds
And scolded them with angry words:
This nest for twenty years kept she
With never such indecency!
Nor been by birds so mortified!
To her the little owls replied,
They weren't to blame for what was done.
Instead, she was the guilty one:
They'd diarrhea out the rear;
Of course that would in nest appear!
She answered, "What you say is so;
It is an easy thing to know:
For I can hatch owl's egg—I sit
And keep it warm and cover it—
But I cannot change nature's course—
Upon such nurturing, a curse!"
An apple, we can likewise see,
Once fell from a sweet apple tree.
Under a bitter tree it lay.
But it can't roll so far away
That someone biting it won't know
The tree that did this apple grow.
From one's kind, one can deviate
But one can never abdicate.

Marie's fable, the earliest recorded version, seems clearly directed toward women's interests—or, at least, toward their duties: the nourishment of one's young, the irritation of finding one's recently cleaned house all messed up, the pride in twenty years of good housekeeping, and the outrage at the present filth, both because it now needs to be cleaned up and because it is an insult to decency.

For all a mother's efforts, however, the fable shows that she must accept nature as stronger than nurture. The hawk bows to nature, leaving her nest to look for food as nature bids ("si cume nature le demande"). The narrative's concluding "nature-nurture" juxtaposition is not this translator's but Marie's own: "Nel poi fors mettre de nature— / Maudite seit tel nureture!" This fable speaks directly to mothers, and especially foster and stepmothers, who should thus realize biological limitations when caring for the young of another. The foster parent issue may have had special significance for Marie and her audience in light of the feudal custom of sending young children away to learn warfare and "courtoisie" in the manor of a great lord and his lady (Kelly 116).

The limits of nurture and of parental effectiveness are central issues in specifically instructional fables, those which present, within the narrative, a parent teaching her child (for in three of these four fables the parent is distinctly a mother). The instructional process, with its different forms for different ages of children, seems to have been of particular interest to Marie. One might expect to find many such instruction-related fables among those in the school curriculum, but for three of Marie's fables (#90, 92, and 93) hers is the earliest recorded version (though all three are included in LBG). In these fables nature and nurture seem to be in delicate balance: one can instruct one's young, but only so far. These fables of instruction also show an understanding of different ages of children: the younger child follows instruction even without understanding it; the older child may well understand but not heed.

In the fable "The Wolf and the Kid" (#90), the young kid follows his mother's advice and does not allow the wolf into his house:

> A she-goat wished, in olden days,
> To find a field where she could graze.
> She called her kid to her and said
> To heed her well: for she forbade
> His letting any beast inside—

By this, on pain of death, abide!—
No matter what their prayers or talk,
Not until she herself came back.
Then as she reached the forest land
Wolf marked her disappearance and
Went to the kid, there to implore
The kid to open wide the door.
He tried to sound like mamma goat.
The kid, in his reply, made note,
While he heard mamma loud and clear,
He did not see her body there:
"Get out of here! You plunderer!
You're not my mamma—That I'm sure!"
However, had the kid said yes
And let the wolf into his house,
On kid wolf would have had a feed! (ll. 1–22)[16]

This fable seems well suited to young children and may serve as an example that all parents can present to their children. Here is a good kid. He follows his mother's directions, even with his childlike partial comprehension of them. It is striking how convincingly this kid thinks and behaves like a child. His response to the wolf's attempted disguise is simple and innocent: He does not see mamma; therefore it is not mamma. This simplicity is lacking in a Latin analogue; there the kid responds with conclusions well beyond his years: "What I hear is my mother's voice, but you are a deceiver and an enemy trying to ensnare me by means of my mother's voice so as to drink my blood and eat my flesh" (Hervieux II, 153; Perry *Aesopica* 572). Even more striking is the parallel in the slightly later Hebrew version of Berechiah Ha-Nakdan, a collection which almost certainly included Marie's fables among its sources.[17] Here the little kid becomes a Hebrew sage: "The voice seems to be that of my mother, but I am afraid that *Lo-'Ami* [a reference to Hosea I 9; II 25] is now lying in wait beyond our walls. . . . Nobody will persuade me that the prophecy about the Wolf dwelling with the Lamb, and the Leopard lying down with the Kid [Isa. XI 6] is now to be finally substantiated! . . . Let not him that girdeth on his harness boast himself as he that putteth it off [I Kings XX 11] (Berechia XXI).[18] These mature responses not only fail to sound convincingly childlike, but they have probably left the children far behind; the simple and important message of Marie's fable—to mind your mamma, no matter what!—is likewise lost.

Of course not all little ones mind their mammas. In a fable that follows soon after, "The Doe and Her Fawn" (#92), Marie tells of a fawn who stupidly resists his mother's advice:

In olden days there was a doe.
She warned her fawn, who was in tow,
That he must keep watch everywhere,
And of the hunters must stay clear
And of all others he might meet
Who'd kill him for a bite to eat.
As they went walking, talking thus,
They saw a man who roving was,
With bolts and arrows and a bow.
The fawn called to the mother doe
And asked her who this man could be.
In answer to her fawn, said she:
"Of him you should be most in dread;
Fear him with all your might," she said.
"Look very closely at that man,
So if you meet him once again
You'll know to watch out when he's near."
Said fawn, "We have no need to fear.
I'm sure that he no harm intends.
Out of our sight he now descends,
Gets off his horse and tries to hide.
He sees us and is terrified."
"Oh no, dear son, you're wrong," said she.
"At first he watches carefully,
Preparing arrows all the while—
The tips of which indeed are vile.
If he should send one over here,
We'd feel it, certainly, my dear!
It's better that we run away."
The fawn replied to her this way:
"Until his bow's drawn, I won't flee—
No matter what my fate may be!"
For many men these words are apt:
Fools do not cry until they're trapped.

When fools don't heed what wisdom says,
They're dupes of their own stupid ways.

This fable is clearly intended to instruct the young. Even the introduction to the narrative is presented as a lesson: the doe is in the middle of teaching her fawn about the dangers of men in the forest when they happen upon a man who can be used as a living example of the day's lesson. The body of the fable then begins with the child's simple question of who that strange man might be. The language is childlike; the advice is given in carefully worded directions appropriate to the young. Here the mother has given sensible instruction crucial for survival—Beware of men!—but the fawn simply refuses to care even as he narrates the news of the hunter hiding and preparing his bow and arrow. The fable thus makes clear that the child both hears the warning and sees the danger; yet he does not heed. The moral, a contemporary proverb, addresses not just the children but all those who persist in stupid stubbornness (Morawski 788).[19] Marie's is the earliest known version of this fable. The Latin LBG omits the fawn's final reply, his obstinate refusal to run away, and thus leaves the impression that the fawn does not have the final and defiant word (Hervieux II, 611; Perry *Aesopica* 678).

In another fable of parental instruction, "The Kite and the Jay" (#87), it is not the child who stubbornly refuses to heed advice but the mother who refuses to do the child's bidding. This fable is also presented as an instructive dialogue between parent and child; the bird child seems older than the fawn of fable 92, for it is identified as simply a kite, not a young or baby bird:

A kite was lying in his bed;
He was quite ill, and so he said.
A jay had made his nest near by
Whom kite did frequently annoy.
Here's what the kite now thought about:
He planned to send his mother out
To beg for pardon of the jay
And ask that he, for kite's sake, pray.
"Mother, I ask you now," said he,
"Go beg the jay to pray for me!"
And she replied, "How can I go?
I don't know how to beg him so.
His nest you frequently have dirtied

And defecated on his birdies."
With foolish people it's like this:
Exactly where they've gone amiss
They cry for clemency and grace
Before they try to mend their ways.

Here the lesson appears to be directed to older children: your mother cannot be responsible for everything you do, nor can she fix all your mistakes. While this fable is found in Babrius (78), Marie's is significantly different. In Babrius the young bird has sinned against the gods, robbing their altars. There can be no remedy for such a crime—his mother weeps for his sin and for his impending and inevitable death. Marie's mother kite does not weep; we cannot tell from her attitude the seriousness of her son's illness or of his misdeed. In changing the crime from sinning against the gods to dirtying the jay's nest, Marie changes the tone of the fable. Indeed (and alas!) dirtying a nest is an act with which any child (and parent) can identify. The young kite is naughty, but not irrevocably wicked. Marie's mother kite does not weep for her young one, for he does not seem to be on his deathbed. There is hope. The final words of the moral suggest that the young kite can and should "mend his ways"! He, not his mother, should apologize to the jay, and he, not his mother, must stop dirtying the jay's nest and defecating on the little jays.

It is interesting that Marie's contribution to the tale, the dirtying of the jay's nest, presents an act similar to that in the fable discussed above, "The Hawk and the Owl," and again raises the question of nature and nurture. While the former fable noted that owls by nature will dirty a nest, here it seems equally clear that kites should not. What also seems important to Marie here is that the mother should distance herself; she should know when to help her child and when to be clear that he should be responsible for himself.

This question of independence, of parental withdrawal and letting go, is central to Marie's final parent and child fable in her collection, "The Crow Instructing His Child" (#93).

Next is a story of a crow
Who taught his fledgling long ago
He must not hang about with men
Lest they should maim and seize him then.
If he sees someone bending down

To grab a stick or find a stone,
He'd better fly off instantly—
Lest the man do him injury!
"If I don't see him stooping and
If I see nothing in his hand,
Then do I have to run away?"
The crow replied, "Enough, I say!
So fly away! Take care, my dear!
For of your life I have no fear.
And I," he said, "must go see how
To help my other birdies now."
A lesson from my tale now hear:
When someone does an infant rear,
Then sees him grow up shrewd and smart,
He should be happy, glad of heart!
Let him manage his own affairs,
And go help others cope with theirs.

This fable is similar to "The Doe and Her Fawn," the fable it immediately follows. Both present a parent giving advice to a child with the child apparently rejecting it. Both are in the form of a dialogue: the parent advising, the child questioning. The subject of both is the dangers of man and how to beware of him. And for both these fables, Marie's is the earliest known version. Yet there is one important distinction between them. In "The Doe and Her Fawn," the moral, although broadened to include all men (*hum*), is directed to the lesson which the child should learn—the child who would not heed the wisdom of his mother. In "The Crow Instructing His Child," however, the lesson is addressed to parents, to anyone who "does an infant rear / Then sees him grow up shrewd and smart." The child in this fable seems oldest of them all; Marie makes clear that now it is time for the parent to let go, to let this offspring "manage his own affairs."

Yet while the moral seems clear and sounds like the wisdom of experience, this fable is wonderfully ambiguous. The young crow's question in response to his parent's advice is puzzling and rings true for that reason. It is not at all clear what the young one understands or intends to do. Is his question that of a smart aleck? Is he playing with the warning, or does he truly understand and fear men? By contrast, in the Latin LBG the ambiguity is resolved; that young crow responds with commendable caution, "Even if he doesn't bend over, I'll fly away when he comes near" (Hervieux II, 612; *Aesopica* 679). Just as Marie's young crow is realistically noncommittal, the advice in her fable seems well suited to both parent and child: you can give your children the lessons they need to hear, but you cannot force good judgment upon them.

Marie's lively portrayals of childhood and the process of growing up, from infancy to maturity, suggest that her fables, even more than those in other early collections, would have been heard (and perhaps read), remembered, and enjoyed by a young audience. Her compassion and understanding of both children and parents —especially mothers—seem not only identifiably Marie's but also appropriate to her time. The twelfth-century rise of a courtly aristocracy had produced great secular interest in culture and the arts, an interest pursued by several important women. It was also a time for exploring the nature of the individual, with a sense of a growing tension between an inner quest for personal fulfillment and a public commitment to one's institutional obligations (see Benson and Constable, Dronke, Hanning, Morris, Ullman). Of course these fables cannot be read as a psychological blueprint for Marie or the age; indeed, practically nothing is known about the historical Marie who wrote these fables.[20] Yet the distinctive compassion found in her fables, particularly toward women and children, seems akin to the compassion for unfortunate lovers, victimized women and children in her *Lais*.[21]

While Marie's fables cannot strictly be considered "children's literature" in the modern sense of stories written and marketed specifically for children, some of them certainly qualify in the broader sense formulated by Gillian Adams for her examination of ancient Sumerian literature: "an imaginative literature which may or may not have been composed for younger children or directed at them, but which was considered particularly suitable for them and to which they were regularly exposed" (26). Although the nature of Marie's courtly audience can finally only be conjectured, albeit with some confidence, her extraordinary empathy with mothers and her perceptive portrayal of the various stages of childhood and childhood education suggest that at least some of these fables were specifically directed to children or written with particular awareness of their presence in a general audience. This in itself invites a new perspective on these remarkable poems.

Notes

Translations of fables reprinted courtesy of the publisher from *Marie de France: Fables*, ed. and trans. Harriet Spiegel, © 1987 by University of Toronto Press.

1. Wooden considers three works, Caxton's *Aesop* (1483), John Foxe's *Acts and Monuments* or *Book of Martyrs* (1563), and the *Orbis Pictus* of Comenius (1657), hoping "to illumine the tradition and suggest the surprising potentialities of picture and text coordination which prepared the ground for the flowering of children's picture books in eighteenth-century England" (2).

2. Marie's fables were first printed in 1820, edited by John-Baptiste-Bonaventure de Roquefort. The first complete critical edition was published in Germany in 1898 by Karl Warnke. The fable texts and translations cited in this paper are from Harriet Spiegel (1987). The Anglo-Norman text is based on Harley 978; the English translation is intended to render the octosyllabic French couplet in an equivalent meter and rhyme.

3. For an excellent introduction to the fable and its background, see Perry, *Babrius and Phaedrus*. All citations of fables and translations of Babrius and Phaedrus in this paper are from this edition and are identified by fable number.

4. While Caxton wrote with didactic intent "to shewe al maner of folk what maner of thyng they ought to ensyewe and folowe and also what maner of thyng they must and ought to leve and flee," he probably did not envision a specifically juvenile audience but rather, as he says, "al maner of folk" (Lenaghan, ed. *Caxton's Aesop*, Preface, Book Two).

5. There has been considerable speculation about Marie's source, if indeed she had a single one. She claims in her Prologue and Epilogue to be translating from an English collection of Aesop, in turn a translation from a Latin translation of Aesop's original Greek. Not only was Marie, along with her contemporaries, mistaken about the existence of a historical Aesop, no English manuscript collection of fables survives or is even known before Marie's time; I doubt its existence (see Spiegel 6–11). It was commonplace in the Middle Ages to attribute one's work to an authority, both as a sign of respect for tradition and as a way to establish credibility.

6. Similarly, in the Prologue to her *Lais* Marie claims to be recording Breton tales she has heard.

7. For a discussion of the literature medieval children may have known, see "A Symposium on Children and Literature in the Middle Ages," *Children's Literature* 4 (1975), 36–63, which, in addition to Barstow's article, includes those of William Robert McMunn, Meradith Tilbury McMunn, and Bennett A. Brockman.

8. While this fable may not be directed to children, the sympathy for the victimized bear is striking, and markedly Marie's. An analogue in the nearly contemporary Latin beast epic *Ysengrimus* ends the rape episode with the comment, "The book tells how she enjoyed these tricks" (Gauisam scriptura referet his lusibus illam) (*Ysengrimus* V, 181.17).

9. Marie's first forty fables are derived from a branch of Romulus called the *Romulus Nilantii*. These fables can be found in Hervieux II, 653–755; subsequent references are to this edition. While this paper considers the fables in the order in which they appear in Manuscript A (Harley 978, generally considered the best and most complete manuscript), it should be remembered that Marie was only partially responsible for establishing the order of the fables. The first forty fables in her collection follow the order of the *Romulus Nilantii*, and even for the rest it is possible that later scribes rearranged the fables to suit their own tastes, or that manuscript leaves or quires might have been scrambled (the earliest extant manuscripts are from approximately one hundred years—one, likely two, transcription generations—after she wrote them; no manuscript survives from her lifetime). Nevertheless,

the emphasis given to pregnancy in the early fables, despite their inherited order, is hers. It is also important not to take Marie's translation claim too literally. Translation in the Middle Ages was a loosely applied term, merely establishing one text's relationship, however broad, to an earlier text—"derived" might be a closer modern term. Even for the fables translated, or derived, from *Romulus Nilantii*, Marie adds her own details, her own emphasis, her own interpretation.

10. I am grateful to Howard Needler for pointing this out in his recent talk, "The Animal Fable among Other Literary Genres," presented at the New England Medieval Conference on November 22, 1987.

11. Marie's word for weaning, *espeldri*, seems to have mystified scribes who, to judge by the variety of nonsense words appearing in the manuscripts, did not recognize the word (or the process?).

12. That men should not be present at childbirth is a folk motif attested to by Stith Thompson (C 151); most of Thompson's citations are to the Child ballads.

13. This moral is problematic, for neither the wolf nor the sow seems to have said anything untrue. Other manuscripts of Marie's fables have here, instead of "merely to avoid a lie" (que pur sulement mentir: literally, solely for [the sake of] a lie), "only to save their own skins" (pur sulement lurs cors guarir), a line neither less nor more satisfying. See Spiegel 269.

14. Although the parent crow in fable 93 is grammatically male, and is therefore translated as a father, he is not identified specifically as a father in the fable.

15. Hervieux II, 610; Perry 676. Reference is to a collection of Latin fables, found in manuscripts in London, Brussels, and Göttingen and accordingly labeled LBG by Warnke (xlviii–ix), a collection slightly later than, related to, and derived in part from Marie's collection. These fables are in Hervieux II, 564–649, and Perry, *Aesopica* (660–692). Reference to Perry is to the number of the fable; these numbers also identify fables from *Aesopica* in the appendix of *Babrius and Phaedrus*, where they are given in translation.

16. Here the appended moral seems only loosely to support the fable; the kid wisely heeded his mother's advice and rejected the wolf's lies, and the moral generalizes from this situation to all people and all advice:

> Smart people therefore should take heed:
> Do not believe in bad advice,
> Nor, feigning truth, should you tell lies.
> For all can give advice, indeed,
> But not all of it should we heed.
> And men of falseness, men of vice,
> Will always give you bad advice.

17. For a discussion of the relationship of Berechiah's fables to Marie's, see the Introduction by W. T. H. Jackson to Hadas, *Fables*, and Schwarzbaum xxxii–xxxv.

18. The translation is Schwarzbaum's, as are the Biblical references (119).

19. "Fous ne crient devant qu'il prent." Reference is to the proverb as numbered by Morawski.

20. Unfortunately, we know very little about Marie herself beyond what can be garnered from her writing, the three literary works generally accepted as hers: the *Fables*, the *Lais*, and the *Espurgatoire Seint Patriz*, her translation of a Latin saint's life. There is no record of her life, of any marriage, children, or property. Well educated and probably a woman of means, she may have lived in a convent with a good library, as would have been appropriate for a single (if indeed she was) woman of her social position.

21. A good example of her sympathetic portrayal of women and children is the discovery of the abandoned infant girl in the lai "La Fresne."

Works Cited

Adams, Gillian. "The First Children's Literature? The Case for Sumer." *Children's Literature* 14 (1986): 1–30.

Barstow, Allen M. "The Concept of the Child in the Middle Ages: The Ariès Thesis." *Children's Literature* 4 (1975): 41–44.

Benson, Robert L., and Giles Constable, eds. *Renaissance and Renewal in the Twelfth Century*. Cambridge: Harvard University Press, 1982.

Brockman, Bennett A. "Children and Literature in Late Medieval England." *Children's Literature* 4 (1975): 58–63.

Darton, F. J. Harvey. *Children's Books in England: Five Centuries of Social Life*. 3d ed. Cambridge: Cambridge University Press, 1987.

Dronke, Peter. *Poetic Individuality in the Middle Ages: New Departures in Poetry, 1000–1150*. Oxford: Oxford University Press, 1970.

Hadas, Moses, ed. and trans., with an introduction by W. T. H. Jackson. *The Meslai Shu'alim: Fables of a Jewish Aesop*. New York: Columbia University Press, 1967.

Hanning, Robert W. *The Individual in Twelfth-Century Romance*. New Haven: Yale University Press, 1977.

Hervieux, Leopold. *Les Fabulistes latins, depuis le siècle d'Auguste jusqu'à la fin du moyen âge*. 2d ed. Paris: Firmin-Didot, 1893.

Kelly, Joan. *Women, History, and Theory*. Chicago: University of Chicago Press, 1984.

Lenaghan, R. T., ed. *Caxton's Aesop*. Cambridge: Harvard University Press, 1967.

McMunn, Meradith Tilbury. "Children and Literature in Medieval France." *Children's Literature* 4 (1975): 51–58.

McMunn, William Robert. "The Literacy of Medieval Children." *Children's Literature* 4 (1975): 36–41.

Morawski, Joseph. *Proverbes français antérieurs au XVe siècle*. Paris: Champion, 1925.

Morris, Colin. *The Discovery of the Individual, 1050–1200*. New York: Harper and Row, 1972.

Perry, Ben Edwin. *Aesopica*. Urbana: University of Illinois Press, 1952.

———. *Babrius and Phaedrus*. Cambridge: Loeb Library, Harvard University Press, 1965.

Riggio, Milla B. "The Schooling of the Poet: Christian Influences and Latin Rhetoric in the Early Middle Ages." *Children's Literature* 4 (1975): 44–51.

Schwarzbaum, Haim. *The Mishle Shu'alim (Fox Fables) of Rabbi Berechiah Ha-Nakdan: A Study in Comparative Folklore and Fable Lore*. Kiron: Institute for Jewish and Arab Folklore Research, 1979.

Spiegel, Harriet, ed. and trans. *Marie de France: Fables*. Toronto: University of Toronto Press, 1987.

Thompson, Stith. *Motif-Index of Folk Literature*. 2d ed. Bloomington: University of Indiana Press, 1955.

Thwaite, Mary F. *From Primer to Pleasure in Reading: An Introduction to the History of Children's Books in England*. London: Library Association, 1963.

Ullman, Walter. *The Individual and Society in the Middle Ages*. Baltimore: The Johns Hopkins University Press, 1966.

Warnke, Karl. *Die Fabeln der Marie de France, mit Benutzung des von Ed. Mall hinterlassenen Materials*. Halle: Niemeyer, Bibliotheca Normanica VI, 1898.

Wooden, Warren W. *Children's Literature of the English Renaissance*, ed. with an introduction by Jeanie Watson. Lexington: The University Press of Kentucky, 1986.

Ysengrimus, ed. Ernst Voigt. Halle: Buchhandlung des Waisenhauses, 1884.

Shakespeare for Girls: Mary Lamb and Tales from Shakespeare

Jean I. Marsden

On September 21, 1796, in a fit of madness, Mary Lamb picked up a knife and fatally stabbed her mother. Mary recovered and spent the remainder of her long life looking after her brother Charles and writing children's books, including the popular *Tales from Shakespeare* (1807). Mary's family and friends, it seems, were kinder to her than literary history has been; today she is remembered almost exclusively as the perpetrator of a lurid matricide. As a result, her role in the composition of *Tales from Shakespeare* has been almost completely overlooked. Mary began the project and wrote fourteen of the twenty tales (the comedies and romances), while Charles contributed versions of six tragedies. Although the book was Mary's idea and she was its primary writer, the *Tales* were published under Charles's name well into the twentieth century.[1] By ignoring Mary we overlook not only her contribution to *Tales from Shakespeare*, but, even more important, the ways in which she deliberately directed this project toward a female audience.

The "feminization" of Shakespeare took a variety of forms, for unadulterated Shakespeare was seen as improper for a delicate female mind (hence the publication of the Reverend Bowdler's popular *Family Shakespeare* within a decade of *Tales from Shakespeare*).[2] Where boys might expect to learn courage from Shakespeare's "manly book," girls had to be presented with a version of the plays which would encourage development of feminine graces —modesty, patience, and gentleness. Elements of gender were thus purposely written into the text of the Lambs' *Tales*, elements which previous critics have seemingly refused to see.[3]

Previous studies of *Tales from Shakespeare* have focused on Charles's dislike of heavily didactic children's literature and the ways in which the *Tales* oppose this didactic tradition.[4] While reintroducing imaginative fiction to children may have been Charles's aim, it was not Mary's main goal. In the first two-thirds of the "Pref-

Children's Literature 17, ed. Francelia Butler, Margaret Higonnet, and Barbara Rosen (Yale University Press, © 1989 by The Children's Literature Foundation, Inc.).

ace"—according to Charles written solely by her[5]—she stresses that the tales were designed for a specific audience: "for young ladies, too, it has been the intention chiefly to write" (vi). They are directed at girls, she continues, "because boys being generally permitted the use of their fathers' libraries at a much earlier age than girls are, they frequently have the best scenes of Shakespeare by heart before their sisters are permitted to look into this manly book" (vi). The *Tales* would thus fill a gap in the education of young ladies whose access to challenging imaginative fiction was limited. Boys would have little need for the *Tales*, not only because they were given an education their sisters lacked, but also because they were allowed access to their father's libraries. Mary suggests that these well-read brothers should assist their sisters and, after their sisters had digested *Tales from Shakespeare*, even read them passages of Shakespeare, "carefully selecting what is proper for a young sister's ear" (vi).

The *Tales* reveal in their emphases and omissions which aspects of Shakespeare the Lambs, their publisher, and their reviewers felt would benefit young ladies, and which they deemed inappropriate for them. The public agreed with Mary's description of the deficiencies in the education of girls, and when the second edition was published in 1809, it included a new "Advertisement" acknowledging its predominantly adolescent female audience: "It has been the general sentiment, that the style in which these Tales are written, is not so precisely adapted for the amusement of mere children, as for an acceptable and improving present to young ladies advancing to the state of womanhood" (iii). The *Tales* were "acceptable" because of their propriety and "improving" both in their tone and in their status as a young lady's introduction to Shakespeare; the advertisement also stresses that in the *Tales from Shakespeare* there was nothing to make a young lady blush.

Mary Lamb knew firsthand of the limitations girls faced. Although her brothers John and Charles spent several years in private schools, she herself was less fortunate. After six months of afternoon classes in a London day school, her parents took her home because of financial difficulties, and for much of her early life Mary supported the family by working as a seamstress while her brother Charles was in school. As a result, she learned only the rudiments of grammar and spelling (a failing she and Charles joked about frequently in later years). Her frustration over her lack of education was a key factor in the composition of *Tales from Shakespeare*.

This frustration is clearly articulated in the autobiographical story "Margaret Green," published in the Lambs' second children's book, *Mrs. Leicester's School* (1809), written shortly after *Tales from Shakespeare*.[6] Because this story deals explicitly with the issue of girls and reading, it serves as a useful gloss to Mary's goals in *Tales from Shakespeare*. An account of the dire effects of locking little girls away from books, the story presents a parable of the problems which Mary Lamb hoped that *Tales* would remedy.

In "Margaret Green" the title character tells of her childhood experiences living in a lonely old house where her mother worked as a paid companion to an elderly lady. Margaret finds herself isolated in this claustrophobic environment and cut off from all intellectual stimulation, not being allowed to read for more than a few minutes a day because of bad eyesight. Ignored by her mother, Margaret finds a locked door which, despite all her efforts, she cannot open. It is, of course, the library. Finally, after several days of hard work, she pries open the door and wanders inside, pulling down books at random. One particular volume, *Mahometanism Explained*, attracts her interest. Enthralled by the story, Margaret concludes she must be a Mahometan "because I believed every word I read" (51). In retrospect, Margaret comments that if she had it to do over, she would tell her mother "and ask her to permit me to read a little while every day in some book that she might think proper to select for me," but her mother rarely speaks to the little girl who "scarcely ever heard a word addressed to me from morning to night" (50). Locked in her isolation, Margaret does not dare admit that she has been reading without permission. Her estrangement is complicated by fears that her mother will perish unless she too can be converted to Mahometanism, but Margaret knows of no way to break through the wall of silence.

These conflicts bring on an attack of hysteria and fever.[7] A kindly doctor and his wife cure Margaret of her "Mahometan fever" by bringing her out of seclusion and giving her strong doses of amusement and education; along with the pincushion and work basket that Margaret is given, the doctor's wife buys Margaret a geographical game. (Sewing is obviously permissible for girls with weak eyesight—but not reading.) The combination effects a quick cure, and the doctor explains the real nature of the "fatal book"—the author really meant to expose the fallacies of the Mahometan faith, but so many pages had been excised that the message had become garbled.

In "Margaret Green" Mary Lamb outlines both the problems resulting from a girl's enforced lack of mental stimulation and the disasters of unsupervised reading. Forbidden to read more than the snippets approved by her elders, Margaret is driven to surreptitious reading which results in hysteria; as Mary Lamb suggests, hiding books from girls can be dangerous. The preface to *Tales from Shakespeare* states openly that the book is an attempt to combat such problems. While it may not be possible for girls to read independently, Mary stresses that properly supervised reading is a necessity. Shakespeare might be too strong for the sensibility of a young lady (as such moralists as Bowdler believed), but a modified version of Shakespeare could serve the same healthy educational purpose as Margaret Green's geographical game and the reading which she was denied. As author, Mary Lamb thus takes the place of the kindly doctor and his wife, while the uninterested mother can be seen as a representative of a tradition that sought to hold girls back not only from Shakespeare but from education in general.[8] Although *Tales from Shakespeare* cannot open the library door, it should at least fill a void in the intellectual life of a nineteenth-century young lady whose mother, like Margaret's, might fail to select wisely for her. The effect of reading *Tales* would be very different from that of reading *Mahometanism Explained*; the imagination would be satisfied while appropriate moral education was instilled.

The question of authorship must be addressed before any discussion of *Tales from Shakespeare* can begin. As the preface indicates, the Lambs divided up Shakespeare's plays along strict gender lines with Mary responsible for the comedies and romances and Charles handling the tragedies (presumably a more masculine subject). But such rigid distinctions distort the actual composition process, for, unlike the later *Mrs. Leicester's School* where the tales were written separately, the brother and sister collaborated closely on *Tales from Shakespeare*. As Mary writes to her friend Sarah Stoddard: "You would like to see us as we often sit writing on one table (but not on one cushion sitting) like Hermia & Helena in the Midsummer Night's Dream, or rather like an old literary Darby and Joan. I taking snuff & he groaning all the while & saying he can make nothing of it" (II, 229). Writing was a communal process. They may have worked initially on separate sheets, but they then passed these sheets across a shared table. As a result it is difficult (if not impossible) to distinguish precisely where Mary's work stops and Charles's begins; we know they began with different topics, but no significant distinctions exist in the finished product of collaboration.[9] I would argue that Mary was the informing presence; Charles disclaimed credit for the comments on audience (he claims Mary's part of the preface "hath a more feminine turn and does hold me up something as an instructor to young Ladies; but upon my modesty's Honour I wrote it not" (II, 256–7), yet his tales reveal the same patterns of feminization as Mary's.

Both Lambs were attentive to the moral effect their book would have on its young readers. Charles concludes the preface by suggesting that the *Tales from Shakespeare* will provide instruction and enhance its readers' lives as the plays themselves will do later: "What these Tales shall have been to the *young* readers, that and much more it is the writers' wish that the true Plays of Shakespeare may prove to them in older years—enrichers of the fancy, strengtheners of virtue, a withdrawing from all selfish and mercenary thoughts and actions, to teach courtesy, benignity, generosity, humanity: for of examples, teaching these virtues, his pages are full" (vii). This stated goal is particularly interesting when we remember that the "young reader" who would have been exposed to these tales and their moral lessons was a young *girl*. Charles's words echo those of Hannah More on educating girls: "She is to read the best books, not so much to enable her to talk of them, as to bring the improvement which they furnish, to the rectification of her principles and the formation of her habits" (I, 363). Young ladies are to garner moral lessons, not poetry, from reading. (As Mary admits in the preface, the greatest weakness of the tales is the loss of Shakespeare's language; yet, she feels, the essential instruction remains.)[10] *Tales from Shakespeare*, like the books More's young lady is to read, should encourage the reader to participate in appropriate social behavior rather than in literary discourse. Presumably, "talking of books" is a male activity unsuited to the polite young lady; Hannah More's strictures for women or girls against indulging in literary conversations seem to imply a transgression out of the perceived female realm. Along with censoring the aspects of Shakespeare which were too "manly" for a young female audience, then, the *Tales* were designed to instill lessons regarding proper female behavior.

The table of contents, with its emphasis on comedy and romance, immediately evokes the needs of the specialized audience. The omissions are notable—no Roman plays and no histories. The reason for these omissions lies in the plays' subject matter; standard fare for boys and young men with their vivid battle scenes and emphasis on politics, the plays concern subjects outside the "proper" feminine sphere. Instead, the works selected represent the private sphere and focus on either love (the romantic comedies) or family issues (as in *King Lear, Hamlet*). Only Charles's versions of *Macbeth* and *Timon of Athens* move outside of these categories to portray a more public, "masculine" realm, and *Macbeth* is, of course, also a play about marital influence.

Within the plays selected, many excisions were made. Although these omissions were necessary, as even summarizing Shakespeare's plays in their entirety would have been ungainly, the cuts follow a specific pattern. Like the eighteenth-century adapters of Shakespeare, Charles and Mary Lamb eliminated all examples of low comedy and most subplots. Bottom and the other workmen disappear from *A Midsummer Night's Dream*, the Gloucester subplot is cut from *King Lear*, and all clowns, fools, or other elements of slapstick farce vanish. As the Lambs admit in the preface, the task of representing these characters was more than they could handle; these figures would not translate well from drama into narrative. Even more important, these low comedy figures often spoke in crude terms and laced their speeches with sexual innuendo. Because such bawdy humor was believed to incite blushes rather than laughter in a female audience, Shakespeare's comedies had to be redefined for young ladies so that they became indistinguishable from his romances. In effect, love and the happy resolution of a marriage plot replaced humor.

As a result, love became the major focus for almost every tale. While love is central in many of the plays adapted, the omission of subplots and minor characters highlights its presence in several others, for love is the one element of the plot which is never abridged. The foregrounding of love also reflects the influence of the proposed female audience; according to common wisdom, women were constitutionally subject to love and other "soft" passions: "Their hearts are naturally soft and flexible, open to impressions of love and gratitude; their feeling tender and lively; all these are favorable to the cultivation of a devotional spirit. Yet while we remind them of these native benefits, they will do well to be on their guard lest this very softness and ductility lay them more open to the seductions of temptation and error" (More I, 368).

Such feminine softness demanded a revised view of both comedy and tragedy. All harsh edges—comic or tragic—had to be smoothed away in order to protect the perceived audience. Raucous humor or rough emotion threatened to coarsen feminine softness and thus destroy the precarious ideal of femininity. Love, the innate predisposition of the soft female nature, was the perfect antidote to such indelicacies. In "A Midsummer Night's Dream," for example, the absence of the clowns leaves only the central plot of the four lovers. A more extreme case appears in "The Tempest," where the tale becomes the story of Miranda and Ferdinand's developing love —Prospero creates the storm to net an appropriate lover for his daughter. Little remains of the other shipwrecked sailors (Sebastian and Trinculo vanish completely; only Gonzalo and Antonio are mentioned by name). In other plays, the Lambs similarly overemphasize the presence of love, especially if, in Shakespeare, this love plays a minor role. Hamlet's seemingly unloverlike behavior is carefully explained as hidden affection for "his dear mistress":

> Though the rough business which Hamlet had in hand, the revenging of his father's death upon his murderer, did not suit with the playful state of courtship, or admit of the society of so idle a passion as love now seemed to him, yet it could not hinder but that soft thoughts of his Ophelia would come between, and in one of these moments, when he thought that his treatment of this gentle lady had been unreasonably harsh, he wrote her a letter full of wild starts of passion, and in extravagant terms, such as agreed with his supposed madness, but mixed with some gentle touches of affection, which could not but show to this honoured lady that a deep love for her yet lay at the bottom of his heart. [270]

Hamlet thus becomes a lover struggling with two conflicting desires: love for Ophelia and the need to revenge his father's death. As a result, the play becomes a romantic tragedy, just as in other tales comedy and romance merge into comic romance.

Even questionable pairings are modified to conform to the ideal of romantic love. Macbeth and Lady Macbeth, bad role models in all other respects, are a loving couple. Any hint that marriage is less than happy, or that factors other than love motivate marriage, is carefully avoided. In "The Merchant of Venice," no mention is made of the three caskets or of Bassanio's interest in a rich heiress. Instead, Bassanio has long loved from afar and Portia marries him because she "loved him for his worthy qualities" (100). Similar modifications appear in "Measure for Measure." Whereas in Shakespeare's play Isabel does not respond to the Duke's offer of marriage, the Lambs' version tells us that she accepts "with grateful joy" the "honour" he offers her and that the two live happily ever after as "the mercy-loving duke long reigned with his beloved Isabel, the happiest of husbands and of princes" (213). More extreme changes are found in "All's Well that Ends Well." The disconcerting quality of Helena's marriage with the weak and peevish Bertram vanishes as Bertram comes to love and value his virtuous wife. The Lambs gloss over the unsavory elements of Bertram's nature; he does not sleep with the disguised Helena, nor does the play end with her pregnancy and his hesitant acceptance of his marriage. Instead, he comes to love Helena during a midnight conversation where "the simple graces of her lively conversation and the endearing sweetness of her manners so charmed Bertram, that he vowed she should be his wife" (166).[11] When he is confronted with the deception, he readily capitulates and happily agrees to love Helena. This expurgation manages to topple the original improbabilities of the bed trick into absolute impossibility.

Helena's revised relationship with Bertram is only one of numerous pieces of censorship. As Bowdler was to do only a decade later in his *Family Shakespeare*, incidents that could not with propriety be read aloud are carefully removed or altered. Mariana is married, not betrothed, to Angelo; Imogene carries a distinctive mole on her neck, not her left breast; the brothel vanishes from "Pericles"; and Timon of Athens encounters a solitary Alcibiades unaccompanied by whores. Where improprieties cannot be completely avoided, the Lambs skim lightly over them: in "Much Ado about Nothing," Hero is punished for being a "naughty lady, who talked with a man from her window" (57), and Desdemona's loss of Othello's handkerchief is described as "doing so naughty a thing as giving his presents to another man" (292). Except for "naughty" characters, sexuality vanishes from Shakespeare, thus reinforcing the emphasis on love.

More subtle changes appear in the moral lessons the *Tales* suggest. Although Charles and Mary—unlike other authors for children—rarely attach explicit morals to the tales,[12] they carefully construct a framework consistent with conventional morality, "a lesson of all sweet and honorable thoughts and actions." The tales' most radical alterations appear in the ways the Lambs shape the stories so as to teach this "sweet and honorable" behavior to a female audience. Following the lead of such educators as Hannah More and Mary Wollstonecraft, the Lambs emphasize humility, modesty, and gentleness, the virtues traditionally assigned to women.[13] The startling result is that, with the exception of "Macbeth" and "Timon of Athens," every tale details and highlights the experiences of women; even in "Hamlet" almost one-third of the tale is devoted to Ophelia's tragic life. In general, these female characters are presented as positive role models, their noble behavior highlighted by what the Lambs choose to summarize and by their editorial comments. For example, in "The Merchant of Venice," Portia's "graceful modesty" is stressed by the Lambs' praise for the way she "prettily dispraise[s] herself" (100). In "The Two Gentlemen of Verona," Julia fears she will lose her defining feminine features, her "noble maiden pride and dignity of character" (90) if she adopts male attire and follows her lover. Like Julia, the Lambs are acutely aware of what is befitting a well-bred young lady. Their characters establish standards for proper behavior in composite speeches and descriptions portraying a feminine ideal.

Improper role models are even more carefully pointed out and their improper behavior flagged for the innocent reader. The aggressive Lady Macbeth is a "bad, ambitious woman" (145) who comes to a terrible end, haunted by guilt for her evil deeds. Even essentially good characters, such as Olivia or Beatrice, are occasionally censored for unladylike behavior. Beatrice's verbal aggressiveness does not sit well, and through Benedict the authors point out that "it did not become a well-bred lady to be so flippant with her tongue" (51). Olivia makes a more serious error and forgets the "noble maiden pride" which Julia and the authors value so highly. Her infatuation with Caesario causes her to ignore both social rank and "the maidenly reserve which is the chief ornament of a lady's character" (220). In each case, the characters go against the ideal of the gentle, patient, and above all meekly passive woman. Only desperate circumstances, such as those faced by Portia or Rosalind, could justify breaking away from this ideal.

Following the examples set by contemporary educators, the *Tales* portray uncontrolled love as the greatest threat to a young lady's character.[14] It makes Helena in "A Midsummer Night's Dream" behave "foolishly" (25) and arises as a "hasty and inconsiderate passion" (246) in Juliet which leads her to a highly improper conversation with Romeo in the orchard:

> A crimson blush came over Juliet's face, yet unseen by Romeo by reason of the night, when she reflected upon the discovery which she had made, yet not meaning to make it, of her love to Romeo. She would fain have recalled her words, but that was impossible: fain would she have stood upon form, and have kept her lover at a distance, as the custom of discreet ladies is, to frown and be perverse, and give their suitors harsh denials at first; to stand off, and affect a coyness of indifference, where they most love, that their lovers may not think them too lightly or too easily won. [248]

This passage sends an unmistakable note of warning, a message emphasized by the shift from past tense, when describing Juliet's embarrassment, to present tense, when describing the preferred behavior of "discreet ladies." In the Lambs' world, standards for proper female behavior dictate against falling in love as Juliet did.

Although no comments are made concerning the male role in marriage, discussions of wifely duty appear throughout the *Tales* along with the guidelines for appropriate courting behavior. These discussions rest on the fundamental assumption that proper feminine behavior necessarily involves submission to masculine authority. Both "The Taming of the Shrew" and "The Comedy of Errors" provide cautionary tales of the disasters which can occur when women—married or unmarried—forget this standard. Katherine and Adriana nearly lose their chance of domestic happiness through their aggressive behavior; only when the two women repent of such unfeminine conduct are they awarded a happy ending. "The Taming of the Shrew" goes even further than its Shakespearean original in emphasizing wifely obedience, for its sense of closure depends upon stating what Shakespeare leaves implicit—Katherine's future status as the good wife. The tale ends: "Katherine once more became famous in Padua, not as heretofore, as Katherine the Shrew, but as Katherine the most obedient and duteous wife in Padua" (181). In other tales, such characters as Portia and Desdemona are praised for their willingness to submit to their husbands' authority. Despite Portia's learning and general good sense, she admits "with a meek and wife-like grace" to "submit in all things to be governed by [her husband's] superior wisdom" (102). She acts out of "the sole guidance of her own true and perfect judgement" (103) only in Bassanio's absence when she feels "called forth into action" by the "peril of her honoured husband's friend" (102).

Even the male characters in this retelling have feminine traits. The qualities stressed in the portrayal of male characters are predominantly such "feminine" traits as gentleness or patience. Although courage is identified as a specifically "manly" trait—as Ganymede, Rosalind attempts to project a "manly courage" (69)—courage is not as important, seemingly, as more feminine qualities. Only Macbeth, Othello, and Hamlet, all characters in Charles's tales, are described as courageous. Even in these cases the importance of courage is downplayed; Macbeth represents a bad example of courage, while Hamlet's courage is of less importance than his gentleness. The *Tales* lack almost any reference to the specifically masculine traits one would expect, had the work been directed at both boys and girls. Instead, male characters are either gentle (Orlando, Hamlet, Romeo, Imogen's brothers, and even Timon's servant Flavius) or patient (Pericles and Duke Senior). Thus the men in *Tales from Shakespeare* are refashioned so that they also can act as role models for the female audience.

But the readers must not be allowed to forget that important distinctions separate the sexes, and the *Tales* emphasize these distinctions by portraying the difficulties women encounter when they attempt to enter the male world. As Imogen discovers, simply changing from female to male attire does not affect womanly weakness: "She was with weariness and hunger almost dying; for it is not merely putting on a man's apparel that will enable a young lady, tenderly brought up, to bear the fatigue of wandering about lonely forests like a man" (118). Not only can women not put on a man's strength with a man's clothes; like Julia in "The Two Gentlemen of Verona," they find that the mere act of slipping out of their feminine attire threatens to destroy their femininity. Only extreme hardship can justify such a radical movement away from conventional female behavior, as in the case of Viola: "It was a strange fancy in a young lady to put on male attire, and pass for a boy; but the forlorn and unprotected state of Viola, who was young and of uncommon beauty, alone, and in a foreign land, must plead her excuse" (215). As it was highly unlikely that any of the Lambs' readers would find themselves in such a perilous situation, they should avoid such otherwise suspect conduct.

Even while disguised as boys, the female characters in the *Tales* remain explicitly feminine, a point which the Lambs stress through their repeated use of the adjective "pretty." "Pretty" appears throughout the *Tales* as a general synonym for feminine. The word rarely relates to appearance but rather to behavior; Julia speaks with a "pretty Ladylike childishness" (84) when she receives Proteus's letter, just as Cordelia "prettily express[es]" (141) her concern for her father in the closing pages of "King Lear." The word reestablishes the femininity of characters who might otherwise seem to be conducting themselves in a notoriously unfeminine manner. Women masquerading as boys are almost universally labeled as pretty: when Orlando meets Rosalind in disguise he is "much pleased with the graceful air of this pretty shepherd-youth" (74); Julia describes herself "with a pretty equivocation" (91), while Portia enters the courtroom "prettily disguised by her counsellor's robes and her large wig" (103). Even indirectly masculine behavior, such as swearing, is qualified by the feminine adjective, so that Desdemona responds to the account of Othello's adventures by swearing "a pretty oath" (282).

The *Tales* reinforce the importance of virtuous behavior through a gentle, but pervasive, moral tone. Divine justice overtly prevails in these stories so that virtue is rewarded while evil suffers. Laertes is "justly caught" in his own treachery (279), and the famous stage direction in *The Winter's Tale* is glossed "a bear came out of the woods, and tore him to pieces; a just punishment on him for obeying the wicked order of Leontes" (141). Readers are assured that heaven will not let virtue be unjustly punished so that the "justice of Heaven" (61) establishes the innocence of Hero in "Much Ado about Nothing." Divine providence even guides the feet of the characters; where chance might seem to lead Imogen to her brothers' cave in "Cymbeline" or the evil Duke to a hermit and subsequent conversion in "As You Like It", these coincidences, like the meting out of reward or punishment, are the province of a benevolent deity.

The Lambs use moral commentary in the same way that they use the happy resolution of love stories, as a means to effect closure, particularly when adapting plays whose endings were dark or difficult. Helena's patience gains her a reformed and sanitized Bertram, and the questionably happy ending of *Measure for Measure* is reshaped into triumph of love and virtue:

> Isabel, not having taken the veil, was free to marry; and the friendly offices, while hid under the disguise of a humble friar, which the noble duke had done for her, made her with grateful joy accept the honour he offered her; and when she became duchess of Vienna, the excellent example of the virtuous Isabel worked such a complete reformation among the young ladies of that city, that from that time none ever fell into the transgression of Juliet, the repentant wife of the reformed Claudio. And the mercy-loving duke long reigned with his beloved Isabel, the happiest of husbands and of princes. [213]

The Lambs' conclusion carefully ties up all loose ends, giving the tale a sense of closure conspicuously absent in Shakespeare's play. Not only does a joyful Isabel marry the Duke, but this resounding romantic conclusion leads to widespread moral order as Isabel's virtue works the changes neither the Duke nor Angelo could effect. Isabel represents the paradigmatic Lamb heroine, a figure whose virtuous example should reform the young ladies of the audience, as well as those of Vienna.

Even the bleak conclusion of *King Lear* is worked into the framework of virtue rewarded and vice punished. Evil is summarily quashed as the "justice of Heaven" overtakes both Lear's wicked daughters and Edmund (142); the fate of Cordelia and Lear presents more problems. Unlike the Tate adaptation of the play, still popular on the London stage at this date, the Lambs' version does not change the ending; the tale closes with the deaths of Lear and Cordelia. As many have observed, the Lambs admit that heaven is not always just:

> While the eyes of all men were upon this event [the death of the evil sisters], admiring the justice displayed in their deserved deaths, the same eyes were suddenly taken off from this sight to admire at the mysterious ways of the same power in the melancholy fate of the young and virtuous daughter, the lady Cordelia, whose good deeds did seem to deserve a more fortunate conclusion: but it is an awful truth, that innocence and piety are not always successful in this world. [142]

But the Lambs end the paragraph with moral commentary which links them once again with the long tradition of didactic children's literature: "Thus, Heaven took this innocent lady to itself in her young years, after showing her to the world an illustrious example of filial duty" (142). Cordelia is pointed to as an example of virtuous behavior, and the Lambs suggest, not that such behavior is its own reward, but that Cordelia reaped a heavenly reward, a happy ending outside of earthly confines.

As in "Measure for Measure," "King Lear" presents the female heroine as an "illustrious example," a figure whose behavior is designed to be emulated. (In this tale the Lambs provide divine authority for the idea of the role model as heaven itself "show[s]" Cordelia "to the world" as an example.) This discussion of Cordelia's exemplary nature epitomizes the function of the heroines in most of the tales. The passage also illustrates the *Tales*' insistence on poetic justice within the structure of the plot. These two features—the characters' function as role models and the stress on reward and punishment—work together through the implication that virtue will be rewarded at some level. "King Lear" represents the aims of the *Tales* as a whole; they are shaped to appeal to a specific audience, and, through the use of good and bad examples, they teach this audience an acceptable code of behavior.

Mary Lamb reached her goal of giving girls the access to Shakespeare that they might otherwise never have had. But the "Shakespeare" they were to read was not the literature their brothers knew. Rather, it represented the nineteenth-century ideal of what young ladies should learn from England's greatest poet; they were not to read his actual poetry for fear of moral contamination. Although the *Tales from Shakespeare* provided previously unavailable imaginative literature, the requirements of proper ladies' reading material demanded a certain adherence to moral expectations—regardless of the cost to Shakespeare's texts. In this the works of Shakespeare are not unique; they are merely the most prominent example of a gender-based division (and revision) of literature. For girls of Mary Lamb's time, the study of literature was subordinated to learning the dictates of feminine behavior. The library door was unlocked, but the books themselves were still out of reach.

Notes

1. Scholars have contributed to this neglect by focusing on Charles's tales; for example, although Joseph Riehl admits in his study of Charles Lamb's writings for

children that "it is impossible to disentangle their achievement and give credit to one and not the other" (84), he spends less than a page of his study discussing Mary's "achievement."

2. First published in 1818, *The Family Shakespeare* is subtitled "In which nothing is added to the original text; but those words and expressions are omitted which cannot with propriety be read aloud in a family." Bowdler states in his preface that the members of this "family" about whom he is most concerned are the women: "It certainly is my wish, and it has been my study, to exclude from this publication whatever is unfit to be read aloud by a gentleman to a company of ladies. . . . I can hardly imagine a more pleasing occupation for a winter's evening in the country, than for a father to read one of Shakespeare's plays to his family circle. My object is to enable him to do so without incurring the danger of falling unawares among words and expressions which are of such a nature as to raise a blush on the cheek of modesty" (x).

3. U. C. Knoepflmacher, in his article "The Return to Childhood through Fairy Tale in Ruskin's 'King of the Golden River,'" examines another example of feminization of children's literature in the nineteenth century. But, as Knoepflmacher argues, Ruskin's feminization of his protagonist arises from his own psychological makeup, not from a larger attempt to appeal to a female audience.

4. As, for example, the discussion of *Tales from Shakespeare* in *A Critical History of Children's Literature*. The emphasis on Charles's interest in imaginative stories for children appears as early as the late nineteenth century in such articles as "Battle of the Babies" by Agnes Repplier. In support of this argument, Charles's comment to Coleridge is cited almost more often than the *Tales* themselves: "Mrs. Barbault['s] stuff has banished all the old classics of the nursery; & the Shopman at Newberry's hardly deign'd to reach them off an old exploded corner of a shelf, when Mary ask'd for them. Mrs. B's and Mrs. Trimmer's nonsense lay in piles about. Knowledge insignificant & vapid as Mrs. B's books convey, it seems, must come to a child in the *shape* of *knowledge* . . . instead of that beautiful Interest in wild tales, which made the child a man" (*Letters* II:81). In reality, the *Tales* also bear a strong resemblance to the moral tradition of children's literature outlined and discussed by Mitzi Myers in her article on Mary Wollstonecraft.

5. As Charles notes in a letter to Wordsworth, "My part of the Preface begins in the middle of a sentence, in last but one page after a colon thus:—which if they be happily so done &c" (II, 256). Mary's section deals with style and audience; Charles's section, with the lessons to be learned from the *Tales*.

6. *Mrs. Leicester's School* consisted of ten stories, seven by Mary and three by Charles. The book was published anonymously and was very popular, running through eight editions in two decades.

7. Margaret's illness can be seen as an extreme example of the mental disorders that Florence Nightingale would later characterize as the result of holding women back from education. In *Cassandra*, Nightingale laments the direct and indirect social restrictions on women's education. She comments: "Women often strive to live by intellect. . . . But a woman cannot live in the light of intellect. Society forbids it. Those conventional frivolities which are called her 'duties,' forbid it" (37). Nightingale continues: "Women long for an education to teach them the laws of the mind and how to apply them—and knowing how imperfect, in the present state of the world, such an education must be, they long for experience, not patch-work experience, but experience followed up and systematized." When "starved" of such education and experience, women fall into daydreaming, at best, and at worst "incurable infancy" or even suicide.

8. It is tempting to read "Margaret Green" as a symbolic representation of Mary Lamb's own bouts with madness. Like Margaret, Mary was given sewing instead of reading to occupy her time. Her limited schooling gave way to the work as a

seamstress with which she supported her family until the breakdown occurred when she killed her mother. In reality, however, Mary suffered throughout her life from manic-depressive illness. Although the lack of intellectual outlet clearly contributed to the 1796 fit, the pressure of supporting her family economically coupled with her mother's indifference (and, according to some reports, continual nagging) were even more important factors.

9. I had hoped when studying the *Tales* to discover such a distinction, but, despite my efforts, I found that it was impossible to draw a clear line between Charles's and Mary's contributions. In the end I was forced to conclude that any attempt to draw such a line would create a distinction where none exists.

10. Mary comments that although she and Charles attempted to retain some of Shakespeare's own language, the tales cannot approach the beauty of the original works: "Faint and imperfect images they must be called, because the beauty of his language is too frequently destroyed by the necessity of changing many of his excellent words into words far less expressive of his true sense, to make it read something like prose; and even in some few places, where his blank verse is given unaltered, as hoping from its simple plainness to cheat the young readers into the belief that they are reading prose, yet still his language being transplanted from its own natural soil and wild poetic garden, it must want much of its native beauty" (vi). And if Bowdler is to be believed, even as grown women the readers of *Tales from Shakespeare* would encounter an abridged version of Shakespeare's language. He comments that in Shakespeare "many words and expressions occur which are of so indecent a nature as to render it highly desireable that they should be erased" before women read or hear the plays (viii).

11. Although the Elizabethan connotation of "conversation" as sexual intercourse still existed in abbreviated form in legal documents (adultery was referred to as "crim. con.," or criminal conversation) at the time the Lambs wrote, here the reference is clearly to the word's more common meaning of "talk."

12. The only exceptions to this rule are "The Winter's Tale," which reminds readers that Hermione's patience reaps a reward, and "Pericles." In "Pericles," however, the lengthy moral outlined in the tale's final paragraph is a close paraphrase of the speech with which Gower concludes Shakespeare's *Pericles*.

13. In *Thoughts on the Education of Daughters*, Wollstonecraft emphasizes all three qualities: "A constant attention to the management of the temper produces gentleness and humility, and is practised on all occasions, as it is not done 'to be seen of men'" (62). Commenting on female manners, Wollstonecraft states, "How bewitching is that humble softness of manners which humility gives birth to, and how faint are the imitations of affectation!" (31). She stresses the importance of such meek and self-effacing behavior when she praises the "shrinking" girl as the ideal standard for a young lady's conduct (20).

14. As cited above, More warns that the very softness which inclines a woman to love also can lead her into "temptation and error." Wollstonecraft goes even further, and in the lengthy chapter on love in *Thoughts on the Education of Daughters*, she identifies love as a great threat to stability and reason. Love causes normal people to behave improperly and induces much misery, especially for women. She advises young ladies to focus on good principles rather than attachment.

Works Cited

Bowdler, Thomas. *The Family Shakespeare*. [In which nothing is added to the original text; but those words and expressions are omitted which cannot with propriety be read aloud in a family.] 10 vols. London: Longman, Hurst, Rees, Orme, and Brown Paternostêr Row, 1818.

A Critical History of Children's Literature. Ed. Cornelia Meigs et al. London: The MacMillan Company, 1969.
Knoepflmacher, U. C. "The Return to Childhood through Fairy Tale in Ruskin's 'King of the Golden River.'" *Children's Literature* 13 (1985), 3–30.
Lamb, Charles and Mary. *The Letters of Charles and Mary Lamb*. Ed. Edwin W. Marrs, Jr. 3 vols. Ithaca: Cornell University Press, 1976.
———. *Mrs. Leicester's School and Other Writings in Prose and Verse*. New York: A. C. Armstrong and Son, 1900.
———. *Tales from Shakespeare*. 1st ed. London, 1807. Page references in this article are to *Tales from Shakespeare*. Ed. Sylvan Barnet. New York: New American Library, 1986.
———. *Tales from Shakespeare*. 2d ed. London, 1809.
More, Hannah. *The Complete Works of Hannah More*. 2 vols. New York: Harper and Brothers, 1836.
Myers, Mitzi. "Impeccable Governesses, Rational Dames, and Moral Mothers: Mary Wollstonecraft and the Female Tradition in Georgian Children's Books." *Children's Literature* 14 (1986), 31–59.
Nightingale, Florence. *Cassandra: An Essay*. Old Westbury, N.Y.: The Feminist Press, 1979.
Repplier, Agnes. "Battle of the Babies." (1895.) In *Children and Literature: Views and Reviews*, ed. Virginia Haviland. Glenville, Ill.: Scott Foresman and Company, 1973.
Riehl, Joseph E. *Charles Lamb's Children's Literature*. Salzburg: Salzburg Studies in English Literature, 1980.
Shakespeare, William. *The Riverside Shakespeare*. Ed. G. Blakemore Evans. Boston: Houghton Mifflin Company, 1974.
Wollstonecraft, Mary. *Thoughts on the Education of Daughters*. London, 1787.

Cleanliness and Class in the Countess de Ségur's Novels

Marie-France Doray

Translated by Margaret R. Higonnet

> *There is no such thing as absolute dirt: it exists in the eye of the beholder.*
>
> —Mary Douglas, *Purity and Danger*

In the mid-nineteenth century, even before Louis Pasteur's discoveries rationalized the struggle against dirt, dirtiness became a major preoccupation of the French bourgeoisie, who wove new links among filth, stench, poverty, and vice.[1] Uncleanliness became emblematic of immorality in a perceptual code of value that run-of-the-mill children's literature helped transmit. From its first years, the principal children's weekly, *La Semaine des enfants* (The Children's Week),[2] published numerous stories whose leitmotif was "poor but clean." In these stories the concern for cleanliness both masked and expressed the bourgeoisie's apprehensions about the "dangerous" working classes.

Only one of the authors who wrote that year for the *Semaine des enfants* is still known and read by French youth: the Countess de Ségur. Her nineteen novels, written between 1858 and 1869, shed special light on a critical moment in the formation of class relations and social values. This exceptional author rejected the new descriptive code, according to which cleanliness plays an essential *moral* role. Her sense of propriety in effect harks back to aristocratic definitions of manners that predated nineteenth-century bourgeois efforts to neutralize corporal excretions and exhalations; inner virtues take precedence over outer traits. For her, filth could be an undesirable result of physical circumstances or (on rare occasions) could even serve as a catalyst of hearty humor. As a realist, she charted the newly reinforced distaste of the bourgeoisie for the dirt of the lower classes. But she condemned the simplistic equation

Children's Literature 17, ed. Francelia Butler, Margaret Higonnet, and Barbara Rosen (Yale University Press, © 1989 by The Children's Literature Foundation, Inc.).

of dirt with vice; as a profoundly religious woman, she believed this moral arithmetic threatened the peaceable coexistence of rich and poor and undermined charity.[3]

As nineteenth-century adults struggled to repress the evidence of our natural drives, a split appears to have developed between parents and their children. The children, who only gradually internalized adult repugnance for dirt, natural functions, and odors, seem to have remained closer to the manners of an old Russian aristocrat than to the newer bourgeois mores.[4] What was true then is probably still true today. Ségur's treatment of these themes helps explain her persistent success among children.[5] At the same time, her explicit discussion of taboo material, especially bodily excretions (and corporal punishment), brought her condemnation by adults, including even Freud.[6]

"Poor but Clean"

There is no French proverb equivalent to the English Protestant "cleanliness is next to godliness," and yet by the mid-nineteenth century, this message was conveyed by many stories in the *Semaine des enfants*. The originality of the Countess de Ségur clearly emerges, if one considers the fiction in this weekly. A study of the narratives published in 1859 (a year when one of her novels also appeared there) indicates that, as a broadly accepted social norm permitting us to judge chance acquaintances, cleanliness displaced vulgar language and manners. Subtly, this new index of value led readers to reconcile the socially useful principle that "poverty is not a vice" with its subliminal opposite, a general suspicion of the poor or the nearly destitute. In later years, the encoding of dirt as vice in this journal became even more pronounced.

Even more than an author addressing adults, a children's writer must be careful to indicate whether new characters introduced into a narrative are good or evil. Concise moral adjectives may furnish this information ("the honest," "the sly") or physiognomic descriptions ("open-faced," "shifty"). Or a simple physical description may do: "A little boy of nine or ten years, modestly but cleanly dressed" (Plemeur 212), where "modest" is a measure of wealth, not character. To describe a character as "cleanly" dressed is to signal a "nice" person (and "nice" in English carries just this ambiguity), but the clue is valid only if the individual is poorly dressed—or even covered with rags. For the well-dressed person, cleanliness is a matter of course and cannot indicate moral value; yet within this logic, the poor upkeep of good clothes reveals moral weakness, as in a story about two children "in schoolboy uniforms." They loiter in the street on a school day; passersby judge them on their outfits: "Look how dirty their clothes are. Their caps are covered with dust. I bet they are idlers" (Jarry 117).[7]

In the nineteenth century much of the population bought its clothes secondhand, as Charles Aubin explains to his young readers: "The greatcoat disdained by the elegant gentleman and thrown out by his valet may still tempt the worker who wants cheap Sunday finery. . . . When old clothes have finished their city service, they close their working career in the country" (80). Thus, among those of modest income, it is not the style of clothing but the way clothes are maintained that tells us about an individual. When an author with the pen name "Marcel" wishes to present a couple of honest workers, he observes that the woman "wore the same dress four years long, but since she was very clean, she always seemed well dressed" (186). Her attractive appearance is plausible since the couple work regularly, have only two children, and live in proper lodgings.

Many narratives convey the impression, however, that cleanliness is always possible, even in extremely wretched conditions. One story, which elsewhere shows an avaricious and dishonest farmer's forehead bound with a "sordid" handkerchief, introduces an admirable poor family: "In a cramped hut, whose thatched roof was disintegrating in the rain, its door broken, on damp beaten earth, lived a young mother and her four children of whom the oldest was not yet six." Having lost their father, these wretches scarcely stave off starvation, and yet "all were charming in spite of their rags, and, a rarity among the poor, all were exquisitely clean" (Frank 183). Writers assume that even the most impoverished have the means to keep clean, as one story implies by showing a mother who washes and irons her children's only clothes while they lie naked in bed, so that they will be "fine" for church (Carraud, "L'Enfant" 43). Dirtiness, then, is a sign not of poverty but of negligence, of idleness. The rarity of cleanliness among the poor proves for writers like Frank and Carraud their lack of merit.

In these narratives, descriptions of the poor who are worthy of charity (which the sequel invariably awards them) are much more common than portraits of the undeserving poor. When a picture of the latter is drawn, it is invariably embellished with dirt. Thus in a tale set in Lyons, a rapidly industrializing city with a swelling population of workers, a beggar girl, whose mother has sent her out into the street with her ragged baby brother, reluctantly leads the charitable heroines back to her home. They pass through "dreadful narrow streets to a low door, which led into a courtyard like a deep well. There they found a dark, noisome den. Everything was dirty and in disorder in this awful hovel, where a drunken woman lay stretched out on a bed" (Carraud, "La Mendiante" 411). After reading this vivid description, we are grateful to the heroines for placing the children with a religious order.

The rarity of such detailed evocations of filth suggests just how offensive dirt had become. To make explicit for children such disgusting realities was not only shocking but immoral. Adult literature gives a much more precise idea of the new sensitivities and repulsions. Like doctors or social researchers, Honoré de Balzac, Victor Hugo, and Eugène Sue all drag their readers into dreadful narrow streets, noisome dens, and obscure hovels and give the painful impressions of such places in detail (see Chevalier 99–124 and passim; Corbin 146, 155–56, 168). Narratives for children convey the sensory changes that were distancing the honest bourgeois from the putrid poor more indirectly and tacitly. Yet even this elision exposes the new moral code, by which the poor merit their fate if they can't wash themselves. An unclean being either does not yet belong to civilization or no longer does; bourgeois and statisticians alike in the latter half of the nineteenth century perceive the working classes as "savages" or "degenerates" (Chevalier 359–417).

The moral value generally attached to cleanliness increased over the years. "Do you want people to think well of you at first glance? Be clean and decent; even the poorest can always manage it" (Bruno 26). This advice from the most famous of the Third Republic's manuals effectively summarizes dominant late nineteenth-century opinion. The evolution of the Countess de Ségur's work took the opposite course. If in her first novels she was content as a rule simply to avoid the equation between dirt and immorality, she actively sought in one of her last novels, *Diloy le chemineau* (Diloy the Tramp, 1868), to expose the falsity of these views.

Ségur's Perception of Cleanliness

In the last issues of 1859, *La Semaine des enfants* began to serialize the *Mémoires d'un âne* (Memoirs of a Donkey), and in these pages we find the only passage where Ségur used the theme of cleanliness as her contemporaries did—as a moral gauge that enables readers to judge characters they have just met. Even then, the information is immediately supplemented by other traits indicating character: "I saw a little isolated house that was quite *clean*. A simple old woman sat spinning at its doorstep. I was moved by her appearance. She looked sad but good." Preceded by his "soft voice," there appears a "handsome six- or seven-year-old boy. He was poorly but *cleanly* dressed" (ch. 3, p. 15, my italics).[8]

The passage is noteworthy because Ségur did not use cleanliness as a moral standard in the three novels she had previously published or in her sixteen later books of fiction. Her avoidance of the theme is all the more striking if we bear in mind Ségur's intensely realistic technique. She was careful, ordinarily, to describe the clothes of her characters, their diet, their income, and their furniture (Bleton). But Ségur drew the line when she came to the hygienic circumstances in which her numerous more humble characters might live. Thus, in the *Petites Filles modèles* (Model Little Girls, 1858), Madame de Fleurville organizes a search of the miller's home to find Marguerite's doll, but we get no clue as to the domestic skills of the thieving miller's wife. The butcher Hurel offers the visiting ladies from the château a glass of cider, but did he give them clean or dirty glasses? We remain uninformed. When the child Sophie wishes to help a poor woman, her house is described in unhurried detail, but once again, hygiene is not on the author's agenda. Sophie spends much effort in portraying the woman's tiny size and upright carriage, her ninety years, and her bed of ferns laid in an oven—but nothing beyond. The opportunity to describe moral worth through a reading of cleanliness is not taken up.

Household "virtues" were, to be sure, of interest to this writer-pedagogue. In her book on children's health, *La Santé des enfants* (1855), she gives detailed instructions on washing and powdering the folds of an infant's skin to prevent rashes and cracks. Her concern there is purely hygienic. And in the *Petites Filles modèles*, while Camille will teach the newly arrived child Marguerite to read, Madeleine proposes to show her "how to work, to arrange everything, and to put each object in its place" (ch. 4, p. 29). For upper-class girls, we may remember, cleanliness was a matter of course. Regardless of rank, however, good little girls in Ségur's social universe learn not only how to sew but how to do the wash and keep an orderly house.[9] Yet the key point is that these skills are treated as social, not moral, values.

Tellingly, cleanliness mediates relationships between the classes. When little James arrives at Madame Blidot's home, he asks for a chance to clean up his little brother (*L'Auberge de l'ange gardien,* ch. 2, p. 24). Or again, before going to the château at Blaise, the porter's son runs to a water barrel to wash his hands and face: "He rejoined Jules and the Count after he had washed and combed his hair" (*Pauvre Blaise,* ch. 3, p. 25), just as Julien washes and puts on a "faded but clean shirt" before visiting M. Georgey (*Le Mauvais Génie,* ch. 7, p. 58). What distinguishes these descriptions is Ségur's suggestion that the lower orders clean themselves in order to please their superiors—which leaves us to imagine their condition at other times, including moments when we clearly see them as virtuous. Ségur ordinarily introduces the reader to a poor character's propensity for clean living after having indicated other, more important traits of piety, affection, or skill. Cleanliness for Ségur was not the cornerstone of character, not a determining sign of virtue, as it was for her contemporaries.

Scatology

It would be wrong to suppose that Mme de Ségur's comparative reticence about matters of cleanliness arose from the usual desire to shield young readers of delicate sensibility. Paradoxically, the aristocratic countess describes scatological incidents which must surely have offended her bourgeois readers. Indeed, one wonders how these passages escaped the vigilant eye of her regular publisher, Louis Hachette. In 1857, Hachette had launched the *Bibliothèque rose* (Pink Library), a cheap but well-illustrated series for children, within the framework of his monopoly on books for the train system. The public function of the railroad "libraries" necessitated respect for the proprieties; they fell under imperial censorship, like the peddled chapbooks that they resembled by their price and broad public. Perhaps her success as the best-selling author of the series (Mistler 211–28) enabled her to avoid censorship.

Take, for example, the story told by Monsieur de Rugès in *Les Vacances* (Vacation Time, 1859). Asleep in a supposedly haunted room, the Marshal de Ségur dreams that a knight has revealed to him where to find a hidden treasure. How to mark the spot? "While musing, the Marshal felt sharp pangs in his entrails, caused by the anxiety of the knight's visit. He laughed, 'It's my guardian angel telling me how I can deposit a memento on this very precious stone.' . . . No sooner said than done, recounted a chuckling Monsieur de Rugès." The Marshal soon awoke, and "ill at ease in bed, got up. Everything had vanished, phantom and treasure, except the memento he thought he had left on the floor, which was in his sheets." How would he face his landlady? Oh, he reflected, a fire will solve my problems. I'll tell my hostess that spirits took the sheets, and I'll pay her for them ten times over (ch. 11, pp. 229–40).

The context in which the story is told gives some clues about the claims a respectable author for children makes to justify violating taboos. Signaling the unusual nature of this tale, Mme de Ségur introduces it by the remarkable observation, "This is a true story, which really happened to the Marshall de Ségur and was told to me by his son." (Rugès is an obvious anagram for the name of her husband's family.) A laconic footnote emphasizes that the anecdote is "historical" (ch. 11, p. 229). Her claim of historical truth might appease the censors.

A modern reader, however, may be surprised to learn that the noble Marquis Henri Philippe de Ségur, an important personage in the cabinet of Louis XVI, should himself have retold this story to amuse his children, or that the Countess de Ségur included it among those she passed on to her model granddaughters (Herz 12). The Burkean incivility of nobles, filtered from our consciousness today, was still a living presence for the Countess de Ségur. Born a Russian noblewoman, Ségur (née Rostopchine) described with some skill the impulsiveness and violence of her Russian milieu; imbued with French culture, as were all Russian aristocrats, she could also record the manners of the French aristocracy she married into. She was well aware of differences between a bourgeois and a noble sense of decency, whether French or Russian. Though the aristocracy no longer initiated social change or dictated the code of manners, it retained its social prestige in the Second Empire. We can infer that the Countess de Ségur relied on the bourgeois reader's respect for the aristocracy (Benjamin 148). By appealing to the aristocracy of her narrator, she smuggled her scatological material past the threshold of censorship.

The spirit of the time would not permit many more such bravura pieces, but there are traces of a similar taste for scatological jokes in a few of the Countess de Ségur's other works. Later, in *Les Mémoires d'un âne*, for example, Cadichon, the four-footed narrator, knocks the wicked boy Augustus into a ditch, which, as it happens, carries kitchen effluvia: "All sorts of sweepings were pushed into that ditch, where they rotted in the used dishwater and turned into a black and stinking mud, . . . the dirty water filled his mouth; he was up to his ears in the stuff" (ch. 21, p. 131). In 1859 it was already quite improper, as we have seen, to evoke cloaca or to describe noisome odors to children, but undoubtedly this comeuppance amused children just as much then as it does now.

Even more revealing are the mishaps of Georgey, a sympathetic and worthy English guest, which also provoke comic delight. As he clutches a turkey at arm's length, to avoid any accident, the poor animal realizes his worst fears (ch. 3, p. 26). Nor is this the end of it, since this symbol of fastidious Albion trips headfirst into liquid manure: "The Englishman got up, dripping with the black and fetid liquid. 'Oh! my goodness! Oh! my God,' he moaned lamentably (in English), unable to move" (ch. 4, p. 30). Since Georgey is fundamentally a positive character, his involuntary bath sharply distinguishes Ségur's rough-and-tumble comedy from the prudery and rigid descriptive codes of contemporaries.

As Alain Corbin has shown, the Europeans' sense of smell has not been constant. The enlightened and modern bourgeoisie made new demands of both flowers and perfumes, displaying a sudden and extreme intolerance for bodily and excremental smells. But as Corbin also shows, the lower classes resisted efforts at sanitation and deodorization, and the aristocracy treated such bourgeois injunctions with insouciance (211–21). The gap that sets Mme de Ségur apart from her bourgeois contemporaries shows up in her brisk description of the third-class compartment of that archetypally modern fixture, the railway: "The swaddled babies cried out, at times alone, at times together. The nurses fed the one, sang to the other, and shook yet another. Soiled diapers fell onto the floor, where they dried out and lost their repulsive odor" (*Les deux nigauds*, ch. 3, p. 256). One cannot miss the contrast, both of smells and of class consciousness, between such a passage and one in a letter from Flaubert to Mme Bonenfant: "The journey back was excellent, apart from the stench exhaled by my neighbors on the top deck of the coach, the proletarians you saw when I was leaving."[10]

A transitional figure, Mme de Ségur reveals in her attitudes toward dirt the continuities between aristocratic attitudes and popular "loyalty to an ancien régime of sensory values" (Corbin 211). Already in M. de Rugès's ghost story we can see a link between excrement and money that echoes such folktales as "The Wishing-Table, the Gold-Ass, and the Cudgel in the Sack." The connection between these themes and popular traditions interests her. For many humble people whom she respects, dirt and excrement have their place in a system of popular values and remedies, contributing perhaps to popular resistance to the new hygiene (see Loux 115–29). The father of Blaise successfully nurtures plant stems which Jules has broken by wrapping them in cow dung. His wife is no less successful in applying "Valdajou's cataplasm." "'Do you have what you need?'" inquires the Count de Trénilly. "'Why yes, thank you sir,'" she replies, "'I take some bran and put it in a pot, and I pour into it some . . . some . . . well, I just can't tell you what the liquid is. . . . I put it on the fire and when it's hot, I melt a candle into it. That's all!'" (*Pauvre Blaise*, ch. 19, p. 274). Not surprisingly, (literary) experience proves the good woman's cure to be more efficacious than the remedy proposed by the count's physician. Ségur uses this woman's deferential ellipsis, comically, to underscore an actual distance between classes. At the same time, her aristocratic lack of squeamishness leads her to treat the scatological elements of folklore sympathetically.

Odors of Sanctity

A religious concern helped Ségur resist the new bourgeois condemnation of squalor, lice, and bodily odors.[11] Take the following episode: The fourteenth chapter of the *Mémoires d'un âne* sketches the tale of an abandoned female child who is pitied by the little girls who own the donkey. This waif needs help; a hungry and homeless orphan, with ill-fitting wooden shoes, she lives by begging. Only when she is brought back to the château by her benefactresses do they notice her extreme dirtiness, on account of which the castle's servants reject the child. Little Thérèse, for whom a bath has been drawn, asks her mother for permission to bathe the waif instead: "She is so dirty that she is disgusting. So, maman, if you will allow it, she can bathe in my place. To spare my maid, I will undress her myself. I'll soap her. I'll cut her hair, which is full of rats' nests and white lice too, though they're not jumping about." Her mother wonders if the child can face it, and Thérèse answers, "If I were like her, I would be so happy if some one would take care of me" (ch. 14, p. 75).

To understand this scene we should know that Ségur profoundly admired the celebrated curé d'Ars, a man who refused to change his cassock since he cared more for God's housework than his own. Nauseous odors were for him an omen of our mortal decay (Corbin 218). He helped clean his school's cesspool and even followed the cleaners' vats to their dumping place. Scatological spirituality was not new, since the Church had encompassed also Benoît Labre's devotions, Luther's belief in the therapeutic value of excrement, and the practices of the "fathers of the desert," who were fascinated by their droppings and had eaten their own vermin (Guerrand 22). While not morbid herself, indeed known for her personal cleanliness (Hédouville 194), Ségur drew on these forms of religious feeling as a shield against the new disgust, which to her mind prevented contact with part of humanity and denied identification with ostensibly subhuman individuals.

Ségur's piety leads to physical pleasures and comforts, not self-mortification. The waif attracts charity, but she is also cleaned. "All four little girls took the orphan to the bathroom, where they undressed her, in spite of their extreme disgust for the child's filthy state and for the odors her rags gave off. They hurried to immerse her and to soap her from head to toe. They found pleasure in the amusing operation, and the waif for her part was enchanted. They soaped her down and held her in the water longer than they need have done. At the end, the orphan had had enough and was quite glad when her four guardians let her get out. They rubbed her down, and dried her so hard that her skin turned red. She was as dry as a ham when they slipped onto her a shirt, petticoat, and dress of Thérèse" (ch. 14, p. 77). Here as elsewhere, Mme de Ségur, rigorous Catholic though she may have been, was hardly impervious to the sensuous charms of the body.

Social Gaps or Harmonious Inequality?

We must distinguish Ségur's own set of moral values from her realistic representation of changes in moral values in the world around her. Even more than novelists who accepted the new code, she was attentive to its details and consequences. Her novels highlight two social transformations taking place in her world.

The first change concerns the desire of domestic or "body" servants to become refined, a desire for *embourgeoisement* that lends special value to such emblems as filth and stench—paradoxically so, since the same bourgeois phobias stigmatize servants and mark their distance from their masters (Guiral). Significantly, when Thérèse and the waif emerge from the washroom, the family's servants are impressed: "'It can't be the same horror that we saw a minute ago'"(77). The cook for his part exclaims, "'I would not have touched her if you gave me twenty francs.'" The kitchen maid, too, has acquired an olfactory sensibility like that of her masters: "'She really did smell bad.'" When an annoyed coachman reproaches her for her "too sensitive" nose (had she forgotten the grease and all the dirt from the pots she handled?), the maid, undaunted, replies to this servant who works outside the home, "'My grease and pots don't smell like manure, as do a lot of people I know'"(78). These servants, then, discern a hierarchy of odors, not just between rich and poor but among themselves, and they go so far as to attribute their own superiority to their ability to discern that hierarchy.

Precisely because social distances were in flux, those who wished to guarantee their own relative superiority on the ladder tried to reinforce social distances by physical separation.[12] The kitchen maid's distinction between house servant and stable servant underscores this point, as do several episodes in *Diloy le chemineau* (Diloy the Tramp, 1868). The new bourgeois elite insisted on its olfactory and perceptual distance from mere manual workers. Once again, Ségur aligns herself against what she perceives as the negative impact of the new refinement. Her portrayal of the hero Diloy, a deracinated railroad worker (*cheminot*), could even be described as a somewhat unsophisticated portrait of the new proletarian. His story unfolds against the backdrop of a struggle between two rich families: the ancient noble family of d'Orvillet, with their governess, and the recently ennobled and basically dishonest Castelsot (Foolcastles). The revealing figure here is Félicie d'Orvillet (aged eleven), the only member of her family who is seduced by the easy manners and pretensions of the Castelsot.

From the outset, Félicie finds it difficult to be with the poor and drags her feet when the family set out to visit some farmers.

Though it is half the distance to the Castelsot property, the farm, she thinks, "is so far." Félicie finds it humiliating to be gracious with "people of no account" (ch. 1, p. 248) and can't stand their proximity: "It displeases me, it annoys me. Their dirty hands disgust me; they smell bad; their hair isn't combed. I just hate it when they touch me" (ch. 24, p. 401). Félicie's speech makes explicit what the *Semaine des enfants* dares not say.

She is encouraged in these ways by her false friend, Cunégonde de Castelsot, who proposes to Félicie that if they must go to a peasant wedding, they will dance together "so as not to touch their dirty hands" (ch. 10, p. 305). Cunégonde's family and Félicie demand to have their own table set apart. A comic dialogue with the brother of the peasant groom reveals the social gap created by the new code of manners. Félicie complains that she does not have a fork (ch. 12, p. 317).

> MOUTONET: Excuse me, missy, there is one beside you.
> FÉLICIE: That's a dirty fork.
> MOUTONET: Excuse me, missy, Mother Robillard has just put a clean one.
> FÉLICIE: But I just ate with it.

When Moutonet objects that a "clean miss" can't soil a fork by eating with it, Félicie answers that the sauce certainly can soil it.

> MOUTONET: Oh, missy! All that isn't dirty! On the contrary, it's good!
> FÉLICIE (impatiently): How stupid this peasant is! Do give me a clean fork.

Predictably, Moutonet wipes the fork clean on a rag he finds in a corner and earns only the wrath of the prissy miss, as two radically different codes of cleanliness collide.

Félicie's own family (and Ségur) do not approve of her behavior: on the way home, her uncle denies that the Robillard home was dirty. "It was very clean and good; but . . . you played fastidious and squeamish like your friends. Next time you will behave better" (ch. 15, p. 336). The d'Orvillet may change settings between meals, but they do not disdain a meal or a dance with their farmers. Indeed, the uncle believes the social snobbery of the nouveaux riches Castelsot is a contagious influence: "Those people are a plague for you, and you know one should flee the plague-stricken" (ch. 15,

p. 335). The maid agrees: "Pride can be caught, like skin diseases" (ch. 2, p. 257). Ségur engineers the defeat of the Castelsot and their rejection by Félicie. The fact that Félicie cannot completely shake off this negative influence underscores Ségur's attention to early behavioral instruction. That Félicie is only partially enlightened suggests as well Ségur's perception that the French nobility was gradually being corrupted by the materialist values of a new age that fostered arrogance toward the people.[13]

Diloy le chemineau intimates that the scorn of the possessing classes may unleash a workers' revolt. In an early episode, Félicie meets Diloy, who offers to help her jump over some bundles of firewood blocking the path through the forest. "'Don't touch me, dirty old man!'" she cries and wrenches her hand away, only to fall down. As he bends to help her, she "kicks him right in the face, yelling, 'I don't want a peasant to touch me; let me alone, you unclean, gross, disgusting man!'" Then she spits in his face. Overcome—and his judgment impaired by a bit too much drink—Diloy explains that he broke a stick and "corrected" her (ch. 3, p. 263).[14] Although Félicie has been terribly humiliated, her family does not consider Diloy guilty, and the dedication goes so far as to call him "THE GOOD TRAMP." Against the current of the times, they never propose the reform of Diloy to greater temperance or cleanliness, but rather reward him with an occasional bottle of old wine.

Children's literature offers a very particular evidence for the history of mentalities. A period's taboos are inscribed there silently, while new, positive norms are often stated more explicitly than in literature for adults. Yet the contrast between the general tenor of *La Semaine des enfants* and the works of the Countess de Ségur suggests that part of her strength lies in her ability to escape this function of social reinforcement and conformism. Her reputation as a reactionary Catholic has kept us from rereading her works with care, and she has been condemned for legitimizing social inequality —or perhaps simply for showing social difference. Doubtless her reformism was reactionary, but her works are remarkable for their depiction of not only infantile drives but a broad social dynamic. She expressed physical realities that her contemporaries silenced as a first step toward converting infantile pleasures into shame and distaste and a further step toward guaranteeing the social order. In significant ways, she was not conformist at all.

The split reception of her work, her success among children and discredit among adults, suggests that she may have used, deliberately or not, anamorphosis, a technique that would be more systematically and consciously developed by her younger contemporary, Henry James (see Jean Perrot 332).[15] In children's literature, we may speak not only of successive generations of adult readers who assume new perspectives on a text (Nières 53) but of socially repressed material that remains closer to the threshold of perception for children, distinguishing their angle of vision from that of adult readers. Indeed, every writer for children may present one sense for adults, another for children.[16] Visibly, in an incident like the ghost story of M. de Rugès, Ségur ushers taboo material, guarded by codes of realism and aristocratic manners, past the threshold of censorship by her publisher and adult public. The code of realism indeed makes fecal clues "readable" as something other than what they are; perhaps her original readers, once grown, also repressed their memory of materials that formerly amused but might later shock. Today, a further shift in our perspective on infantile drives has reopened our eyes to Ségur's anamorphosis.[17] We are able to see that in her subversive approach to themes of dirt and filth, her refusal to equate dirt with moral disorder, she legitimates for her young readers their first, sensuous world, in which human relationships can cross class barriers and complexly intertwined feelings and perceptions are acknowledged rather than reduced to simplistic codes of value.

Notes

The author wishes to extend her thanks to Margaret Higonnet for what was more a collaboration than a translation.

1. In his historical study of changing customs, Norbert Elias shows that external constraints join interiorized interdictions to dictate the way our sensations are interpreted: *The Civilizing Process: The History of Manners* (1939, tr. 1978). The perceptual revolution between 1750 and 1850 concerning dirt and odors is the subject of Alain Corbin's *Fair and the Foul* (1982, tr. 1985). Pasteur's discoveries accentuated this trend at the end of the century, giving a scientific basis for the supervision of bodies and people.

2. This weekly published by Louis Hachette and the printer Lahure appeared starting January 3, 1857. In 1876 it fused with *Le Magasin d'éducation et de récréation,* edited by Hetzel (begun in 1863). Other weeklies of the period are more religious.

3. On the links between Ségur's belief in a paternalistic but providential Christianity and the duty to perform deeds of charity, see Herz 13.

4. Elias comments on the growing privatization of certain natural functions. Society gradually begins "to repress the positive pleasure component in certain func-

tions" by arousing anxiety and cultivating "displeasure, revulsion, distaste." "But precisely by this increased social proscription of many impulses, by their 'repression' from the surface both of social life and of consciousness, the distance between the personality structure and behavior of adults and that of children is necessarily increased" (142–43).

5. Only three French children's authors of this period have been regularly reprinted: the Countess de Ségur, Hector Malot, and Jules Verne. Only the last still interests adults. The best critical studies of Ségur are by Hédouville, Guerande, Bleton, Soriano, Caradec, and (unpublished) Muller. She continues to draw attention, as recent studies by Beaussant, Kreyder, and Vinson indicate.

6. In 1919 Freud held that the *Bibliothèque rose*, in which her books were prominent, stimulated children's beating fantasies ("A Child" 180*n*). Her "sadistic tendencies" were also condemned by Dr. Pichon, who thought parents should protect children from "certain stories ostensibly at their level that incessantly discuss corporal punishment; particularly the nefarious writings of Madame de Ségur née Rostopchine, dripping with sado-masochism, have had a fatal role in the genesis of libidinal perversions, and should be absolutely proscribed" (317). Isabelle Nières notes that adults like Ségur for their own conservative purposes but repress the elements of anguish and passion they find in her, as they cling to a myth of nineteenth-century bowdlerizing.

7. A printing error in the same story by Edme Jarry permits us to see how significant such means of discrimination may be. Jarry writes, "A rather cleanly dressed woman was seated on a bundle of mattresses," but the caption for the engraving reads, "A rather poorly dressed woman was seated on a bundle of mattresses." A printer has replaced "proprement" by "pauvrement," a slip encouraged perhaps by the qualifying "assez." The distinction is essential in this narrative economy: the woman, who awaits on her mattresses the arrival of the bailiff's wagon to carry away her furnishings, would deserve the charity of rich passersby if she were *cleanly* dressed; if she were *poorly* dressed, her furniture would be carried off without the author bothering to tell us about it.

8. Since there are so many competing reeditions of Ségur's novels, chapter numbers as well as page numbers are cited.

9. Among the many examples we may count Hélène de Trénilly (*Pauvre Blaise*), Natasha (*Générale Dourakine*), Lucie (*Les Petites Filles modèles*), and Caroline (*La Soeur de Gribouille*).

10. *Correspondance*. Paris: Pléiade ed. 1: 103. May 2, 1842.

11. On Ségur's religiosity, Herz comments, "She does not . . . shrink from scenes of violence," but she is also not a Jansenist who would guide children by fear; hers is "a gentleman's God" (19).

12. The French enforced such separation later than the English (see Guiral 90). One can make the same observation about the social geography of the Southern plantation house.

13. Through Félicie's incomplete reform Ségur indicates the importance of habits formed early while lending a realistic note to her moral tale.

14. Muller insists on a symbolic rape in this scene, whereas I find a suggestive rape fantasy. Diloy not only inverts the old feudal right of nobles to use violent punishment but challenges the new assignment of that right to the state. In another scene, Félicie and the Castelsot children provoke a mass reaction by little villagers and must be rescued by the adults.

15. In anamorphosis the artist may represent key material in such a way that its significance does not become apparent unless perceived from a particular angle; thus Holbein's "Ambassadors" reveals from the proper perspective that an amorphous object in the foreground is a death's-head.

16. I am grateful to Jean Perrot for leading me to this insight.

17. If today's writers are less overtly moralizing about matters of cleanliness than most nineteenth-century authors, what this means is less clear. Certain taboos (against spitting, for example) have not disappeared but have been widely internalized. The social contrasts have become inverted: families with modest incomes may be more strict, while members of the professional classes are inclined to be more relaxed, buying naughty rhymes for their children. Indeed, such scholars as Gaignebet study children's obscene folklore. Yet adult readers are still shocked by these features in Ségur, perhaps because they repress their memory of pleasurable childhood reading, or perhaps because she violates the norms of her own age.

Works Cited

Aubin, Charles. "Le Marchand d'habits." *Semaine des enfants* 62 (6 March 1858): 80.

Beaussant, Claudine. *La Comtesse de Ségur ou l'enfance de l'art.* Paris: Laffont, 1988.

Benjamin, Walter. *Reflections: Essays, Aphorisms, Autobiographical Writings.* Ed. Peter Demetz. Trans. Edmund Jephcott. New York: Schocken, 1978.

Bleton, Pierre. *La Vie sociale sous le Second Empire, un étonnant témoignage de la Comtesse de Ségur.* Paris: Editions ouvrières, 1963.

Bruno, G. [Mme Alfred Fouillée, née Augustine Tuillerie]. *Le Tour de la France par deux enfants.* Paris: Belin, 1877.

Caradec, François. *Histoire de la littérature enfantine en France*, ch. 8. Paris: Albin Michel, 1977.

Carraud, Zulma. "La Mendiante." *Semaine des enfants* 156 (24 Dec. 1859): 410–11.

———. "L'Enfant adoptif." *Semaine des enfants* 110 (5 Feb. 1859): 43–46.

Chevalier, Louis. *Laboring Classes and Dangerous Classes in Paris during the First Half of the Nineteenth Century.* Trans. Frank Jellinek. French original, 1958. New York: Howard Fertig, 1973.

Corbin, Alain. *The Foul and the Fragrant: Odor and the French Social Imagination.* French original, 1982. Cambridge: Harvard University Press, 1986.

Douglas, Mary. *Purity and Danger: An Analysis of the Concepts of Pollution and Taboo.* 1966. London: Ark, 1985.

Elias, Norbert. *The Civilizing Process: The History of Manners.* Trans. Edmund Jephcott. German original, 1939. New York: Urizen, 1978.

Frank, E. "Le Frère et la soeur." *Semaine des enfants* 131 (2 July 1859): 179–84.

Freud, Sigmund. "A Child Is Being Beaten." In *The Standard Edition of the Complete Psychological Works*, vol. 17, ed. James Strachey et al. London: Hogarth, 1955.

Gaignebet, Claude. *Le Folklore obscène des enfants.* Paris: Maisonneuve et Larose, 1974.

Guerande, Paul. *Le Petit Monde de la Comtesse de Ségur.* Paris: Les Seize, 1964.

Guerrand, Roger-Henri. *Les Lieux: Histoire des commodités.* Paris: La Découverte, 1985.

Guiral, Pierre, and Guy Thuillier. *La vie quotidienne des domestiques en France au dix-neuvième siècle.* Paris: Hachette, 1979.

Hédouville, Marthe de. *La Comtesse de Ségur et les siens.* Paris: Conquistador, 1953.

Herz, Micheline. "The Angelism of Madame de Ségur." *Yale French Studies* 27 (1961): 12–21.

Jarry, Edme. "Causeries après l'étude." *Semaine des enfants* 117 (26 March 1859): 98–104.

Kreyder, Laura. *L'Enfance des saints et des autres: Essai sur la Comtesse de Ségur.* Fasano, Italy: Schena-Nizet, 1987.

Loux, Françoise, and Philippe Richard. *Sagesses du corps.* Paris: Maisonneuve et Larose, 1978.

Marcel [pseud.?]. "Georges le jaloux." *Semaine des enfants* 128 (11 June 1859): 186–87.
Mistler, Jean. *La Librairie Hachette de 1826 à nos jours*. Paris: Hachette, 1964. 211–28.
Muller, Simone. *La Thématique de la stabilité dans l'oeuvre romanesque de la Comtesse de Ségur*. (Thesis "third cycle.") University of Strasbourg, 1978.
Nières, Isabelle. "De la métamorphose à l'anamorphose: Quelques adaptations des *Malheurs de Sophie*." *La Revue des livres pour enfants* 101 (1985): 52–60.
Perrot, Jean. *Henry James, une écriture énigmatique*. Paris: Aubier, 1982.
Perrot, Michelle. *De la Révolution à la Grande Guerre*. Vol. 4, *Histoire de la vie privée*. Ed. Philippe Ariès and Georges Duby. Paris: Seuil, 1987.
Pichon, Edouard. *Le Développement psychique de l'enfant et de l'adolescent*. 1936. Paris: Masson, 1947.
Plemeur, Charles. "Paul et Guillaume." *Semaine des enfants* 131 (2 July 1859): 211–15.
de Ségur, Sophie, Comtesse. *L'Auberge de l'ange gardien*. 1863. Grandes Oeuvres. Paris: Hachette, 1983.
———. *Les deux nigauds*. 1868. Grandes Oeuvres. Paris: Hachette, 1983.
———. *Diloy le chemineau*. 1868. Grandes Oeuvres. Paris: Hachette, 1983.
———. *Les Malheurs de Sophie*. 1859. Grandes Oeuvres. Paris: Hachette, 1982.
———. *Le Mauvais Génie*. 1867. Grandes Oeuvres. Paris: Hachette, 1985.
———. *Les Mémoires d'un âne*. 1860. Grandes Oeuvres. Paris: Hachette, 1982.
———. *Pauvre Blaise*. 1861. Bibliothèque rose illustrée. Paris: Hachette, 1888.
———. *Les Petites Filles modèles*. 1858. Paris: Librairie Générale Française, 1983.
———. *La Santé des enfants*. Paris: Hachette, 1855.
———. *La Soeur de Gribouille*. 1862. Grandes Oeuvres. Paris: Hachette, 1983.
———. *Les Vacances*. 1859. Paris: Librairie Générale Française, 1983.
Soriano, Marc. "Bibliothèque rose et Série noire." Preface to *La Fortune de Gaspard*, ix–lxiii. 1964. Paris: J.-J. Pauvert, 1972.
———. *Guide de littérature pour la jeunesse*. Paris: Flammarion, 1975.
Vinson, Marie-Christine. *L'Education des petites filles chez la Comtesse de Ségur*. Lyons: Presses Universitaires de Lyon, 1987.

Bibliographic Appendix

Aside from adaptations of *Les Malheurs de Sophie* and *Mémoires d'un âne*, there have been comparatively few translations of Ségur's work into English. Listed in chronological order, they are:

Fairy Tales for Little Folks. Trans. Mrs. Chapman Coleman and her daughters. Philadelphia: Porter and Coates, 1869.
The Adventures of a Donkey. Trans. "P. S." Baltimore: The Baltimore Publishing Company, 1880. Philadelphia: H. L. Kilner, 1880. Later translated as *Memoirs of a Donkey*. Trans. Marguerite Fellows Melcher. Illus. Lauren Ford. New York: MacMillan, 1924.
The Little Hunchback. Trans. C. Mulholland. Dublin: Gill and Son, 1884.
Sophie's Troubles. Trans. "P. P. S." New York and Philadelphia: P.J. Kennedy and Sons, 1889.
Princess Rosette and Other Fairy Tales. Trans. Virginia Olcott. Illus. Ben Kutcher. Philadelphia: Macrae Smith, 1930.

Only one translation is currently in print:

The Angel Inn. Trans. Joan Aiken. Illus. Pat Marriott. London: Jonathan Cape, 1976. (The preface, giving biographical information, was published in *The Horn Book*, December 1976.)

A Portrait of the Artist as a Little Woman

Beverly Lyon Clark

Alcott as submissive, Alcott as subversive, Alcott as ambivalent—these are dominant themes in recent reflections on Louisa May Alcott.[1] The same themes appear in Alcott's own writing about writing, when she writes about Jo March. Though Alcott gives some play to subversive ideas of self-expression, her overt message is that girls should subordinate themselves and their language to others. A little woman should channel her creativity into shaping the domestic space or shaping her soul. She can enact *Pilgrim's Progress* and learn to live as a Christian—to live by God's Word, or by John Bunyan's word, not by her own.[2]

Nineteenth-century male authors send a very different message to their readers. Jan B. Gordon notes that in works as diverse as the Alice books, Mill's *Autobiography*, and *David Copperfield*, the child "must reverse or otherwise overturn a prescriptive text that had kept him in a figurative prison" (179). The opposite is true for the girls in *Little Women*. Laurie may complain that "a fellow can't live on books" (62), rebelling against prescribed texts as other males do, but Jo must learn to stifle her rebelliousness and to forgive Amy for burning the only manuscript of her book, Jo's attempt to find her own voice.

In her other works Alcott shows a similar reluctance to rebel. Her adult novel *Work* may in effect rebel against its predecessor *Jane Eyre*, but only in the service of a higher submission. The heroine, Christie, objects to Charlotte Brontë's portrayal of Rochester: "I like Jane, but never can forgive her marrying that man, as I haven't much faith in the saints such sinners make" (80). Then Christie enacts her objection to *Jane Eyre* by marrying not the Rochester-like Mr. Fletcher but David Sterling, a type of St. John Rivers, with whom she undertakes missionary work at home; and a symbolic bedroom fire is caused not by the madwoman in the attic but by Christie's dangerous penchant for books. Alcott rebels against the romance of *Jane Eyre* not so much to find her own voice as to submit

Children's Literature 17, ed. Francelia Butler, Margaret Higonnet, and Barbara Rosen (Yale University Press, © 1989 by The Children's Literature Foundation, Inc.).

herself to the divine and masculine allegory of *Pilgrim's Progress*. Christie's very name recalls those of Christian and Christiana, and in her progress through temptations she eventually achieves a state of grace, with the help of a character compared to Mr. Greatheart. Thus Alcott's rebellion against a predecessor text is not so rebellious after all: it is a reworking of the secular *Jane Eyre* in order to submit to the higher truths of *Pilgrim's Progress*, a reworking that underscores the searing dangers of books to women. She rebels not to find her own voice but to modulate it in the heavenly chorus.[3]

In *Work* Alcott stifles her predilection for the lurid and sensational, much as she has suppressed her blood-and-thunder tales (first by publishing them anonymously or under a pseudonym and then by turning instead to juveniles). In a telling entry in her diary, at age eighteen, she notes, "Reading Miss Bremer and Hawthorne. The 'Scarlet Letter' is my favorite. Mother likes Miss B. better, as more wholesome. I fancy 'lurid' things, if true and strong also" (Cheney 63). Eighteen years later, in her own writing, Alcott has submitted to the preferences of her mother, the arch-representative of the family, giving up the gothic for domestic realism, banishing the "skeleton in the closet." Or hiding "behind a mask," as so many of Alcott's strong gothic heroines do, concealing her passions and longings behind the passionless and virtuous facade of her "marble women."[4] Alcott's reworking of *Jane Eyre* (one of fifteen items in an 1852 list of books she liked) is more a self-chastisement for her sneaking fondness for things gothic, more an act of penitent submission to Christian godliness than a rebellion against a predecessor text.[5]

In *Little Women*, too, Alcott stifles the sensational—or at least hides it. In the first volume it still lurks just below the surface. Thomas H. Pauly points to the contrast between the romantic literature that the girls read and their plain lives, a contrast that signals both Alcott's innovation, the way she calls "attention to the drama and impact that could attend the commonplace," and also the "notable deficiencies that Alcott perceived in the very environment she strove to recommend" (123). Or perhaps in *Little Women* the two tendencies are in creative tension, the sensational not yet as fully repressed as it will later be: Ann Douglas suggests that "Alcott hoped to let sensational and domestic fiction educate each other" (238).

Still, the surface message in *Little Women* is that the March sisters should aspire to domesticity and moral goodness. *Little Women* may not enforce submissiveness as much as some of Alcott's other books for girls do—Jo is remarkably rebellious for a nineteenth-century girl. And some of her eventual taming may result from Alcott's sense that fiction for girls ought to teach feminine virtues—Alcott may simply have been acceding to the constraints of the form. Yet she chooses to submit to these constraints (and also to the constraint of writing popular books that will earn money for her family). Jo, too, eventually submits to the constraints of what her culture considered seemly feminine behavior.[6]

According to this cultural definition of the feminine, art and fiction are suspect, self-control preferable to self-expression. Such self-control requires control of language; and, significantly, the two girls with artistic aspirations, Amy and Jo, are also the two who need to learn greater control of their language. Janice Marie Alberghene has suggested that each tries "to forge a personal style," Amy having too great a weakness for the ornamental, Jo for the sensational (21). Certainly Jo is fond of slang and strong language, of saying "pegging away" for "studying," and of using phrases like "desperate wretches," making Meg chide her for using such "dreadful expressions." Later, in volume two, Jo is largely cured of her weakness, perhaps in part because she has acted out its extreme manifestation by becoming Mrs. Malaprop at a masquerade party (much as she seems to be cured of writing partly from having sampled the extremes of thrillers and virtual sermons).

Amy, too, is guilty of excess in both art and language in volume one but overcomes both excesses by the end of volume two. Early on, she tries to use impressive words but commits malapropisms, using "label" for "libel," "samphire" for "vampire," "fastidious" for "fascinating." Likewise, she is fond of drawing ludicrous caricatures, which "came fluttering out of all her books at unlucky moments" (49). By the end of the first volume, though, she has learned to control her language and to channel her creativity into religion, to model her life after *Pilgrim's Progress*, to meditate in front of a picture of the Madonna instead of drawing one herself. What creativity she does allow herself is a tribute to domestic bliss: she sketches the engaged Meg and Mr. Brooke. By the end of the second volume she recognizes her own lack of genius and happily submerges personal in domestic achievement, tastefully arranging curtains rather than an artist's draperies. She may be allowed the indulgence of molding a model of her baby, but only in case this second Beth dies, "so that, whatever happens, I may at least keep the image of my little angel" (531).[7]

Much as art should not be Amy's supreme goal, writing should not be Jo's. Jo should outgrow it, like her strong language and her tomboy exuberance.[8] Alcott undermines the value of writing, yet she cannot dismiss it altogether, for she herself is Jo, she herself is writing. Initially, Alcott endorses writing; especially in the first volume, fiction allows Jo to enact her masculine fantasies of power. She can assume male roles in the plays that she writes and in meetings of the Pickwick Club, where, as Augustus Snodgrass, she gives her word as a gentleman. Writing fiction gives her an arena where she can express herself, express her anger, instead of just tightening her lips to suppress it as her mother teaches her.

The other girls, too, though less strikingly, find in the stories they invent an outlet for self-expression—and also self-revelation—before they submerge themselves in domesticity. For *The Pickwick Portfolio*, the family newspaper, Meg writes a romantic story of the Lady Viola's wedding to an apparently impoverished suitor, unconsciously anticipating her own marriage to John Brooke. Housewifely Beth writes a homely tale of the life of a squash, grown by a farmer, baked by a little girl, and eaten by the Marches. Irresponsible Amy writes a note of apology for not writing anything.

Stories similarly allow self-expression and self-revelation when a group of young people plays Rigmarole, a game in which players take turns telling a story, one picking up the thread where another leaves off. Although the game affords Alcott a chance to display stylistic virtuosity—the segments are variously romantic, gothic, adventurous, humorous, or Polonius-like combinations thereof—it also sheds light on the characters. It reveals the tellers' literary tastes and hints at matters important to them. Mr. Brooke, for instance, tells of a poor knight who tames a colt and longs for a captive princess, much as he has been taming Laurie and longing for Meg. Shy Beth characteristically prefers not to participate—as if she knows the dangers of fiction and chooses not to indulge.[9]

The game also celebrates creativity and self-expression, as becomes clearer if we compare it to a similar game in Charlotte Yonge's popular family story, *The Daisy Chain* (1856). Quite possibly Alcott wrote her episode in response to the British one, for Alcott's game is introduced by a British visitor, and the whole chapter plays Britain against America: the American friends, as if inspired by "the spirit of '76," defeat the British family at croquet, even though one of the British boys has cheated; nor is the British young lady's tendency to condescend to young women who earn money, as Meg does, endorsed. On some level, it seems, Alcott wants to show how the American family story can outdo the British, and how accepting money for one's writing (instead of channeling it to religious and other charitable causes, as Yonge did) is worthy. In any case, while all the players of Alcott's Rigmarole have been influenced by their favorite reading, the segment told by the boy who cheated at croquet is even more derivative, jumbling together phrases and facts from a single book—from *The Sea-Lion*, as Laurie recognizes. And it's clear that such plagiarism is not praiseworthy.

In *The Daisy Chain*, however, a kind of plagiarism is endorsed. The story game is, to begin with, rather different: various people tell someone stories incorporating an agreed-upon word until the person can guess what the word is. The story segments are related semantically rather than syntactically, metaphorically rather than metonymically. The game thus invites allegorical stories, focused on the key word, rather than the wide-ranging inventiveness fostered by Rigmarole. The young girl Flora tells of a girl who becomes the first woman to achieve the glory of ascending Mont Blanc; the story is a thinly veiled allegory of Flora's own ambitions, particularly her later political ambitions for her dullard husband. Her father tells of a hummingbird who considers itself "vain and profitless" but whose master tells it that by valuing its own bliss and praising its master it "conduces to no vain-glory of thine own, in beauty, or in graceful flight, but . . . art a creature serving as best thou canst to his glory" (287, 288). As for the heroine, Ethel, an engaging and lively girl like Jo, she too tells a story distinguishing between worldly and heavenly glory, about princes competing to serve the ladies Vana Gloria and Gloria: the one prince, trying to conquer worlds, finally discovers Vana Gloria to be vain and ugly; the other, staying at home and being good to his subjects, finds his Gloria, still lovely, as he dies. Here is an allegory particularly apt for Ethel, who learns to seek her glory—to glory in her duties—close to home.

Significantly, Ethel does not invent her story; she has modified a tale from an old French book. Yet such plagiarism does not call forth censure here, implicit or otherwise, as it does in *Little Women*. Far from it. Ethel has enacted what the story preaches—by not seeking earthly glory through her own originality but, in a devout and womanly fashion, assimilating the moral in another's work.

As for the secret word in Yonge's story game, it is, of course, "glory." And much as we have learned its true meaning in these transparent allegories, so do we learn it in the book as a whole. The young people are not to pine after earthly glory, we are later told, but to discover that "charity is the true glory" and that letting God's will be done can release an exulting "cry of Glory" (600, 641).

Thus is the reader invited to read *The Daisy Chain*, more chained by religious allegory than *Little Women*, just as its language game is more constrained. For, compared to Ethel, Jo is granted considerable freedom; Ethel is more willing than Jo to accept her constraints, more willing to give up her writing. The differing imports of their nicknames are emblematic. Josephine lays claim to male prerogatives when she becomes Jo. Ethel, on the other hand, is short for Etheldred. As a younger child she had been nicknamed King Etheldred the Unready—King for short—the overt significance being her childhood tendency to be a little slapdash with household duties. Yet the nickname is also male, appropriate for someone who chafes more than her sisters do against traditional expectations for women. She finally settles, however, for the feminine Ethel, thus reversing Jo's progress, outgrowing the male and becoming female. Or rather, Jo's progress is a little more complex, for when in later volumes Jo becomes Aunt Jo or Mrs. Jo, both gender oxymorons, she highlights the tensions between the two tendencies toward domestic and literary creativity that she continues to embody.

Not all the stories in *Little Women* are as self-expressive as the Rigmarole ones are; some are constrained by allegorical shaping. In the chapter called "Burdens" each girl tells a story, or rather a vignette, of her experiences that day. These stories are not so much outlets for self-expression as reflections on each pilgrim's progress. The girls are morally shaping their lives, allegorizing them, rather than creatively expressing their feelings. Jo tells of interesting Aunt March in *The Vicar of Wakefield* in lieu of Belsham's Essays; Meg tells of a disgrace in the society family where she works as a governess; Amy tells of the embarrassing punishment meted out to a fellow pupil; Beth tells of seeing Mr. Laurence's act of kindness to a poor woman. True, the stories are expressive insofar as the girls reveal aspects of themselves. It is fitting that Jo tell a story about the attractions of fiction, that Meg tell a story about the attractions of society, that Beth tell a story of selfless generosity, that Amy tell a story of the horrors of embarrassment (anticipating her own experience later at school). Yet the girls are learning, in their monitory stories, to channel their feelings in socially acceptable ways: they are learning both how to behave (like Mr. Laurence, not like the fellow pupil) and how to channel storytelling.

The culmination they should aim for is the selflessness of Marmee —a selflessness and devotion she then enacts by glossing their stories. For Marmee tells a transparent allegory about four girls who learn to become happy by counting their blessings: "One discovered that money couldn't keep shame and sorrow out of rich people's houses; another that, though she was poor, she was a great deal happier, with her youth, health, and good spirits, than a certain fretful, feeble old lady, who couldn't enjoy her comforts; a third that, disagreeable as it was to help get dinner, it was harder still to have to go begging for it; and the fourth, that even carnelian rings were not so valuable as good behavior" (54). Just as the girls tell stories here to shape their lives more than to express their feelings, Marmee provides a final shaping, one that unifies the stories, much as she unifies the family. Furthermore, she subtly revises the moral of Jo's potentially subversive story—from the pleasures of fictional escape to the advantages of Jo's own lot—much as she subtly revises, redirects, Jo herself.[10]

Writing is thus double-edged, enabling expression or repression, or both. Some of Jo's other fictions likewise aim not so much at self-expression as at accommodation: they allow her, as she grows older, to come to terms with domesticity. She works through her adjustment to domesticity, in part, by writing of it in "A Song from the Suds." The poem joins the virtues of domesticity and moral goodness. She can physically "wash and rinse and wring" and wants further to "wash from our hearts and souls / The stains of the week away" (190). Her writing here has been tamed to laud domestic and moral virtues—as has Alcott's own in *Little Women*. And again Jo follows a male model, Bunyan, for she creates an allegory out of the ordinary. Yet for all its surface compliance the poem is subtly subversive. There's humor in the mere idea of "A Song from the Suds" as moral literature. And instead of simply living *Pilgrim's Progress*, as Marmee has enjoined, Jo is rewriting it, much as Alcott herself has done.

Thus Alcott remains ambivalent—about writing, about self-expression, and about gender roles. A key emblem of her ambivalence is Jo's cutting of her hair, ambiguously masculine and feminine. The daring action itself may be "masculine," as may the shorn hair, but the sacrifice of a prized possession for the benefit of others—so that Marmee can travel to her ailing husband—is "feminine." Further complicating the gender valence is the echo of Samson and Delilah. For Delilah was active, not passive, and Samson's shorn hair became a sign of masculine weakness. The traditional gender boundaries were blurred, decisive action associated with the female, long hair associated with physical strength. Moreover, Jo plays Delilah to her own Samson—she is ambiguously, perhaps ambivalently, both artist and art object, both Samson and Delilah.[11]

By the end of the first volume, though, Jo becomes more object than artist, more conforming, less wildly imaginative: her father is proud of her for becoming "a young lady who pins her collar straight, laces her boots neatly, and neither whistles, talks slang, nor lies on the rug as she used to" (294). Jo learns to restrain her exuberance, in both writing and action, and to submit to her proper role—and to God: to submit both to the Word and to the words of Bunyan's text. She must learn to curb her "abominable tongue"; she must channel her creativity into living, "replac[ing] her pen with a broom" (137); she must forgive Amy for burning a precious manuscript. Thus Jo's writing recedes into the background, eventually stopping. At the end of the first volume she is presumably still writing, but we see less of it and its fruits. It could be that she no longer needs to act out her melodramas and instead channels her earlier public exuberance into writing done behind the scenes. More likely, though, Alcott simply had to submerge this self-expressive writing since, according to the ethic she wanted to espouse, submerging the self and caring for others are more suitable to a little woman than self-dramatization and self-expression.

Jo's submersion in domesticity can be gauged, in part, by the submersion of her fictions, including her dramatic fictions. On the first Christmas the melodramatic adventures of Don Roderigo and Zara are so compelling that both stage scenery and "dress circle" collapse. Even here, though, Alcott feels the need to justify staging Jo's play: "It was excellent drill for their memories, a harmless amusement, and employed many hours which otherwise would have been idle, lonely, or spent in less profitable society" (24). She is not altogether comfortable about giving free reign to creativity. Certainly such exuberant self-expression is not appropriate for the grown women the little women want to become. As

Karen Halttunen suggests, the play "permits Jo's theatrical violation of true womanhood only within a larger ritual of family harmony," enabling Jo to act out "the moral struggle raging within her" and thereby "to control the destructive potential of her inner demon" (244, 245). The following year the drama is muted and more fully absorbed into the life of the family—the girls seem to follow Marmee's early advice and recognize that *Pilgrim's Progress* "is a play we are playing all the time in one way or another . . . not in play, but in earnest" (17). The melodramatic romance of Don Roderigo and Zara has become the more prosaic one of John Brooke and Meg. The play is absorbed not only into the plot but also into metaphor: the volume has become "the first act of the domestic drama called 'LITTLE WOMEN'" (258). Much as Jo learns to suppress anger, all the girls—and the narrator—learn to suppress melodramatic fictions.

And much as drama gives way to drama metaphor, fiction gives way to fiction metaphor: the stories of the Pickwick Club and the game of Rigmarole dwindle, by the end of the first volume, to story metaphors. Meg no longer needs romantic fictions because she lives her own novel: she "felt like the girls in books"; John might act "like the rejected lovers in books"; he then "looked decidedly more like the novel heroes whom [Meg] admired" (229, 249, 251). As the narrator tells us, "Now and then, in this work-a-day world, things do happen in the delightful story-book fashion" (241). The volume concludes when "Father and Mother sat together, quietly re-living the first chapter of the romance which for them began some twenty years ago" (258).

This taming of exuberance, this attempt to control it through metaphor, reverses the movement of the contemporary *Alice's Adventures in Wonderland* (1865). Lewis Carroll did not attempt to justify his excursion into fiction by making it moral. He simply sought to entertain Alice Liddell and to find a means of self-expression. Thus the book literalizes metaphor: "mad as a hatter" engenders a Mad Hatter; "mock turtle soup," a Mock Turtle. The book is profoundly liberating, granting the imagination creative freedom—even if Carroll does try to recant at the end, making the adventure just a dream. *Little Women*, on the other hand, metaphorizes the literal. It grounds Jo's early imaginative flights, and it similarly grounds the dangerously fictive, constraining it in metaphor. Like the budding poet in Alcott's "Mountain Laurel and Maidenhair," Jo "put her poetry into her life, and made of it 'a grand sweet song' in which beauty and duty rhymed so well that the . . . girl became a more useful, beloved, and honored woman than if she had tried to sing for fame which never satisfies" (158–59). Still, the mere existence of the fiction metaphors may remind us of the earlier fictional flights, of the potential for imaginative, not just imaginary, freedom.

The effects of this shift in *Little Women*, this absorption of fictions into the plot, are several. One is to show the domestication and maturing of the little women: they have outgrown their childish reliance on stories and now live them, as they try to live *Pilgrim's Progress*. Another is to lift the book itself into the never-never land of story: the book loses some of its reality, becoming more of a romance, receding from our everyday world in part because of its saccharine sweetness but also because of its metamorphosis into the fiction it has previously enclosed. The fiction metaphors may remind us that we are, after all, reading a fiction—and thereby give us enough distance to call the pronouncements it seems to endorse into question. In any case, because of the shift from fiction making to living, Jo is no longer primary author and mover; she can no longer direct Meg in a play or in life. And her loss of authority may account for some of her indignation that Meg wants to marry and leave her sisters.

The devaluation of writing continues in the second volume. For here writing is a means, not an end. It is, first of all, a means of earning money, to send Beth and Marmee to the seashore. Writing is more womanly if its goal is self-sacrifice and kindness to others, if self-expression is subordinate to self-abnegation. Alcott's ambivalence is nowhere so clear as in the kind of writing that she allows herself and Jo to pursue—"popular" writing to earn money for others, not "serious" writing for the selfish purposes of art.

Elsewhere in the second volume writing is similarly a means, though not always unambiguously so. When Jo is feeling despondent, Marmee urges her to write to make herself happy—a therapy that largely works. Some degree of self-expression is permissible, it seems, as medicine, though the line dividing therapy and creativity is not entirely clear. But the two samples of Jo's writing that we see in the second volume, both poems, are less ambiguous: both achieve crucial nonartistic ends, their artistry subordinated to utility. Compared to the lively pieces in the first volume, these two are plodding and pedestrian. The first, Jo's poem about Beth's dying, allows Jo to express some of her grief and to tell Beth that she has not lived in vain, that others have benefited by her example. The second, a meditation on four trunks in the garret, revealing some of Jo's loneliness and longing for love, appears in a publication that Professor Bhaer reads—and it brings him courting. Jo acknowledges that it is "very bad poetry," but the Professor points out that "it has done its duty" (519), beauty once again subordinated to—made to rhyme with—duty.

Even more striking is how dangerous art has become. At first, in volume two, the effects are relatively benign. Jo's overdeveloped imagination leads her to believe Beth in love with Laurie, "and common sense, being rather weakened by a long course of romance writing, did not come to the rescue" (354). The consequences here are trifling. Later, as Jo is lured to write thrillers for the sake of money, a worse danger looms: "She thought she was prospering finely; but, unconsciously, she was beginning to desecrate some of the womanliest attributes of a woman's character. She was living in bad society; and, imaginary though it was, its influence affected her, for she was feeding heart and fancy on dangerous and unsubstantial food, and was fast brushing the innocent bloom from her nature by a premature acquaintance with the darker side of life, which comes soon enough to all of us" (381). Beyond such possible excesses, though, writing is simply not what a little woman should aim for. Jo's beloved Beth urges her to follow the claims of love and duty: "you'll be happier in doing that than writing splendid books or seeing all the world; for love is the only thing that we can carry with us when we go, and it makes the end so easy" (455).[12]

Jo essentially does stop writing when she marries, and she channels her creativity into telling stories to her household of boys and composing a song for a festive occasion. True, bookishness has brought Jo and her Professor together: they read Hans Christian Andersen; he gives her a volume of Shakespeare; they attend a literary dinner. Yet the Andersen is simply sugarcoating for Jo's German lessons, the dinner a disappointment. Books are insufficient in themselves, but they may serve a useful end. And that end is marriage and domesticity. Early on, Jo is bookish, with a metaphoric family: her stories are "dutiful children whom good fortune overtakes"; she herself, a "literary spinster, with a pen for a spouse, a family of stories for children" (474, 478). She ends, though, with a true family, and bookishness is metaphoric; when the Professor becomes intimate with Jo he will read "all the brown book in which she keeps her little secrets" (519). The metaphoric family becomes actual, the actual bookishness metaphoric. At the end of volume two as at the end of volume one, fiction is channeled into metaphor. Jo does state, "I haven't given up the hope that I may write a good book yet, but I can wait, and I'm sure it will be all the better for such experiences and illustrations as these" (530). Such a teasing reminder of Jo's earlier bookishness may subvert some of Alcott's surface message—and may also remind us that we are reading a book, only a book, and can thus question its pronouncements. But the surface message remains clear: as long as she is happy and busy and dutiful—as a proper woman, a wife and mother—Jo should feel no great call to write.

In the first continuation of *Little Women*, in fact, she feels none. The only writing she does in *Little Men* is in her Conscience Book, where each week she records the virtues and follies of the boys at Plumfield. Again, the writing is instrumental, here (as in Alcott's own works) an instrument of moral growth. Not until *Jo's Boys*, published nearly twenty years after *Little Women*, does Alcott allow Jo the writing she allowed herself. And then it is only because Jo has been fretting for something to do while sick, has hoped to lighten her family's financial burdens, and has wanted to buy Marmee some peace and comfort at the end of a hard life. Furthermore, it's not dangerous gothic tales that Jo indulges in but domestic realism. Still, Alcott calls this return to writing "Jo's last scrape"—and not just because Jo's popularity makes her the prey of autograph hounds. Despite all the rationalizations, writing remains morally dubious. Later, Jo and Laurie collaborate on a Christmas production, one far different from the melodrama of Don Roderigo and Zara in *Little Women*. For this one is a tribute to motherhood: "I'm tired of love-sick girls and runaway wives. We'll prove that there's romance in old women also" (243). The play thus provides closure to the family saga that began with a Christmas play so long ago. But the tenor of the final play exalts the everyday rather than the exotic, the dutiful rather than the beautiful, echoing the shift in Alcott's own writing from the gothic to the domestic.[13]

Fortunately, even if she was dubious about its justification, Alcott herself continued to write. She could justify her writing by doing it out of a sense of duty: she earned money to feed her family, and her fiction was an instrument of good, teaching girls how to become proper women. Alcott may have espoused women's rights, including suffrage, but in her books as in her life the greatest good was not individual rights and self-fulfillment but loyalty and service to the family; she was a "domestic feminist," seeing the family as the key to reforming society (see, for example, Strickland 145). Though she sometimes needed to escape her family in order to write and rented a room in Boston, the family almost always took precedence over her liberal causes, over herself, over her writing.

Alcott couldn't write just for the sake of writing, for the joy of creating. She may have continued beyond the point of financial necessity partly because she liked indulging in writing, but her avowed goal was always security for the family. Perhaps the only way she could permit herself to write was to pretend, even after her family was secure, that she was writing only for the sake of the family (see Strickland 56, Elbert 132). Or, to put it another way, the act of writing itself may have been liberating, but Alcott paid for such self-indulgence by making the writing instrumental, by sacrificing herself and her writing to duty. The liberating pen was also its homonym: confinement could give birth to creativity but could also abort it.

Notes

Even though my title echoes one of Elizabeth Keyser's, "Alcott's Portraits of the Artist as a Little Woman," I came up with it independently and can't resist the temptation to use it. Perhaps my slight swerve from her wording can be taken as a sign of my swerve from her reading. I read Alcott as less intentionally subversive; Keyser concludes "Portraits" by suggesting that although Marmee can hope for nothing better than marriage for her daughters, "the artist who conceived *Little Women* has wished something better for us" (457). Perhaps, too, the similarity of my title to Keyser's can be taken as a sign of my indebtedness to her, both to her published work—her bracing reminders that "instead of offering facile or partial solutions to social problems, [Alcott] exposed their complexity and the imperfect nature of all solutions, not excluding her own" ("Domesticity" 174)—and to her careful and generous reading of this essay.

1. See, for instance, Habegger and Kaledin, who stress submissiveness, the former suggesting that Alcott's fantasies are politically regressive; Janeway and Keyser, who emphasize subversion, the latter with more sophisticated, potentially deconstructive readings; and such proponents of ambivalence as, in their varying ways, Fetterley, Halttunen, Langland, and O'Brien.

2. Even a male character may say, in Alcott's story "Psyche's Art," that "Moulding character is the highest sort of sculpture, and all of us should learn that art before we touch clay or marble" (65). With respect to the March sisters' game of imitating the *Pilgrim's Progress*, Keyser notes "that the women's pilgrimage is merely a game, an imitation of men's" ("Portraits" 446). For a more general examination of domesticity

and Christian redemption in sentimental fiction, demonstrating the convergence of the two by means of typology, see Tompkins.

3. Or (in contrast with Gilbert and Gubar's notion of women seeking rather than rebelling against female predecessors out of an "anxiety of authorship") Alcott is not so much seeking a predecessor in Brontë as disavowing her, rejecting her in the name of God.

For further discussion of *Work,* one that assesses its radical aims and its failure to convey moral development convincingly, see Yellin.

4. In her Introduction to *Plots and Counterplots,* Madeleine Stern discusses the theme of the marble woman, which appears in such Alcott thrillers as "Behind a Mask" and "A Marble Woman."

Only once after publishing *Little Women* did Alcott indulge in the gothic—to write and publish the anonymous *Modern Mephistopheles* in her publisher's No Name Series. The novel also gives curious expression to some of Alcott's ambivalence about authorship. Not only did she publish it anonymously, but the plot hinges on the Mephistophelian Jasper Helwyze's power over the young Felix Canaris: the former allows the latter to publish Helwyze's work as his own and to bask in the ensuing fame and success, which the young man is reluctant to give up. Alcott seems to be expressing some of her ambivalence about fame, about owning one's own work, about the satanic power an author can have. For further discussion of Alcott's exploration of such issues, see Cowan xi–xii.

5. A similar message, though it stresses domestic virtues more than religious ones, appears in Alcott's *Rose in Bloom.* A woman like Phebe may sing in public for a while, to prove her self-restraint and worthiness of Archie, but a woman should not write. When Rose bemoans her lack of talent for poetry or singing or painting, her uncle assures her that she has "one of the best and noblest gifts a woman can possess" —"the art of living for others so patiently and sweetly that we enjoy it as we do the sunshine, and are not half grateful enough for the great blessing." He adds that "the memory of a real helper is kept green long after poetry is forgotten and music silent" (322–23). Likewise, in "Mountain Laurel and Maidenhair," a young girl is encouraged to "Write your little verses, my dear, when the spirit moves—it is a harmless pleasure, a real comfort, and a good lesson for you; but do not neglect higher duties or deceive yourself with false hopes and vain dreams" (150). It's true that *An Old-Fashioned Girl* contains women characters—minor characters—who are allowed some measure of success as artists. But the writer looks sick and overworked. And the sculptor's statue of the coming woman includes not only a symbolic ballot box, pen, and palette, but also a needle and a broom. It's likewise true that the fragmentary *Diana and Persis,* which Alcott never published, holds out some hope for women artists, while exploring the possibilities for uniting art and domesticity. Will Percy be able to pursue her art after becoming a mother? Will Diana's art be enriched by a budding relationship with a fellow sculptor and his son? Alcott's inability to finish the novel suggests her inability to resolve such questions—much as the death of her sister May, the model for Percy, soon after the birth of her child curtailed any resolution in her own family. And perhaps the differences among critics about the sequencing of chapters, with significant implications for the resolution of the story (see Showalter xxxviii, xli), hints that such perplexity continues to resonate.

6. Nina Auerbach explores the subversive qualities of *Little Women*—how it subverts cultural prescriptions by validating the March family's community of women. True, the book is subversive in this respect. But belonging to a community of women is not necessarily liberating for an artist: the family's communal values may allow a little woman to deviate somewhat from the values of the larger community, but they do not foster individual self-expression. As Keyser suggests, "Jo's sisterhood . . . means loyalty to the patriarchal family, and far from strengthening her in her

unconventionality, it compels her to conform" ("Portraits" 458). Or as Halttunen suggests, "Through the character of Jo March, Alcott performed literary penance for her greatest sins against the cult of domesticity: her flight to Washington, her Gothic period, her consuming literary ambition, and her refusal to marry" (243).

7. It's true that Laurie, a male, submerges his own yearning for musical achievement, but we've never sensed that he is as accomplished as Amy. His dabbling at a requiem and an opera seems more an attempt to overcome Jo's rejection than a whole-hearted commitment to music. In other novels Alcott allows men to be artists —in *Jack and Jill*, for instance, Ralph receives no censure for becoming a sculptor, and Mac of *Rose in Bloom* becomes a successful poet. Even in the fragment *Diana and Persis* we may see Diana as a talented sculptor, yet in her budding relationship with the well-known sculptor Stafford it is clear who is metaphorically the master and who the pupil, whose genius is established and whose is not, at least not yet. Although it could be that Alcott wants to distinguish between talented dabbling and professional genius—those who are merely talented dabblers should subordinate their talents to serving others—there does seem to be a gender bias. For further discussion of the ambiguities of Amy's artistry, see Keyser, "Portraits" 455–56.

8. Sharon O'Brien provides an illuminating discussion of the contradictions inherent in the nineteenth-century encouragement of tomboyism.

9. In her other works as well Alcott hints at the dangers of fiction. The one story that Rose of *Eight Cousins* tries to tell has disastrous consequences. She tells a pointed story of a little girl who takes a rolled bandage from a basket, without asking permission—thus making guilty little Pokey, who has behaved like the girl in the story, overwhelmingly remorseful and confused. It's bad enough that Dr. Alec then chides Rose for publicly embarrassing Pokey, but Pokey's champion Jamie also tells Rose's secret—that she has had the vanity to pierce her ears. The moral is not just that Rose should beware of embarrassing others, but that she shouldn't tell stories. She may marry a poet, not become one.

10. Yet Marmee can't erase the traces of the original stories, traces that are potentially subversive: Keyser suggests that "Alcott, by having Meg laughingly accuse Marmee of turning their stories against them in order to extract a moral, indicates her recognition that each story, far from pointing up the girls' good fortune, exposes something about the unfortunate condition of women, a condition in which they all share" ("Portraits" 448).

11. See Madelon Bedell: "In this modern female version, the legend of Sampson and Delilah is . . . turned upside down. To shear a woman's hair is to give her power" (xxi). Elizabeth Langland suggests that the episode "equates Jo's cutting her hair with a masculine assertion of responsibility. Jo not only acts like the man of the family in this episode, but she now looks 'boyish.' Yet, she cries for the loss of her beauty, and this detail endears her to us as a woman" (122).

12. I agree with Anne Hollander that Alcott "demonstrates that to achieve a good character the practice of patience, kindness, discretion, and forbearance among one's fellows must totally absorb one's creative zeal. Such zeal may not be expended on the committed practice of any art, or any intellectual pursuit which might make the kind of demand that would promote the unseemly selfishness of the creative life" (38). But I disagree with her argument that, for Alcott, the driving force of creativity is sexuality, and that Jo cannot become a true artist until she accepts her sexuality. Hollander claims, for instance, that "Jo can write as a true artist only later, when she finally comes to terms with her own sexual self and thus rather belatedly grows up. . . ." (34). But when Jo marries she stops writing.

In any case, the praise of duty reverberates throughout Alcott's fiction. In *Jack and Jill* a mother knows "that it was better for her romantic daughter to be learning all the housewifery lessons she could teach her, than to be reading novels, writing verses, or philandering about with her head full of girlish fancies, quite innocent in themselves, but not the stuff to live on" (201–02). In *Eight Cousins* Dr. Alec tells Rose that housekeeping "is one of the most beautiful as well as useful of all the arts a woman can learn. Not so romantic, perhaps, as singing, painting, writing, or teaching, even; but one that makes many happy and comfortable, and home the sweetest place in the world" (185). In *Under the Lilacs* a young girl follows the advice of a young woman and loses an archery contest to a boy, sacrificing her own achievement for that of another: "Losing a prize sometimes makes one happier than gaining it" (247). Even in "Psyche's Art," in which a woman's art is not stifled but enriched by attending to home duties, and in which Alcott allows the possibility that the heroine may not marry the hero, the hero wins "fame and fortune" as an artist while the heroine grows "beautiful with the beauty of a serene and sunny nature, happy in duties which became pleasures, rich in the art which made life lovely to herself and others, and brought rewards in time" (83)—not happy and rich in the art of sculpture.

13. Although most of the young women in the novel end up marrying, Alcott does allow one to become a doctor and to remain a spinster. For a discussion of Jo's ambivalence about her own achievements and those of the next generation of women, see Keyser, "Women and Girls."

Works Cited

Alberghene, Janice Marie. "From Alcott to *Abel's Island*: The Image of the Artist in American Children's Literature." Ph.D. diss., Brown University, 1980.

Alcott, Louisa May. *Eight Cousins; or the Aunt-Hill.* 1875. Illus. Ruth Ives. Garden City, N.Y.: Doubleday, 1958.

———. *Jack and Jill: A Village Story.* 1880. Boston: Little, Brown, 1910.

———. *Jo's Boys, and How They Turned Out: A Sequel to "Little Men."* 1886. Boston: Roberts, 1890.

———. *Little Women: or Meg, Jo, Beth and Amy.* 2 vols. 1868–69. Boston: Roberts, 1893.

———. "Mountain Laurel and Maidenhair." *A Garland for Girls.* 1886. Rpt. in *Glimpses of Louisa: A Centennial Sampling of the Best Short Stories by Louisa May Alcott.* Ed. Cornelia Meigs. Boston: Little, Brown, 1968.

———. "Psyche's Art." *Proverb Stories.* 1882. Boston: Roberts, 1896. 55–83.

———. *Rose in Bloom.* 1876. Illus. Hattie Longstreet Price. Boston: Little, Brown, 1927.

———. *Under the Lilacs.* 1877. New York: Grosset and Dunlap, 1919.

———. *Work: A Story of Experience.* 1873. Introd. Sarah Elbert. New York: Schocken, 1977.

Auerbach, Nina. *Communities of Women: An Idea in Fiction.* Cambridge: Harvard Univ. Press, 1978.

Bedell, Madelon. Introduction. *Little Women.* By Louisa M. Alcott. New York: Modern Library, 1983. ix–xlix.

Cheney, Ednah D., ed. *Louisa May Alcott: Her Life, Letters, and Journals.* Boston: Roberts, 1891.

Cowan, Octavia. Introduction to *A Modern Mephistopheles*, by Louisa May Alcott. Toronto: Bantam, 1987. v–xiii.

Douglas, Ann. "Mysteries of Louisa May Alcott." *New York Review of Books* 28 Sept. 1978. Rpt. in Stern, *Essays.* 231–40.

Elbert, Sarah. *A Hunger for Home: Louisa May Alcott and* Little Women. Philadelphia: Temple Univ. Press, 1984.

Fetterley, Judith. "*Little Women*: Alcott's Civil War." *Feminist Studies* 5 (1979): 369–83.

Gilbert, Sandra M., and Susan Gubar. *The Madwoman in the Attic: The Woman Writer and the Nineteenth-Century Literary Imagination.* 1979. New Haven: Yale Univ. Press, 1980.

Gordon, Jan B. "Lewis Carroll, the *Sylvie and Bruno* Books, and the Nineties: The Tyranny of Textuality." In *Lewis Carroll: A Celebration*, ed. Edward Guiliano. New York: Potter, 1982. 176–94.

Habegger, Alfred. "Precocious Incest: First Novels by Louisa May Alcott and Henry James." *Massachusetts Review* 26 (1985): 233–62.

Halttunen, Karen. "The Domestic Drama of Louisa May Alcott." *Feminist Studies* 10 (1984): 233–54.

Hollander, Anne. "Reflections on *Little Women.*" *Children's Literature* 9 (1981): 28–39.

Janeway, Elizabeth. "Meg, Jo, Beth, Amy, and Louisa." *New York Times Book Review* 29 Sept. 1968. Rpt. in *Only Connect: Readings on Children's Literature*, ed. Sheila Egoff, G. T. Stubbs, and L. F. Ashley. 2d ed. Toronto: Oxford Univ. Press, 1980. 253–57.

Kaledin, Eugenia. "Louisa May Alcott: Success and the Sorrow of Self-Denial." *Women's Studies* 5 (1978): 251–63.

Keyser, Elizabeth. "Women and Girls in Louisa May Alcott's *Jo's Boys.*" *International Journal of Women's Studies* 5 (1983): 457–71.

Keyser, Elizabeth Lennox. "Alcott's Portraits of the Artist as Little Woman." *International Journal of Women's Studies* 5 (1982): 445–59.

———. "Domesticity versus Identity: A Review of Alcott Research." *Children's Literature in Education* 16 (1985): 165–75.

Langland, Elizabeth. "Female Stories of Experience: Alcott's *Little Women* in Light of *Work.*" In *The Voyage In: Fictions of Female Development*, ed. Elizabeth Abel, Marianne Hirsch, and Elizabeth Langland. Hanover, N.H.: Univ. Press of New England, 1983. 112–27.

O'Brien, Sharon. "Tomboyism and Adolescent Conflict: Three Nineteenth-Century Case Studies." In *Woman's Being, Woman's Place: Female Identity and Vocation in American History*, ed. Mary Kelley. Boston: Hall, 1979. 351–72.

Pauly, Thomas H. "*Ragged Dick* and *Little Women*: Idealized Homes and Unwanted Marriages." *Journal of Popular Culture* 9 (Winter 1975). Rpt. in Stern, *Essays*. 120–25.

Showalter, Elaine. Introduction to *Alternative Alcott*, by Louisa May Alcott. Ed. Elaine Showalter. New Brunswick: Rutgers Univ. Press, 1988. ix–xliii.

Stern, Madeleine B., ed. *Critical Essays on Louisa May Alcott.* Boston: Hall, 1984.

———, ed. *Plots and Counterplots: More Unknown Thrillers of Louisa May Alcott.* New York: Morrow, 1976.

Strickland, Charles. *Victorian Domesticity: Families in the Life and Art of Louisa May Alcott.* University, Ala.: Univ. of Alabama Press, 1985.

Tompkins, Jane P. "Sentimental Power: *Uncle Tom's Cabin* and the Politics of Literary History." *Glyph* 8 (1981): 79–102.

Yellin, Jean Fagan. "From *Success* to *Experience*: Louisa May Alcott's *Work.*" *Massachusetts Review* 21 (1980): 527–39.

Yonge, Charlotte M. *The Daisy Chain[; or, Aspirations, a Family Chronicle].* 1856. Preface Susan M. Kenney. New York: Garland, 1977.

Dismembering the Text: The Horror of Louisa May Alcott's Little Women

Angela M. Estes and Kathleen Margaret Lant

Me from Myself—to banish—
Had I Art—
Impregnable my Fortress
Unto All Heart—

But since myself—assault Me—
How have I peace
Except by subjugating
Consciousness?

And since We're mutual Monarch
How this be
Except by Abdication—
Me—of Me?
—Emily Dickinson

On the floor of an attic room slumps a thirty-year-old woman, stripping off her disguise as a submissive seventeen-year-old governess; removing her false teeth, she takes another swig from a flask and plots a scheme to undermine and conquer an entire family. In another room sits a young girl, laboriously—albeit resentfully—stitching together small remnants of fabric as she learns simultaneously the practical art of patchwork and the womanly virtues of patience, perseverance, and restraint. What possible connection could exist between these two women?

These two scenes—the first from Louisa May Alcott's thriller "Behind a Mask" and the second from her children's story "Patty's Patchwork"—exemplify the apparent extremes that characterize the heroines and plots of Alcott's works. Traditionally, Alcott has been considered a writer of inoffensive, sometimes mildly rebellious children's fiction, but the discovery and republication in 1975 and 1976[1] of Alcott's anonymous and pseudonymous adult thrillers (first published between 1863 and 1869) and the emergence of more

Children's Literature 17, ed. Francelia Butler, Margaret Higonnet, and Barbara Rosen (Yale University Press, © 1989 by The Children's Literature Foundation, Inc.).

thoughtful recent critical approaches to her children's stories have raised significant questions for Alcott scholars: How is the Alcott canon to be reenvisioned to explain the existence of her hidden fictional efforts? How do we account for Alcott's fascination with the lurid, the wild, the unacceptable and untrammeled heroines of the thrillers when we remember the little girls—at least superficially docile—of the children's short stories and the ultimately tamed Jo of *Little Women*? And, most importantly, how do these thrillers, characterized by violence, deceit, infidelity, and licentiousness of every kind imaginable, reshape or enrich our understanding of Alcott's classic children's novel *Little Women* (1868)?[2]

I

The seemingly contradictory aspects of Alcott's fiction can be better understood when we place her in a personal and historical context. She was intimately involved in the transcendental circle of her father and his friends, the literati of Concord, including, of course, its leader Ralph Waldo Emerson. Alcott embraced the transcendental ideals of self-expression, self-reliance, and self-exploration as espoused by both Emerson and her father, Bronson Alcott. In a journal entry (27 April 1882), Alcott affirms Emerson's pervasive influence on her life and thought: "Mr. Emerson died at 9 P.M. suddenly. Our best and greatest American gone. The nearest and dearest friend Father has ever had, and the man who has helped me most by his life, his books, his society. I can never tell all he has been to me . . . his essays on Self-reliance, Character, Compensation, Love, and Friendship helped me to understand myself and life, and God and Nature" (Cheney 345). Alcott insisted, moreover, that the self-reliance and self-awareness so vaunted by the transcendentalists be extended to women as well as men. In a letter to Maria S. Porter, she asserts woman's right to an identity and a life of her own by calling for an exploration and redefinition of "woman's sphere": "In future let woman do whatever she can do; let men place no more impediments in the way; above all things let's have fair play,—let *simple justice* be done, say I. Let us hear no more of 'woman's sphere' either from our wise (?) legislators beneath the gilded dome, or from our clergymen in their pulpits." Alcott goes on to insist that woman be allowed to "find out her own limitations" (Porter 13–14).

But Alcott, well educated in the proprieties of her own time, realized the dangers for a woman of nineteenth-century America in advocating such potentially liberating attitudes too openly. In fact, Alcott seemed to sense the ambiguities inherent, at least for women, in Emerson's position, for it is Emerson, the man from whom she learned the value of self-reliance, whose censure she fears when creating (in the adult thrillers) her most self-reliant and self-assertive female characters:

> I think my natural ambition is for the lurid style. I indulge in gorgeous fancies and wish that I dared inscribe them upon my pages and set them before the public. . . . How should I dare to interfere with the proper grayness of old Concord? The dear old town has never known a startling hue since the redcoats were there. Far be it from me to inject an inharmonious color into the neutral tint. And my favorite characters! Suppose they went to cavorting at their own sweet will, to the infinite horror of dear Mr. Emerson, who never imagined a Concord person as walking off a plumb line stretched between two pearly clouds in the empyrean. [Pickett 107–08]

Alcott was, moreover, reticent about openly advocating self-reliance and assertiveness in her works for children; she was aware of the responsibility she bore her young readers in that they so fully identified with and followed the careers of such characters as Jo. In fact, after the publication of *Little Women*, Alcott seemed quite moved by her young readers' responses to her works: "Over a hundred letters from boys & girls . . . & many from teachers & parents assure me that my little books are read & valued in a way I never dreamed of seeing them" (quoted by Stern in her introduction to Myerson and Shealy, xxxiii). And in a letter of 1872 to William Henry Venable, Alcott expresses gratitude that her stories are "considered worthy to be used for the instruction as well as the amusement of young people" (Myerson and Shealy 172).[3]

In the final analysis, however, it seems clear that Alcott was not unambivalently committed to the creation of "innocent" entertainments (Myerson and Shealy 172) for the young. In fact, her impatience with such works becomes obvious in her more candid moments: she claims in a letter probably written in 1878 that she wrote what she refers to as "moral tales for the young" because she felt pressure from her publishers and because such tales provided her with a much needed income. "I do it," she admits, "because it pays well" (Myerson and Shealy 232).

Louisa Alcott found herself, then, confronted with conflicting impulses: on the one hand, Alcott—educated under the tutelage of Emerson and Bronson Alcott—craves freedom and the power of self-assertion for both herself and her characters; on the other hand, she feels strongly the pressure to meet the needs of her young readers and the demands of her publishers. In Alcott's most famous novel for children, therefore, woman's development toward membership in the acceptable female sphere is rendered in a surface narrative; to reveal the complex, dangerous truths of female experience, the self-assertive drives toward womanly independence, Alcott (resorting to one of the ploys she uses frequently in the thrillers—disguise) must incorporate a subtext. Thus, in *Little Women*, Alcott, employing both a surface narrative and a subtext to disclose an extended vision of feminine conflict, presents a vision of female experience at once innocuous and deadly. What appears at first to be a conventional and somewhat sentimental tale of the innocent trials of girlhood—what we have mistaken for a "feminine" novel of domestic education—is, on closer examination, another of Alcott's lurid, violent sensation stories. For in presenting the conflict between appropriate womanly behavior and the human desire for assertiveness and fulfillment, Alcott finds herself forced to wage war upon her protagonist, Jo. Young Jo—fiery, angry, assertive—represents all that adult Jo can never be, and for this reason young Jo must be destroyed. Thus, while the surface narrative achieves some closure, while it implies a moderately "normal," well-integrated future for Jo, the horrifying subtext of *Little Women* reveals that for an independent, self-determined Jo, no future is possible.

II

The horrors that lurk at the heart of Alcott's novel are, surprisingly, least obvious to those who cherish her work most. Even today, women who as children read *Little Women* remember Jo at her best, that is to say, at her most liberated. Elizabeth Janeway, for example, praises the novel's heroine as "the one young woman in 19th-century fiction who maintains her individual independence, who gives up no part of her autonomy as payment for being born a woman—and who gets away with it" (Janeway 42). Janeway seems to repress her awareness that Jo—who never wants to marry, who values her writing above all else—*does* finally marry and abandon the writing she cherishes, taking up the kinds of writing her family and husband deem suitable for her.

However, two of the most hostile readers of *Little Women*, Leslie Fiedler and James Baldwin, have sensed a certain horror and duplicity in it, and despite their patent distaste for Alcott's novel, their unsympathetic readings of *Little Women* illuminate the work. In comparing Alcott's work to Harriet Beecher Stowe's *Uncle Tom's Cabin*, Baldwin and Fiedler denigrate *both* works, terming them sentimental, self-righteous, dishonest, and inhumane—among other harsh criticisms. Both imply, too, that a secret crime or perversion hides at the center of these two novels. Fiedler finds the "chief pleasures" of *Uncle Tom's Cabin* "rooted not in the moral indignation of the reformer but in the more devious titillations of the sadist" (114). And at the center of these "titillations of the sadist" is Little Eva, "the pre-pubescent corpse as heroine" (114). Fiedler compares Stowe's "orgy of approved pathos" to that created by Alcott in *Little Women*: "Little Eva is the classic case in America, melting the obdurate though kindly St. Clare from skepticism to faith. What an orgy of approved pathos such scenes provided in the hands of a master like Harriet Beecher Stowe, or the late Louisa May Alcott, who in *Little Women* reworked the prototype of Mrs. Stowe into a kind of fiction specifically directed at young girls!" (114). James Baldwin also sees a kind of orgy of "sentimentality" in *Uncle Tom's Cabin*, which he condemns by comparing it with *Little Women*: "*Uncle Tom's Cabin* is a very bad novel, having, in its self-righteous, virtuous sentimentality, much in common with *Little Women*. Sentimentality, the ostentatious parading of excessive and spurious emotion, is the mark of dishonesty, the inability to feel; the wet eyes of the sentimentalist betray his aversion to experience, his fear of life, his arid heart; and it is always, therefore, the signal of secret and violent inhumanity, the mask of cruelty. *Uncle Tom's Cabin*—like its multitudinous, hard-boiled descendants—is a catalogue of violence" (92).

Baldwin and Fiedler have sensed—perhaps because of their antagonism toward these novels and their lack of sympathy with the characters who inhabit these two works by women—the doubleness of *Uncle Tom's Cabin* and *Little Women*. As masculinist critics, however, neither seems capable of sufficiently disengaging himself from the prejudices of his culture to understand or elucidate the complexities of the two novels. For it is true that both novels mask secret crimes and enact hidden violence, and the more open-minded reader must inevitably ask herself why Alcott and Stowe resort to hidden abuses to resolve the conflicts their novels present. And also, if *Little Women* has "much in common" with *Uncle Tom's Cabin*; if Alcott's novel is, in Baldwin's terms, replete with a "dishonesty" that masks some "secret and violent inhumanity," some act of "cruelty," then the reader must ask the nature and source of the novel's "dishonesty," she must discover the act of "inhumanity" and "cruelty" the novel perpetrates.[4]

The answers to these questions begin to surface only when we disinter the protagonist of *Little Women*, Jo March, from the text of the novel. For Jo is an experimental heroine through whom Alcott can explore the tensions of female experience in nineteenth-century America: between being a dutiful member of woman's sphere and being an independent, self-reliant woman. In the surface narrative of *Little Women*, the story suitable for Alcott's young readers, Jo March begins as an unruly, self-assertive girl and gradually learns to become a proper "little woman." But when Leslie Fiedler asserts that Little Eva is the "model for all the protagonists of a literature at once juvenile and genteelly gothic" (114), he again inadvertently points by implication to the true design of *Little Women*, revealed in the novel's disguised text. For the experimental transformation of Jo March into a proper "little woman"—performed and delineated in a textual laboratory which masquerades as an informative and supportive guidebook for children—turns out to be, in fact, a "gothic" study in horror, the very kind of story Alcott so longed to write but which she renounced, or tried to, for the sake of her young, impressionable readers.

In order for Jo to live fictionally, to maintain her position within the narrative framework Alcott has constructed, Alcott must murder Jo spiritually. Given Jo's lust for independence, her devotion to her own power and development, Alcott could *never* have allowed her to marry for love—in other words, to love and marry Laurie—for, as the novel demonstrates with Meg's marriage to John Brooke, marriage for love reduces woman to "submission" (*Little Women* 209). Alcott was vehement in her refusal to allow this to happen to Jo. In a letter to Thomas Niles (1869), she deplores the numerous "pairing[s] off" in *Little Women*, asserting "I don't approve" (Myerson and Shealy 119), and in a letter to Samuel Joseph May (1869), she bitterly complains that "publishers are very *perwerse* & wont let authors have their way so my little women must grow up & be married off in a very stupid style" (Myerson and Shealy 121–22).

Tragically, Alcott's reluctance to sacrifice Jo to convention through marriage ultimately results in Alcott's violence against this very character. In a letter to Elizabeth Powell, Alcott is quite clear on her own desires for Jo and on the conflicting demands she feels from her readers. Alcott's solution is to subject Jo to certain violent narrative abuses: "'Jo' should have remained a literary spinster but so many enthusiastic young ladies wrote to me clamorously demanding that she should marry Laurie, *or* somebody, that I didn't dare to refuse & out of perversity went & made a funny match for her. I expect vials of wrath to be poured out upon my head, but rather enjoy the prospect" (Myerson and Shealy 125).

Like Cassy, the horribly abused slave woman of *Uncle Tom's Cabin*, and like Sethe, the equally besieged black woman of Toni Morrison's *Beloved*, Alcott chooses to murder her dearest child rather than force that child to live in a world hostile to her. Alcott's murder of Jo, then, is the secret violence at the center of *Little Women*. Alcott's response to her fiction seems characteristic of the woman or the woman writer beset by irreconcilable conflicts and demands: Jo finds herself among the good who must die young. In order that she not be corrupted by the adult world of heterosexuality, Jo must be killed while at her zenith of eager and fiery independence.

III

From the beginning of *Little Women*, fifteen-year-old Jo March rebels and refuses to be a "young lady": "'I'm not! And if turning up my hair makes me one, I'll wear it in two tails till I'm twenty,' cried Jo, pulling off her net and shaking down a chestnut mane" (5). Jo's behavior is entirely inappropriate for a proper young female. Her "quick temper, sharp tongue, and restless spirit" are "always getting her into scrapes" (36). And although Jo is devoted to and loves the female community she shares with her mother and sisters—Meg, Beth, and Amy—she acts "in a gentlemanly manner," uses "slang words," and constantly defies her sisters' attempts to admonish and reform her:

> "Don't Jo; it's so boyish!"
> "That's why I do it."
> "I detest rude, unladylike girls!"
> "I hate affected, niminy-piminy chits!" [4–5]

In her arrogation of masculine mannerisms, language, and roles, Jo instinctively and correctly identifies the opportunities for independence, self-reliance, adventure, and assertion as those conventionally reserved for men. Jo realizes, in fact, the awful dichotomy between her own impulses and the expectations held out to her: "I can't get over my disappointment in not being a boy" (5).

Jo March is, thus, a nineteenth-century female caught between the requisite role of the domesticated "little woman," represented by her given, imposed name, Josephine, and her own self-guided impulses, represented by her "masculine" chosen name, Jo. Her conflict is so intense that she has renamed, redefined herself. In spite of Jo's self-reliant acts, however—"I'm the man of the family now Papa is away" (6)—she receives continual reminders from her sisters of her inevitable fate: "you must try to be contented with making your name boyish and playing brother to us girls" (5). But for a brief moment at the beginning of *Little Women*, Jo March resides in an idyllic female community of which she is the "male" head. She is a heroic figure—a young woman intent on maintaining the female community of "woman's sphere" while still acting in accordance with her own self-reliant impulses.

And Jo's heroic balancing act works as long as this "woman's sphere," the matriarchal community of Jo's family, remains entirely self-contained and entirely female. But once a male character—the young boy next door, Laurie, who has been longing to enter this female utopia—successfully penetrates the female community, the plot of *Little Women* and the destiny of Jo are immutably altered.

Laurie, a rich but orphaned young boy, is warmly welcomed into the March family, and at first—with the children still inhabiting a prelapsarian Eden—life appears to go on as before. Because the children are presexual in the early parts of the novel, Laurie (as his name suggests) becomes in effect "one of the girls." He is accepted into the female community and poses no threat to Jo or to the female world she loves. Nevertheless, planted in this female garden now, with the arrival of a male, are the seeds of its own destruction. But before these seeds sprout and take root, Alcott seizes the opportunity provided by this idyllic lull in sexual development; she begins, in a subtext, to reveal the causes of both the disintegration of this female community and Jo's fall from self-reliance.

By using Laurie, a male, as a foil for Jo, Alcott underscores the nature of the conflicts which Jo, as a female, must experience and the fate to which she—unlike Laurie—must ultimately acquiesce. In many ways Jo and Laurie are twins: they are the same age, they are both characterized as untamed animals—Jo as a horse (5, 6, 25) and Laurie as a centaur (59)—and both, hating their given names, have renamed themselves. Even Jo's mother remarks that Jo and Laurie would not be "suited" to each other for marriage because they are "too much alike" (299). And Laurie's grandfather, seeing the influence of Jo on Laurie, thinks how Jo "seemed to understand the boy almost as well as if she had been one herself" (50). So identical are Jo and Laurie, in fact, that in their presexual relationship, even as Laurie becomes "one of the girls," so Jo becomes with Laurie just "one of the boys."

Despite the masculine similarities between Jo and Laurie, however, Alcott emphatically reveals that Jo's fate in life—because Jo is, inescapably, female—will be different from Laurie's. Our recognition of the similar natures, attitudes, and feelings that Jo and Laurie share serves, moreover, only to intensify our awareness of the conflicts Jo must endure. Although both Laurie and Jo hate their given names and rename themselves, only Laurie can actively "thrash" and challenge those who would force a false name and thus a false role on him. Jo must passively "bear it":

> "My first name is Theodore but I don't like it, for the fellows called me Dora, so I made them say Laurie instead."
>
> "I hate my name, too—so sentimental! I wish everyone would say Jo instead of Josephine. How did you make the boys stop calling you Dora?"
>
> "I thrashed 'em."
>
> "I can't thrash Aunt March, so I suppose I shall have to bear it"; and Jo resigned herself with a sigh. [27]

Not only can Laurie, because he is male, actively alter reality in accordance with his own will, but he can also, should his self-reliant acts fail, simply leave those situations which limit him; as Huck Finn, the archetypal masculine hero of nineteenth-century American literature, puts it, he can "light out for the Territory." But when

Laurie, angry at his grandfather, proposes to Jo that they run away from home together, Jo, although filled with the same impulses of flight and freedom, must resign herself to captivity:

> For a moment Jo looked as if she would agree, for wild as the plan was, it just suited her. She was tired of care and confinement, longed for change. . . . Her eyes kindled as they turned wistfully toward the window, but they fell on the old house opposite and she shook her head with sorrowful decision.
>
> "If I was a boy, we'd run away together and have a capital time; but as I'm a miserable girl, I must be proper and stop at home. Don't tempt me, Teddy, it's a crazy plan."
>
> "That's the fun of it," began Laurie, who had got a willful fit on him and was possessed to break out of bounds in some way.
>
> "Hold your tongue!" cried Jo, covering her ears. "'Prunes and prisms' are my doom, and I may as well make up my mind to it." [191]

Interestingly, Jo's frustrations and lack of freedom are characterized specifically in terms of her femaleness and in terms of her relationship as a female to language. Jo, the writer, longs to control language, to make herself independent and her family secure with her use of language. But as a woman, "prunes and prisms" are her lot: her relationship to language *should* be characterized by her desire for beauty. As Nancy Baker points out in *The Beauty Trap*, her study of the American woman's obsession with appearance, women of the nineteenth century, reluctant to wear too much makeup, "pinched their cheeks to make them pinker and . . . practiced repeating sequences of words beginning with the letter p—prunes, peas, potatoes, papa, prisms—in order to effect the small, puckered mouth that was so popular" (Baker 21).

Even within the presexual Eden of childhood, then, Jo's stream of impulses is dammed and divided. Were *Little Women* one of Alcott's short stories for children, this is how we would remember Jo: a young female destined sooner or later to come to terms with being a proper "little woman," but a young female alive with rebellion and wildness, intent on having her own way. Because *Little Women* is a novel, though, an extended fiction, the children—including Jo—*do* grow up, they *do* (at least offstage) become sexual. And each sexual coming-of-age is a blow to the foundations of the female community which has become essential to Jo's self-assertion and sense of self-worth. Only as the reigning "patriarch" and caretaker of this female family—"if anything is amiss at home, I'm your man" (292)—does Jo enjoy any power: that power of self-reliantly protecting and providing for one's family, traditionally reserved for the family's highest-ranking male. Jo's solution to the problems her sisters face in finding worthy husbands is a simple one—"Then we'll be old maids" (90)—and as her sisters are drawn closer and closer to marriage, Jo vehemently protests the usurpation of her power and the fall of her female domain: "I think it's dreadful to break up families so" (225).

Jo's power begins to dwindle as a result of the first sexual coming-of-age in *Little Women*—Meg's attraction and marriage to John Brooke. Jo immediately perceives that her weakened position is a direct result of being female and that this challenge to her territory and power is the inevitable manifestation of male privilege: "'She'll go and fall in love, and there's an end of peace and fun, and cosy times together. I see it all! They'll go lovering around the house, and we shall have to dodge; Meg will be absorbed and no good to me any more; Brooke will scratch up a fortune somehow, carry her off, and make a hole in the family; and I shall break my heart, and everything will be abominably uncomfortable. Oh, dear me! Why weren't we all boys; then there wouldn't be any bother'" (183). As Meg's attraction to John Brooke becomes more certain, Jo grows increasingly anxious, lamenting her feminine powerlessness and asserting a desire to usurp masculine sexual as well as social privilege: "I knew there was mischief brewing; I felt it; and now it's worse than I imagined. I just wish I could marry Meg myself, and keep her safe in the family" (182). Finally, when Jo unexpectedly encounters the "spectacle" of the just-engaged lovers in the parlor, she is overcome with revulsion: "Oh, *do* somebody go down quick; John Brooke is acting dreadfully, and Meg likes it!" (209). The scene of the "strong-minded sister," whom Jo had hoped would reject her suitor, now "enthroned" upon the knee of Jo's "enemy" and wearing "an expression of the most abject submission" (209) is intolerable for Jo.

Jo's "shock" (209) and horror at her sister's transformation suggest that Amy, Beth, and Meg function for Jo as more than mere sisters.[5] They embody experimental alter egos of Jo; they represent the versions of female experience—the ways of reconciling a woman's dual impulses—possible for Jo herself. Meg, in her completely acquiescent marriage and motherhood, manifests the total repression of self-reliant impulses. Through her marriage to John Brooke she learns "that a woman's happiest kingdom is home, her highest honor the art of ruling it not as a queen, but as a wise wife and mother" (361). Meg thus represents for Jo the successful, dutiful member of woman's sphere. But as this first sister departs from Jo's female realm, Jo vehemently rejects the example of submission and marriage which Meg offers: "I'm not one of the agreeable sort. . . . There should always be one old maid in a family" (224). Jo insists that she will never marry—"'I'd like to see anyone try it,' cried Jo fiercely" (138)—and is, in fact, "alarmed at the thought" (203).

At this point in the novel, Jo is still defiantly independent and assertive. She proudly claims that she belongs to the "new" set and that she admires "reformers": "and I shall be one if I can" (269). Thus, when Jo and Amy visit their Aunt March and Aunt Carrol, unaware that her aunt is considering taking her on a trip to Europe, Jo boasts, "I don't like favors; they oppress and make me feel like a slave. I'd rather do everything for myself and be perfectly independent" (270). But the consequences of self-reliant behavior continue to impose themselves on Jo, for her "revolutionary" (269) outburst costs her the trip. Jo is deprived because she has a "too independent spirit" rather than an acquiescent and "docile" (280) nature like that of Amy, who is chosen to accompany her aunt to Europe.

Jo gradually adjusts to her misfortune, to Amy's departure, and to the first assault upon her female community, Meg's marriage, only to be confronted with what for Jo is one of the ultimate horrors in the novel: Laurie reveals to Jo that he loves her—as a lover, not as a buddy. When it is first hinted to Jo that Laurie loves her, she rejects the possibility: she "wouldn't hear a word upon the subject and scolded violently if anyone dared to suggest it" (293). And when Laurie does confess his love, Jo decidedly rejects him and all potential suitors: "I haven't the least idea of loving him or anybody else. . . . I don't believe I shall every marry. I'm happy as I am, and love my liberty too well to be in any hurry to give it up for any mortal man" (329, 330).

Alcott's nineteenth-century readers, who clamored for Jo to marry Laurie, found Jo's rejection—and outright horror and dismissal—of marriage to the handsome and wealthy Laurie inconceivable. Jo's revulsion from marriage to Laurie is not so puzzling, however, if we remember that throughout the novel Jo and Laurie have, in effect, been "brothers," even doubles of the same self. Jo categorically rejects Laurie, then, in part because marriage to Laurie would be tantamount to incest. As Jo confides to Laurie, "I don't believe it's the right sort of love, and I'd rather not try it" (328).

Jo also refuses Laurie because marriage to him would render Jo completely powerless. Jo has already witnessed the self-sacrifice, repression, and submission required of Meg in her marriage to John Brooke, and Jo realizes that she, herself, is eminently unsuited to such a role. Jo's mother, too, astutely observes that Laurie and Jo "would both rebel" in a marriage to each other because both are "too fond of freedom" and both have "hot tempers and strong wills" (299). In other words, a marriage between Laurie and Jo would not work because both are, in conventional terms, masculine. Even more important to Jo, therefore, marrying Laurie would entail the absurd paradox of relinquishing her power to the only male with whom—in her relationship as just "one of the boys"—she has ever had power. To retain any remnant of control over her own life, Jo must refuse to marry Laurie. In an identical act of rebellion and self-assertion Jo's creator, Louisa Alcott, concurs: "Girls write to ask who the little women marry, as if that was the only end and aim of a woman's life. I *won't* marry Jo to Laurie to please any one" (Cheney 201). Despite the repressive and conservative message conveyed in *Little Women*, Jo's refusal to marry Laurie remains—for both Jo and her author—the one act of self-assertion which neither can quell.

When Laurie eventually falls in love with and marries Jo's sister Amy, the relief of being freed from the possibility of marriage to Laurie attenuates Jo's grief over the loss of a second member of her female community. Amy, in her marriage to Laurie, represents another of Jo's alter egos—an additional way of reconciling a woman's divided impulses toward self-reliance and woman's appropriate sphere of activity. As Laurie thinks to himself, "Jo's sister was almost the same as Jo's self" (388). Amy is an especially important alter ego for Jo because she, like Jo, wants to be an artist. At the end of the novel Amy as a wife and mother attempts to combine her "artistic hopes" with life in woman's sphere: "I don't relinquish all my artistic hopes or confine myself to helping others fulfill their dreams of duty" (442). Amy's declaration seems to suggest the possibility of balancing a life of art and a life of appropriate feminine behavior.

Although a wife and mother, Amy has "begun to model" again, but her ability to balance the self-expressive demands of art and the self-repressive demands of marriage and motherhood is undermined by what she models. For Amy creates not out of a fresh encounter of her own self with the world; rather, she repeats, imitates, what is now for her the primary act of creation, biological creation, as she models "a figure of baby." And according to both Amy and Laurie, this "figure of baby" is her ultimate achievement: "Laurie says it is the best thing I've ever done. I think so myself." (442). Amy's ability to balance successfully the demands of art and womanhood becomes even more doubtful when we recall that from the beginning Amy has resolved to be "an attractive and accomplished woman, even if she never became a great artist" (233). Amy is interested in her own art, but is more concerned with what people think of her. By her own admission to Jo, Amy intends to follow "the way of the world": "people who set themselves against it only get laughed at for their pains. I don't like reformers, and I hope you will never try to be one" (269). Thus, although Amy seems to represent a possible alternative for Jo—as both artist and "little woman" —Amy, in fact, follows Meg's example in her willing suppression of self-reliant impulses. But Jo's response to Amy's condemnation of "reformers" is typically undaunted: "We can't agree about that, for you belong to the old set, and I to the new" (269).

Jo's commitment to the "new" has been clear from the novel's beginning; she devotes herself rebelliously to her life-long passion: writing. As she sits in her "favorite refuge" (22)—the "garret" (133)—and writes, Jo embodies a version of Sandra Gilbert and Susan Gubar's "madwoman in the attic," attempting to empower and define herself by engaging in the forbidden (for women) act of writing. Jo's goal, her "favorite dream," is to do something "splendid" and "heroic or wonderful that won't be forgotten after I'm dead" (129). Her chief desire, in short, is to write: "I think I shall write books and get rich and famous: that would suit me, so that is *my* favorite dream" (129). Thus, when Jo publishes her first story and receives both the praise of her family and the promise of payment for future stories, she is ecstatically happy: "I shall write more . . . and I *am* so happy, for in time I may be able to support myself and help the girls" (141). Alcott clearly discloses here that writing is the "key" (130) to a successful life for Jo: "for to be independent and earn the praise of those she loved were the dearest wishes of her heart, and this seemed to be the first step toward the happy end" (141–42).

Jo herself is aware, however, that there may never be a "happy end," a successful merging of her dual impulses toward independence and appropriate feminine behavior: "'I've got the key to my castle in the air, but whether I can unlock the door remains to be seen,' observed Jo mysteriously" (130). And in fact, along with Jo's success as a writer comes a warning to Jo of the dangers, even the impossibility, of committing herself entirely to a self-reliant life of writing. For when Jo proudly sends her first novel out to publishers, she finds that she will have to "chop it up to suit purchasers" (245). Consequently, Jo performs a deed that foreshadows the fate—at the hands of her "authoress," Alcott—of her own self-reliant being: "With Spartan firmness, the young authoress laid her first-born on her table and chopped it up as ruthlessly as any ogre" (246). Finally, Jo receives one further indication that writing (now Jo's primary self-assertive act) and duty toward woman's sphere may not be compatible. Absorbed in her writing, Jo lets her sister Beth nurse their sick neighbors, and when Beth contracts scarlet fever, Jo is filled with remorse: "serves me right, selfish pig, to let you go and stay writing rubbish myself!" (160). As a result of Beth's illness—caused by Jo's devotion to her writing—Beth's already frail nature is weakened, and she eventually dies. And with Beth dies the last member of Jo's female community.

Even before Beth's death, however, and despite Jo's success as an author, Jo suffers from the shock of recognition that Laurie's proposal of marriage has forced upon her. His proposal makes Jo realize that she must now confront not only the loss of her female community through the marriage of her sisters but also the assault on her own self-reliant autonomy. In short, Jo is forced into the realization that she is inescapably female. This realization marks a turning point in the novel, after which Jo as we know her mysteriously begins to disappear—or to be erased—from the story. Just as Jo finds it necessary to mutilate her works to satisfy her publishers, so Alcott must destroy Jo to appease her audience.

From the time that Beth becomes ill, Jo's vibrant personality begins to fade, to weaken, to undergo some horrifying transformation. Just as Alcott has referred to Jo's book as Jo's own offspring, just as Alcott is aware that—to please her readers—Jo must mutilate that offspring, now Alcott herself begins inexorably to mutilate her own text, her own character—Jo. The comparison between Jo as author/parent to her books and Alcott as author/parent of *Little Women* (as well as to her other works) becomes convincingly clear in Alcott's correspondence. In a letter to Lucy Larcom, Alcott refers to some lost manuscripts as "waifs of mine" (Myerson and Shealy 119), and to Elizabeth Powell she writes that she herself is the "Ma" of her "stupid 'Little Women'" (Myerson and Shealy 124). Perhaps Alcott—in the very act of mutilating the energetic and irrepressible Jo—felt some kinship with Jo as Jo bowdlerized her own book.

Jo's growing awareness of what it means to be female is confirmed when her sister Beth dies. Through Beth's death, Alcott depicts a further possible response from another of Jo's alter egos to the female predicament. Beth, who has not even sufficient self-reliant impulses to stay alive, becomes for Jo—and by extension for Alcott —the example of what all women are required by custom to be, the completely perfect woman—passive, acquiescent, dead.[6] Ironically, however, Beth's death is also the sole way to maintain Jo's idyllic female community, for only in death can Beth remain inviolably Jo's. When Beth dies, she is "well at last" (379), and her death discloses one sure way of curing a woman's problems. In contrast to Leslie Fiedler's contention that the "pre-pubescent corpse" functions to provide the "titillations of the sadist," it seems much more likely that for a nineteenth-century woman writer and her audience, a "dead woman" would indeed be the only "safe woman" (Fiedler 114). Fiedler asserts that at the death of Little Eva in *Uncle Tom's Cabin*, "death becomes the supreme rapist" (114). But in *Little Women*, death is the only thing, at least in Jo's eyes, that can save a female from the psychological rape—the violation of self-direction and the disintegration of female community—that await her if she grows up and takes her proper feminine place in the heterosexual world. For Jo, then, and for Alcott as well, the dead woman and the perfect woman become synonymous.

From this point in the novel, Jo's response to her own femaleness in many ways parallels Beth's. But because of the intensity of her self-assertive impulses, Jo cannot simply die. Rather, she is forced to be an accomplice to a crime, to participate actively in her own demise. From its beginning, the text of *Little Women* thoroughly documents the enormous influence that Beth—as an alter ego embodying devotion to woman's sphere—exerts over Jo: "by some strange attraction of opposites, Jo was gentle Beth's. . . . Over her big harum-scarum sister, Beth unconsciously exercised more influence than anyone in the family" (38). Indeed it is through Beth that Jo learns the virtues of woman's sphere:[7] "Then it was that Jo, living in the darkened room with that suffering little sister always before her eyes and that pathetic voice sounding in her ears, learned to see the beauty and the sweetness of Beth's nature, to feel how deep and tender a place she filled in all hearts, and to acknowledge the worth of Beth's unselfish ambition to live for others and make home happy by the exercise of those simple virtues which all may possess and which all should love and value more than talent, wealth, or beauty" (164–65). Beth, in fact, increasingly appears to become a part of Jo as her "submissive spirit" seems "to enter into Jo" (167). And in her sickbed, Beth constantly keeps Jo's cast-off "invalid" (56) doll, "Joanna"—symbolic of Jo's divided and therefore crippled self —at "her side" (165). Even independent Jo finally becomes aware of her affinity with Beth: "Beth is my conscience, and I *can't* give her up. I can't! I can't!" (166).

As Beth grows closer to death, her influence over Jo intensifies, and Jo increasingly identifies with Beth: " 'More than anyone in the world, Beth. I used to think I couldn't let you go, but I'm learning to feel that I don't lose you; that you'll be more to me than ever, and death can't part us, though it seems to' " (378). Just before her death, Beth's influence over Jo and her affinity with Jo are so powerful, in fact, that Beth tells Jo that she must replace her: "You must take my place, Jo" (378). And sure enough, on the morning after Beth finally dies, Jo is gone: "Jo's place was empty" (379). Unlike selfless Beth, strong-willed and defiant Jo must go on living, but—in a children's novel—not as Jo.

IV

Through Beth's death, Alcott performs a literary feat of escape rivaling the marvels of Houdini. By this point in the novel, the character of Jo March has become intensely problematic for Alcott. Because Jo inhabits a fictional environment inhospitable to a fully liberated woman, she can have no radically independent life of her own, but because of the spirited self-reliant nature given to her by her creator, she will not submit to repression. Since the perfect woman, the "true woman" is—as Alcott's experiment reveals—a dead woman, and since Alcott's novel demands the showcasing of a "true woman," Alcott can develop the character of Jo, that intractably independent and *alive* female, no further. Jo can only be replaced. In other words, Alcott discovers through the character of Jo March what, according to Ann Douglas, many other women writers toward the end of the nineteenth century were realizing: that there was no place for a self-aware woman to go, that women were "strangely superannuated as a sex" ("Impoverishment" 17). Thus, having stretched the character of Jo March as far as she can on a rack fastened at one end by Jo's independent impulses and secured at the other end by her need to be a proper member of the female community of "little women," Alcott witnesses the final snap of her experimental creation. But by a fascinating sleight of hand, Alcott hides the failed experimental corpse of Jo and switches the identity of her victim.

In *Little Women*, Alcott (with the help of Jo and her writing) kills Beth and then forces Jo to assume a kind of death in life, to impersonate the dead Beth. And this is why Jo, after the death of Beth, displays none of her former willful and self-reliant behavior and all the selflessness of a zombie. Ultimately, then, deep in the macabre subtext of *Little Women*, Alcott's true victim is Jo; Alcott has, in fact, killed the self-celebratory Jo and replaced her with the self-effacing Beth. And the horror of this corpse switching, this premature burial of the living and impersonation of the dead, is accentuated by the fact that not a scream or moan is uttered. All is executed in this novel for children under the pleasant guise of a young girl's gently guided growth into a "little woman."

Alcott's creation of the new zombielike Jo also helps to explain the incredible change in Jo's character following Beth's death. For Jo's transformation in the final chapters of *Little Women* into the blushing, halting maiden and the dutiful wife and mother are otherwise completely implausible. In hiding the evidence of her fictional crime, the longer form of the novel actually works in Alcott's favor. The length of *Little Women* indeed helps to obscure the reader's memory of the youthful Jo, the girl who vehemently proclaimed that she was "not one of the agreeable sort" and preferred therefore to be an "old maid" (224), the Jo who was "alarmed at the thought" (203) of marriage. Because the reader's memory of young Jo who "carried her love of liberty and hate of conventionalities to such an unlimited extent" (235) is apt to have dimmed towards the end of the novel, that reader may be more likely to accept the authenticity of the new Jo, who is "thrilled" by the possibility of a "tender invitation" to "joyfully depart" with her suitor, the much older Professor Bhaer, "whenever he liked" (410). Confronted with such schizophrenic behavior, however, the reader with a good memory is incredulous.

V

The alert reader's sense of discontinuity results from Alcott's deliberate and somewhat desperate mutilation of both her protagonist and her text. Not only has Jo been dismembered and then reformed as a less threatening version of herself, but the text also has been dismantled, reshaped, and disguised. What was originally a story of Jo's refusal to accede to a repressive feminine role now becomes a story of courtship and marriage. But this courtship and marriage mask the horror tale that lies at the center of the novel—the murder of Jo. At this point Jo, like the speaker in Emily Dickinson's poem, has been forced to abdicate herself. Banished from her own consciousness, Jo finds herself alienated and alone.

The kind old German professor thus shines "like a midnight sun" on Jo in her "darkness" (406), and Jo desperately reaches out to him: "'Oh Mr. Bhaer, I *am* so glad to see you!' cried Jo, with a clutch, as if she feared the night would swallow him up before she could get him in" (406). Through the power of love—Alcott's useful tool for altering her stubborn heroines—Jo is required to embrace the accomplice to her own murder. Although Jo's figurative death is alluded to by Laurie—when he transfers his love from Jo to Amy, he feels "as if there had been a funeral" (383) and later responds to Jo out of the "grave" of his "boyish passion" (402)—the subtext discloses that it is Professor Bhaer who is instrumental in effecting Alcott's scheme. For while Professor Bhaer and Jo covertly admire each other from across the room, Bhaer is discussing "the burial customs of the ancients" (408), and he impulsively moves toward Jo, the text tells us, "just in the act of setting fire to a funeral pile" (409). It is significant, then, that Alcott presents Professor Bhaer as a "birthday gift" (406) to the murdered Jo, for out of the death of her old self, Jo must now enact a new birth, a grisly resurrection.

Since the beginning of Beth's illness, Alcott has stealthily but inexorably erased the authentic Jo from the text. Jo first begins to "take lessons" (308) from Professor Bhaer and then, in an act of self-abdication, forgoes even her own intellectual and moral vision: "Now she seemed to have got on the Professor's mental or moral spectacles also" (322). Through Professor Bhaer, Alcott systematically strips Jo of all vestiges of self until she is indeed "Bhaer," or bare—ready to be clothed and defined by someone else, her husband. When Jo finally agrees to marry Professor Bhaer, the professor looks "as if he had conquered a kingdom" and tells Jo, "be sure that thou givest me all. I haf waited so long, I am grown selfish, as thou wilt find, Professorin" (429). Even the feminized German title chosen for Jo by the professor reveals the extent to which Jo has acquiesced to her proper role and become a female version of the professor himself. Most important, Professor Bhaer—in preparing Jo for her resurrection as Beth—has succeeded in destroying Jo's one authentic means of self-assertion—her writing.

We recall that for the young Jo, writing seemed the key to her independence, success, and happiness, the "first step toward the happy end" (142). And when Jo realized that she could write and sell "sensation" stories (243), she "began to feel herself a power in the house" (244), to regain some of the ascendancy she lost as her female kingdom was destroyed. But the surface narrative clearly indicates that a "sensation" story, the melodramatic but authentic inscription of her autonomous female self, is in opposition to the virtues of woman's sphere: "Unconsciously, she was beginning to desecrate some of the womanliest attributes of a woman's character" (316). Professor Bhaer, therefore—the upholder of social proprieties and agent of Alcott's surface narrative—disapproves of Jo's writing, insists that she stop writing sensation stories, and thereby takes away Jo's power, ensuring that there will be no "happy end" to her story: "'I wish these papers did not come in the house; they are not for children to see nor young people to read. It is not well, and I haf no patience with those who make this harm. . . . They haf no right to put poison in the sugarplum and let the small ones eat it. No, they should think a little, and sweep mud in the street before they do this thing'" (321–22). Jo, now internalizing Professor Bhaer's "shortsighted" (322) moral vision, watches Bhaer burn one of the newspapers which publish sensation stories and moments later imitates his act, destroying all of her writing:

> "They *are* trash, and will soon be worse trash if I go on, for each is more sensational than the last. . . . I know it's so, for I can't read this stuff in sober earnest without being horribly ashamed of it; and what *should* I do if they were seen at home or Mr. Bhaer got hold of them?"
>
> Jo turned hot at the bare idea and stuffed the whole bundle into her stove, nearly setting the chimney afire with the blaze. [322]

Blazing up the chimney along with Jo's writings go the remnants of Jo's independent self. Jo burns her stories to please Professor Bhaer, and henceforth not even a memory of the early self-reliant Jo exists.

Ironically, Jo's last self-assertive act is the burning of her writings, the destroying of her own self—her self-reliant, self-expressive, and self-authenticating being. This ultimate act of self-annihilation comes as no surprise, however, to the reader who has been alert to the subtext of the novel. For this alternate text has foreshadowed the enforced self-mutilation that is Jo's fate. One of Jo's first acts of self-effacement in order to become a proper "little woman" occurs early in the novel when Jo cuts off her cherished long hair, selling it to obtain money for her mother to visit her sick father in the army. Jo's comments about her sacrifice reveal that it is much more than a noble act of charity. For the shearing of her hair is Jo's attempt to atone for her selfish acts—"I felt wicked" (147)—and to curb her self-assertive behavior: "It will be good for my vanity" (146). The subtext reveals, however, the destructive consequences of the attempt to suppress a woman's self-reliant impulses, as Jo relates her feelings after cutting off her hair: "It almost seemed as if I'd an arm or leg off" (148).

Jo is repeatedly associated in the novel, in fact, with self-mutilation. Throughout the novel, Beth cares for Jo's cast-off "invalid" doll—appropriately named "Joanna" (56)—a lobotomized amputee symbolic of the fate of the "tempestuous" Jo herself: "One forlorn fragment of *dollanity* had belonged to Jo, and having led a tempestuous life, was left a wreck in the ragbag, from which dreary poorhouse it was rescued by Beth and taken to her refuge. Having no top to its head, she tied on a neat little cap, and as both arms and legs were gone, she hid these deficiencies by folding it in a blanket and devoting her best bed to this chronic invalid" (36). Here

Beth hides the "deficiencies" of "Joanna" even as Alcott later uses the persona of Beth to "hide" the "deficiencies" of the incorrigible Jo. And twice in the novel Jo must mutilate her writing—the sole means she has to express her true self—in order to conform to the demands of others. First she mutilates her works, her "children," to please her editors, "feeling as a tender parent might on being asked to cut off her baby's legs in order that it might fit into a new cradle" (314). Then she completely destroys her works for Professor Bhaer.

Forced to efface and divorce herself from herself, Jo tries now to write moral children's stories. These products of an impersonating self, however, these "masquerading" (323) stories fail. Since Jo no longer writes her beloved thrillers ("Jo corked up her inkstand," 323), she has finally passed the "test" set up for her by the surface narrative's assistant, Professor Bhaer: "He did it so quietly that Jo never knew he was watching to see if she would accept and profit by his reproof; but she stood the test and he was satisfied; for, though no words passed between them, he knew that she had given up writing" (324). Jo now refrains from writing until after Beth's death when—at her mother's suggestion—she attempts a "simple little story" to relieve her depression and to please her family. Jo creates a surprisingly successful and moving work but a work which is more the result of compliance than creativity. By her own admission, certain aspects of the story—for all its "truth . . . humor and pathos"—are not hers: "If there *is* anything good or true in what I write, it isn't mine; I owe it all to you and Mother and to Beth" (394). Even in her act of creativity, Jo has, to a certain extent, internalized the values of those around her.

By the end of the novel Jo has no rebellion, no self, left. Jo's mind, earlier filled with divided but vital and authentic impulses, is now—like the doll Joanna's head—vacuumed out and replaced with Beth's one-dimensional, selfless personality. Alcott can finally resolve the problems and conflicts engendered by the clash of Jo's independent personality with her required role in woman's sphere only by excising and replacing Jo's character.

Careful to leave no trace of blood in this children's novel, Alcott quietly substitutes for Jo an impersonation of the perfect "little woman," the dead and selfless Beth. And when Jo agrees to marry Professor Bhaer, her words affirm the success of Alcott's endeavor: "I may be strong-minded, but no one can say I'm out of my sphere now" (433–34). Jo has indeed been forced into her proper "sphere," but to do so, Alcott has had to perform a lobotomy on her. While in the surface narrative Jo seems to learn the lessons of little womanhood, the subtext of the novel reveals Alcott's Procrustean intent: Jo may begin life as a young "madwoman in the attic," but Alcott kills off this madwoman, leaving only the "angel in the house" (217).

Early in the novel, when Jo writes to her absent mother to report on the progress of the children, Jo writes of herself, "I—well, I'm Jo, and never shall be anything else" (154). The horror of *Little Women* is that Jo does stop being Jo. She has been replaced by a false Jo, a broken doll, a compliant Beth. This, then, is the act of "cruelty," of "secret and violent inhumanity," which according to James Baldwin lurks behind the "sentimentality" of *Little Women*. In reworking Stowe's "prototype"—as Leslie Fiedler suggests Alcott does —Alcott has transformed "the pre-pubescent corpse as heroine" into the pubescent heroine as corpse.

Thus, *Little Women* hides a secret crime. And like many crimes against women, this one is frequently ignored, overlooked, or dismissed as irrelevant. Even readers respectful of Alcott's novel—as Fiedler and Baldwin are not—disregard the horror perpetrated on Jo, insisting that Jo grows smoothly into the woman she was destined to become; in this way, Anne Hollander can observe: "A satisfying continuity informs all the lives in *Little Women*. Alcott creates a world where a deep 'natural piety' indeed effortlessly binds the child to the woman she becomes. The novel shows that as a young girl grows up, she may rely with comfort on being the same person, whatever mysterious and difficult changes must be undergone in order to become an older and wiser one. Readers can turn again and again to Alcott's book solely for a gratifying taste of her simple, stable vision of feminine completeness" (28). The tragedy of *Little Women* is, of course, that Jo is no longer Jo when she reaches maturity, for the real Jo never could reach maturity.

Torn between her personal loyalty to the original Jo—a lovely, vibrant, lively "New Woman" (as Janeway calls her, 44)—and her commitment to those readers who demanded a sufficiently traditional or comfortable narrative pattern, Alcott faced irreconcilable demands. The crime in *Little Women* is Alcott's brutal resolution of this conflict, and its real horrors emerge when we become aware of Alcott's willingness to finish Jo off (in *Jo's Boys*) as "a literary nursery-maid providing moral pap for the young" (42).[8] Alcott has, at this moment, lost even her own fervid joy in the young woman who promised so much, who shone so brightly for so many readers young and old, but who could not grow into adulthood as herself, as Jo.

Notes

Epigraph reprinted by permission of the publishers and the Trustees of Amherst College from *The Poems of Emily Dickinson*, edited by Thomas H. Johnson, Cambridge, Mass.: The Belknap Press of Harvard University Press, copyright 1951, © 1955, 1979, 1983 by the President and Fellows of Harvard College. By permission also of Little, Brown and Company, from *The Complete Poems of Emily Dickinson*, edited by Thomas H. Johnson, copyright 1929 by Martha Dickinson Bianchi; copyright © renewed 1957 by Mary L. Hampson.

1. Alcott's adult thrillers were discovered by Madeleine Stern and Leona Rostenberg and published by Stern in *Behind a Mask* (1975) and *Plots and Counterplots* (1976).

2. *Little Women* has been both assaulted and acclaimed by contemporary critics. Eugenia Kaledin writes that Alcott's "acceptance of the creed of womanly self-denial as much as her willingness to buy success by catering to middle class ideals aborted the promise of her art and led her to betray her most deeply felt values" (251).

Most recent critics of *Little Women*, however, have found more to admire in Alcott's fiction. Their critical responses to *Little Women* have generally been of two kinds. Some emphasize the independence, autonomy, and rebelliousness of Jo March (Janeway, Russ), while others perceive in the novel a matriarchal "reigning feminist sisterhood" (Auerbach). Historian Sarah Elbert finds Jo's development in the novel to be "the only fully complete one" and views Jo's marriage to Professor Bhaer as a "democratic domestic union" (207).

Other critics focus on the tensions and conflicts inherent in the novel. Alma Payne, for example, views Jo as an embodiment of the struggle between "a sense of duty" and "a strong self" (261). Ann Douglas finds that *Little Women* embodies the conflicts which Alcott inherited from her mother's and father's opposing natures ("Mysteries"). And Elizabeth Keyser argues that in *Little Women* Alcott undercuts the domestic values she seems to assert. Finally, Judith Fetterley, perhaps the most insightful critic of Alcott, finds a conflict within the text of *Little Women* between overt and covert messages "which provide evidence of Alcott's ambivalence" on "the subject of what it means to be a little woman" (370–71, 382).

In contrast to these critics, we argue here that in *Little Women* there is not only evidence of ambivalence but also covert manipulation of the text by Alcott in order to disguise the fate of her experimental, self-reliant heroine.

3. In her study of Alcott's short stories Joy Marsella observes that Alcott acknowledged the socializing effect stories had upon children and that she wrote her own in a way that "formed minds, prepared hearts, and molded characters" in a manner fully acceptable to the conservative editors of children's periodicals (xxi).

4. For a discussion of the "crime" hidden at the center of *Uncle Tom's Cabin*, see Kathleen Margaret Lant's "The Unsung Hero of *Uncle Tom's Cabin*."

5. For other discussions of Jo's sisters and their responses to the demands and conflicts of becoming "little women," see Nina Auerbach, Sarah Elbert, Judith Fetterley, Anne Hollander, Elizabeth Keyser, and Patricia Meyer Spacks. Several of these essays and other critical works on Alcott have been collected by Madeleine Stern in *Critical Essays on Louisa May Alcott*.

6. Fetterley thoroughly delineates this point in "Alcott's Civil War": "Beth's history carries out the implication of being a little woman to its logical conclusion: to be a little woman is to be dead" (380).

7. Fetterley supports this reading of Beth's role in the novel: "One can say that Beth's primary function in *Little Women* is to be a lesson to Jo" (381). In contrast to our thesis here, however, Fetterley argues for Jo's "ultimate acceptance of the doctrines of *Little Women*" (382).

8. See Elizabeth Keyser's "Women and Girls in Louisa May Alcott's *Jo's Boys*" for an illuminating discussion of the adult Jo's continuing frustration and resentment arising from her conflicts between "self-assertion and self-sacrifice" (463). Keyser delineates "the broken fragments of Jo's inconsistent ideology" in the "first layer" of the text of *Jo's Boys* and brilliantly suggests how Alcott's "disposing of her characters —most of them in conventional 'happy' marriages" approximates the "act of violence" Alcott contemplated in her temptation to "engulf Plumfield and its environs so deeply in the bowels of the earth that no youthful Schliemann could ever find a vestige of it" (469–70).

Works Cited

Alcott, Louisa May. "Behind a Mask, *or* A Woman's Power." In *Behind a Mask: The Unknown Thrillers of Louisa May Alcott*, ed. Madeleine Stern. New York: William Morrow, 1975. 1–104.

———. *Jo's Boys: A Sequel to "Little Men."* New York: Grosset and Dunlap, 1949.

———. *Little Women, or Meg, Jo, Beth and Amy*. Boston: Little, Brown, 1968.

———. "Patty's Patchwork." In *Aunt Jo's Scrap-Bag*. Vol. 1. Boston: Roberts, 1872. 193–215.

Auerbach, Nina. *Communities of Women: An Idea in Fiction*. Cambridge: Harvard Univ. Press, 1978.

Baker, Nancy C. *The Beauty Trap: Exploring Woman's Greatest Obsession*. New York: Franklin Watts, 1984.

Baldwin, James. "Everybody's Protest Novel." In *Critical Essays on Harriet Beecher Stowe*, ed. Elizabeth Ammons. Boston: G. K. Hall, 1980. 92–97.

Cheney, Ednah D. *Louisa May Alcott: Her Life, Letters, and Journals*. Boston: Roberts, 1889.

Dickinson, Emily. *The Poems of Emily Dickinson*. Ed. Thomas H. Johnson. Cambridge: Belknap, 1955.

Douglas (Wood), Ann. "The Literature of Impoverishment: The Women Local Colorists in America, 1865–1914." *Women's Studies* 1 (1972): 3–45.

———. "Mysteries of Louisa May Alcott." Review of *Louisa May: A Modern Biography of Louisa May Alcott*, by Martha Saxton, and *Work: A Story of Experience*, by Louisa May Alcott. *The New York Review of Books* 28 Sept. 1978: 60–63.

Elbert, Sarah. *A Hunger for Home: Louisa May Alcott's Place in American Culture*. New Brunswick: Rutgers Univ. Press, 1987.

Fetterley, Judith. "*Little Women*: Alcott's Civil War." *Feminist Studies* 5 (1979): 369–83.

Fiedler, Leslie. "Harriet Beecher Stowe's Novel of Sentimental Protest." In *Critical Essays on Harriet Beecher Stowe*, ed. Elizabeth Ammons. Boston: G. K. Hall, 1980. 112–16.

Gilbert, Sandra M., and Susan Gubar. *The Madwoman in the Attic: The Woman Writer and the Nineteenth-Century Literary Imagination*. New Haven: Yale Univ. Press, 1979.

Hollander, Anne. "Reflections on Little Women." *Children's Literature* 9 (1981): 28–39.

Janeway, Elizabeth. "Meg, Jo, Beth, Amy and Louisa." *New York Times Book Review* 29 Sept. 1968: 42–46.

Kaledin, Eugenia. "Louisa May Alcott: Success and the Sorrow of Self-Denial." *Women's Studies* 5 (1978): 251–63.

Keyser, Elizabeth. "Alcott's Portraits of the Artist as Little Woman." *International Journal of Women's Studies* 5 (1982): 445–59.

———. "Women and Girls in Louisa May Alcott's *Jo's Boys*." *International Journal of Women's Studies* 6 (1983): 457–71.

Lant, Kathleen Margaret. "The Unsung Hero of *Uncle Tom's Cabin*." *American Studies* 28 (1987): 47–71.

Marsella, Joy A. *The Promise of Destiny: Children and Women in the Short Stories of Louisa May Alcott*. Westport, Conn.: Greenwood, 1983.

Myerson, Joel, and Daniel Shealy, eds. Madeleine B. Stern, assoc. ed. *Selected Letters of Louisa May Alcott*. Boston: Little, Brown, 1987.

Payne, Alma S. "Duty's Child: Louisa May Alcott." *American Literary Realism* 6 (1973): 260–61.

Pickett, LaSalle Corbell. "Louisa May Alcott." In *Across My Path: Memories of People I Have Known*. Freeport, N.Y.: Books for Libraries, 1970. 105–11.

Porter, Maria S. "Recollections of Louisa May Alcott." *New England Magazine* 6 (1892): 2–19.

Russ, Lavinia. "Not To Be Read on Sunday." *Horn Book* 44 (1968): 521–26.

Spacks, Patricia Meyer. *The Female Imagination*. New York: Avon, 1972.

Stern, Madeleine B. *Critical Essays on Louisa May Alcott*. Boston: G. K. Hall, 1984.

"If We Have Any Little Girls among Our Readers": Gender and Education in Hawthorne's "Queen Christina"

Laura Laffrado

The strong, dark women who live in Nathaniel Hawthorne's major romances invite us to view their author as sympathetic to what Nina Auerbach has called "the complex life of woman in culture" (2). Hester Prynne, Zenobia, and Miriam all shine as "female representatives of the human creative and passionate forces" (Baym 124). Indeed, Hawthorne's depiction of women and his attitude toward feminist ideas in the romances is strongly sympathetic. Because of this sensitivity, the negative presentation of the title character in the earlier children's story "Queen Christina," part of the *Biographical Stories for Children* collection, raises troubling questions about Hawthorne's handling of genre and gender.

In the preface to *Biographical Stories* Hawthorne stated his belief that to acquaint children with the childhood of "eminent personages of times gone by" (213) would encourage an attachment to the history and literature that surrounded them and would stimulate further learning later in life. Hawthorne thus saw his children's stories, unlike his other writing, as tools for education. This educational intent has set his writings for children apart from his romances and, for the most part, has precluded their consideration in the critical literature.

Biographical Stories, first published 1842, features an authoritative adult, Mr. Temple, telling stories about the childhood of famous people to his son Edward, whose eye disorder keeps him confined, eyes covered, in a darkened room. The audience also includes the boy's mother, Mrs. Temple, his adopted sister Emily, and his older brother George. In the course of the book, Mr. Temple tells stories of Benjamin West, Sir Isaac Newton, Samuel Johnson, Oliver Cromwell, Benjamin Franklin, and finally Queen Christina of Sweden, all of which are meant to enliven Edward's confinement and to

Children's Literature 17, ed. Francelia Butler, Margaret Higonnet, and Barbara Rosen (Yale University Press, © 1989 by The Children's Literature Foundation, Inc.).

educate and entertain the family audience and the book's intended youthful readers.

The last sketch of the collection is markedly different from previous sections, both because its featured historical figure is female and because the story of her youth and adulthood is told in completely negative terms. Earlier stories spotlighted the relationship of father with son, sons who grew to be famous and admired men;[1] this story centers on a girl whose womanhood is best ignored, says Mr. Temple, "for it is neither pleasant nor profitable to think of the many things that she did, after she grew to be a woman" (282). The purpose of this tale, paradoxically, is to entertain "quiet little Emily," who "would perhaps be glad to hear the story of a child of her own sex" (275). Despite Emily's placid exterior, we are forced to conclude that, quiet and small though she may be, she must need the tale of Christina's life, a tale "chiefly profitable as showing the evil effects of a wrong education, which caused this daughter of a king to be both useless and unhappy" (275).

Unlike the boys, who were shown what they could grow up to be, Emily must learn in negatives and somehow locate herself in the stories of several famous men and one—at least in the eyes of a Mr. Temple—infamous woman. And, although Emily has been almost silent during the earlier stories, Mr. Temple apparently cannot rely upon her silent judgment, as he qualifies his understanding of her potential reaction by saying that she would "perhaps be glad." These early admonitory signs color the story to come with similarities to cautionary tales. Jonathan Cott has pointed to "the excrescence in the seventeenth century of the malignant 'Joyful Deaths' tradition of life-denying Puritan children's books" (3), and collections of English translations of German cautionary tales were equally graphic in showing an extreme punishment always exceeding a transgression at which an adult has first expressed disgust and horror. Thus, in *Struwwelpeter*, a German collection of cautionary rhymes, a boy who sucks his thumbs is first warned and then ("Snip! Snap! Snip! the scissors go") has his thumbs clipped off (16). In "Queen Christina," a girl who is not taught the eternal feminine virtues not only dies but dies unloved, unmourned, and without "a single flower upon her grave" (283). Even Hawthorne's spare transition from frame to sketch, "here follows the story" (275), carries an ominous tone, as though something dreadful were to come.

Christina is presented at birth as "remarkably plain" and "by no means beautiful" (276).[2] With "remarkably" and "by no means" stressing her lack of beauty, Christina's appearance apparently borders on the ugly.[3] This ugliness matters a great deal to her mother, so much so that her mother's affection is withheld because of it: "The Queen, her mother, did not love her as much as she ought; partly, perhaps, on account of Christina's want of beauty; and also because both the King and Queen had wished for a son" (276). The Queen's desire therefore was for a son of any physical appearance or, as a distant second choice, a beautiful daughter. Christina's ugliness matters to her mother because Christina, as a female, is a tiny mirror image of her mother and thus should reflect her mother's beauty. From the start, then, Christina and her mother form a sisterhood that is both bound and divided by genes and gender.[4]

Their struggle is intensified when, as a child, Christina is taken ill. The illness solidifies her relationship with her father, who becomes "exceedingly fond" of her and thereafter takes her with him on "all the journeys . . . through his kingdom" (276). As the father-daughter bond is cemented, the Queen subsides into a permanently peripheral role. Cast as an unloving (wicked) mother from the start, the Queen is placed in competition with her daughter for the King's love; when she loses that struggle, she is virtually banished from the story. Christina's socialization, however, becomes even more unorthodox after the Queen's defeat. Having displaced her mother in the King's affections, Christina now becomes a consolidation of the King's desires and is portrayed as a substitute wife as well as a makeshift son.

With the Queen in the background, the King determines to educate Christina "exactly as if she had been a boy, and to teach her all the knowledge needful to the ruler of a kingdom, and the commander of an army" (277). Lest the reader have more than a moment to contemplate such an education for a girl, the King's intention is immediately followed by the narrative admonition, "But Gustavus should have remembered that Providence had created her to be a woman, and that it was not for him to make a man of her" (277). The father's blessing on the child's potential transformation is subordinate here to the rigid gender boundaries established by Providence or the Nature of Things. Gustavus ignores these boundaries, deriving "great happiness from his beloved Christina" (277) as they are shown playing and dancing "along the marble floor of the palace —this valiant King, with his upright, martial figure, his war-worn visage, and commanding aspect" (277–78). Indeed, Christina's rule over her father is such that "she could disarm Gustavus of his sword, which was so terrible to the princes of Europe" (278). Shown together like father and son, husband and castrating wife, Gustavus and his daughter Christina only temporarily avoid the sociosexual consequences of overt defiance of gender and familial restrictions.

When Christina and her father must part so that he can go to war, the King's "greatest affliction was the necessity of parting with his child," and "Christina, too, was so afflicted that her attendants began to fear that she would actually die of grief" (278). Soon after, when the King is killed in battle, Christina is proclaimed a child Queen. Even without her father's misguided influence her education continues, according to Mr. Temple, to go wrong: "All this time, though Christina was now a Queen, you must not suppose that she was left to act as she pleased. She had a preceptor named John Mathias, who was a very learned man, and capable of instructing her in all the branches of science. But there was nobody to teach her the delicate graces and gentle virtues of a woman. She was surrounded almost entirely by men; and had learned to despise the society of her own sex. At the age of nine years, she was separated from her mother, whom the Swedes did not consider a proper person to be entrusted with the charge of her" (281). Her growth affected by the loss of the same-sex parent (a loss that also affected Hawthorne deeply in both his childhood and in his reflections in later years), Christina is left isolated from the virtues that Mr. Temple sees as gender-based. "Separated from her mother," Christina is the orphan she appeared to be as a baby, and without a female model her accomplishments continue to be inappropriate: "She learned to read the classical authors of Greece and Rome, and became a great admirer of the heroes and poets of old times. Then as for active exercises, she could ride on horseback as well as any man in her kingdom. She was fond of hunting, and could shoot at a mark with wonderful skill. But, dancing was the only feminine accomplishment with which she had any acquaintance" (281).

If little Emily is listening closely, she has learned what accomplishments lead to female goodness and happiness. Knowledgeable, athletic, and skilled as Christina may be, only her dancing will be allowed to aid her as she moves from girlhood to womanhood. Even Christina's dancing, which Mr. Temple categorizes in general as a "feminine accomplishment," was portrayed earlier in the story as an enactment of her inappropriate relationship with her father. This somewhat tainted skill, therefore, is insufficient to sustain her on her journey to womanhood since Christina "grew up, I am sorry to say, a very unamiable person, ill-tempered, proud, stubborn, and, in short, unfit to make those around her happy, or to be happy herself" (281), as Mr. Temple triumphantly relates. As a woman, Christina's first duty is to "make those around her happy" before she can "be happy herself."

Unlike Christina, other little girls have "been taught self-control, and a due regard for the rights of others" (282). Like Clara in *Grandfather's Chair*, another one of Hawthorne's children's collections, good little Emily rarely speaks and always listens. The education received from either Grandfather or Mr. Temple imposes a female sense of identity made up of exclusions, because both men tell stories featuring men only or featuring women negatively. Like Lewis Carroll's White Queen, girls must learn backwards or not learn at all, and also like the White Queen they must try to adjust to the restrictions of their world: "The White Queen is trying to justify the intolerable, as if she were master of the world and as if the rules were her own invention. . . . (The White Queen) is in fact inventing the rules, rather as the White Knight invents anklets for warding off sharks, because she is not at all the tyrant in her world, but the victim. The first rule is that there will be punishments; that goes along with 'never jam today'" (Sale 120). Having learned from Mr. Temple's introduction that there will indeed be punishments, Emily must view Christina's behavior from the beginning as deserving of those punishments. In this way, like the White Queen, she can align herself with those in authority.

Although at age eighteen Christina is "a young woman of striking aspect, a good figure and intelligent face," her eyes reveal "a very fierce and haughty look" (282). This physical evaluation of Christina is almost approving, even if her eyes—which, unlike Edward Temple's, are not bandaged—hold emotions antithetical to a good and happy woman. Such a favorable description reveals Hawthorne's latent sympathy with Christina, showing her as an attractive woman on guard against the world. This sympathy is temporary, however, and immediately afterward—as if to make up for such a lapse—we are led by Mr. Temple into a paragraph that sags under the weight of gender distinctions and stereotypes: "When she had worn the crown a few years, she began to consider it beneath her dignity to be called a Queen, because the name implied that she belonged to the weaker sex. She therefore caused herself to be proclaimed King, thus declaring to the world that she despised her own sex, and was desirous of being ranked among men" (282). Categories of men and women, kings and queens, a stronger sex and a weaker sex all bump up against one another in the renewed narrative zeal to denounce Christina.

Born a daughter instead of the desired son, and a plain, sickly daughter at that, Christina had been marked from the start for exclusion from conventional gender categories. As a child she is lost between gender distinctions (a girl raised as a boy), and the gap widens as she ages until she finally falls through it. Mr. Temple's use of "proclaimed," "declaring," and "despised" lends a royal quality to his condemnation. Christina finally becomes a sexless monster, a denier of treasured stereotypes and so an anti-woman. Such labels, harsh though they may seem, are fully exemplified by Mr. Temple's final emphasis on Christina's personal appearance once she resigns the throne at age twenty-eight, escapes her enclosures, and devotes herself to traveling: "She is described as wearing a man's vest, a short gray petticoat, embroidered with gold and silver, and a black wig, thrust awry upon her head. She wore no gloves, and so seldom washed her hands, that nobody could tell what had been their original color" (283).

Ultimately, despite her knowledge, skills, and independence that leads her to resign her throne, Christina must be judged, as she was at birth and at age eighteen, on her appearance. That appearance—masculine, unclean, and ridiculed—is represented as in keeping with Christina's maverick life, as is her death: "None loved her while she lived, nor regretted her death, nor planted a single flower upon her grave. Happy are the little girls of America, who are brought up quietly and tenderly, at the domestic hearth, and thus become gentle and delicate women! May none of them ever lose the loveliness of their sex, by receiving such an education as that of Queen Christina!" (283). Mr. Temple's exclamatory epitaph for Queen Christina serves as a form of intimidation, intended to frighten "the little girls of America" into delicacy, in case the attractions of traditional feminine virtues prove insufficient lure.

In his desire to re-create Christina's place in history solely as a cautionary tale for girls, Mr. Temple's final words return to Christina's education as the catalyst for what he sees as her unfortunate life. Much of his tale, however, has strayed from that education and has stressed that Christina was by nature not gentle, delicate, quiet, tender, or lovely. Mr. Temple wishes that Christina had died rather than have become a woman, especially a woman such as this one. Her birth in plainness marks her as a violation and she continues by her very presence to interfere, to disrupt, and to age, as she displaces her mother in her father's affection, displaces her father as king, and displaces various visions of femaleness. Despite the blame leveled at Christina's education, it is in reality her very existence that Mr. Temple finds disturbing.

"Emily, timid, quiet, and sensitive" seems "shocked at the idea of such a bold and masculine character" (283). "With that love of personal neatness, which generally accompanies purity of heart," Emily tells Mrs. Temple that it troubles her "to think of her unclean hands!" (283). Emily's only other comment on the story, also directed to Mrs. Temple, is, significantly, "I never could have loved her" (283). Despite the sexism, moral bigotry masquerading as piety, anger, and sexual frustration that fuel the telling of the Christina story, the possibility of love has not been banished from Emily's mind. Emily recognizes another woman, another little girl, and considers responding to her with the love that was denied Christina both in her lifetime and in this story. But Emily's judgment is limited by the stereotypes of femininity. She has not been "spoiled" by an overintellectual education as Christina has; she believes instinctively that Christina ought to have pleased those around her by being lovable, that is, clean and neat. Emily's education has been so narrow and ill-managed that, finally, she cannot love Christina because, like Mr. Temple, she believes that character is reflected in unclean hands.

What Emily has learned from the story, however, amounts to more than a rejection of Christina's life. Mr. Temple has unwittingly furthered Emily's education by underestimating the volatile role that history—in this case the history of Christina of Sweden—can play in person's self-knowledge. The story of Christina of Sweden, despite its negative presentation, teaches Emily what one woman has done and thus what a woman can do. Indeed, Christina opens herself to be read (in her behavior and her clothing) and at the same time resists being read, in that she demands a new way of reading. Neither Emily nor Mrs. Temple is capable of that new reading, but their post-story comments reflect the beginnings of a newborn and shared knowledge.

Earlier stories in the collection had received little more than perfunctory commentary from Mrs. Temple. Christina's story, however, prompts her beyond platitudes. Though she disparages Christina as "a sad specimen of womankind indeed," she also maintains that "it is very possible for a woman to have a strong mind, and to be fitted for the active business of life, without losing any of her natural delicacy. Perhaps, some time or other, Mr. Temple will tell you a story of such a woman" (283–84). Perhaps he will, but given the tenor of the story he has just told, it is doubtful, and Mrs. Temple, purposely vague with "perhaps" and "some time or other," is not strong enough even to request that story directly. Emily will have to hear "a story of such a woman" from another woman or create one herself, since Mrs. Temple has not yet learned to be an author and defers the job to her husband. This deference, however, need not be overrated. After all, now that she has heard about Christina's life, Mrs. Temple is able to envision a new sort of biographical story, one that offers revisionist implications with its stress on a strong-minded woman "fitted for the active business of life." Too blurry about the edges to be able to begin to tell this story herself, Mrs. Temple has progressed nevertheless on the path to author-ity.

Unlike the other sketches in *Biographical Stories*, Christina's story refuses to allow an authoritative man, a father and a king, to judge what is proper in his child's transformation; Gustavus's fulfilled wish to educate his daughter as a boy is a transgression that is punished by his death and Christina's monsterhood. It is convenient for the purposes of Hawthorne's story that Gustavus of Sweden was indeed killed during his daughter's youth. Thus, in this version of Christina's life, her historical orphaned state—father dead, mother banished—can be used against her with the implication that she is alone and unloved because she is a plain, masculine, atypical woman, and against her father, because he was responsible for her miseducation.

But the life of Christina overcomes the gender-based rigidities of the story and insists upon visibility. It challenges its modern readers to read it in a new way, to decode it properly, as it may have challenged its nineteenth-century female readers who were not selectively blinded to its implications by the dominant culture.

Despite the questionable female portrayals in "Queen Christina," at the time Hawthorne wrote the story he himself had much in common with little Emily. Like her, he had to locate himself in a world of negatives, a world where a man who worked at the Boston

Custom House or wrote for a living did not earn enough money and respect to sustain himself. In such a world, as the White Queen would have known, there were punishments. By creating a narrator such as Mr. Temple and allowing that narrator to condemn Christina, Hawthorne, like Emily, aligned himself with those in authority, made himself appear as one with the monied, properly employed, unartistic men of the world, the men who seemed to be everything he was not. Indeed, Mr. Temple's harsh treatment of Christina can be seen as a product of Hawthorne's frustration at his own inability to affirm himself as someone eccentric, someone atypical, a creator strong enough to move from alienation and isolation to a declared, defiant identity. In Mr. Temple he externalizes the societally determined figure he feels guiltily he should be.

By turning to children's literature, Hawthorne could change his focus from what he saw as the restrictive expectations of his adult audience. Writing for children allowed him to concentrate on education, and the freedom gained from this genre switch, combined with his "deep sense of responsibility" concerning what he cast "into the fountain of a young heart" (preface 214), resulted in his telling a personal truth: that miseries awaited one whose education led toward estrangement from society, perhaps as an artist, perhaps as a woman.

In his zeal to educate and his temporary genre-based liberty, Hawthorne was free to give children a strongly biased history lesson, free to make that lesson angry and full of displaced hostility in order to convey the urgency of his meaning, the frustration of his life. So much more withdrawn than the woman whose history he told, he could not bring himself then to admire openly the unconventionality in her that he was reluctant to acknowledge in himself and in his writing. The creation of Mr. Temple to narrate and condemn the problematic course of Christina's life allowed him to mediate his ambivalence toward Christina's social estrangement. Hawthorne's sympathy with Christina in her frustration is revealed in his admiration-charged description of her at age eighteen, in his exhaustive catalog of her many accomplishments, and in Mrs. Temple's commentary on the story. After Hawthorne's marriage, the death of his mother, and his attainment of success as an author, he sympathetically portrayed women not unlike Christina and greatly diluted the authority of their male narrators or associates.[5] These portrayals were possible once he had defied the expectations of society that had chafed him for so long.

In this children's story aimed at educating its youthful readers, the combination of genre and subject matter worked to educate the author himself. The history of Christina's life added to Hawthorne's self-knowledge, prepared him not only for his later portrayals of women and his recognition of their complex role in culture, but for his own eventual and overdue break from the cultural expectations that had impaired his art and his life. In writing "Queen Christina," Hawthorne sat in his enclosure, his own form of the darkened room and bandaged eyes, and, like the White Queen, tried to justify the intolerable. Instead of the White Queen's "never jam today," Hawthorne's justification was his pious and harsh glorification of the restrictions he saw preventing his own transformation from bachelor to husband, from unknown writer to literary figure. In "Queen Christina," for the last time Hawthorne savagely refused himself and the future artists, the future women, in his audience the invention of a world that would allow for the unconventional, that would allow a Christina or a Zenobia, the full possibilities of her biographical story.

Notes

1. The corresponding male portraits in *Biographical Stories* are notable for their absence of women. Mothers or mother figures are rarely mentioned, and wives are not mentioned at all. The relation of father with son or, for Oliver Cromwell, of uncle with son, consumes all of Hawthorne's attention in these stories. The guidance given by the fathers consistently results in their sons' achievements later in life.

This steady stream of masculinity is deformed once Hawthorne reaches Christina and Gustavus. Gustavus's masculinity—the masculinity that shapes Christina—is presented as misguided, defiant, inappropriate, and a clear violation of cultural and almost religious restrictions. ("Providence had created her to be a woman, and that it was not for him to make a man of her.") Christina's masculinity—her identification with her father, separation from her mother, physical appearance, and putative denial of her own sex—is also a deformed version of the male responses to fathers in the earlier stories. That Hawthorne chose to highlight Gustavus's and Christina's masculinity negatively helps to reveal his own recoiling from overt masculinity in his art and in his life.

2. Christina's appearance at birth seems to have been noted in virtually all records of Gustavus's reign. Christina herself almost cheerfully corroborates this description, remarking in her autobiography that her mother's classification of her as "a girl and ugly . . . wasn't far from wrong because I was as dark as a little Moor." There is no reason to suspect that Christina's autobiography was Hawthorne's source of information, however. Walter Hart's *The History of Gustavus, King of Sweden* is a much more likely candidate. A copy of Hart's book was withdrawn from the Salem Athenaum in Hawthorne's name twice in 1827 (Kesselring 53). Hawthorne was no longer living in Salem in 1841 while he was writing *Biographical Stories*, and no record of his having consulted Hart's book during that time has been recovered. The skeletal information in "Queen Christina" is close enough to that in Hart's book (which subscribes to commonly held views of Christina as both plain and eccentric) to render it likely that this was Hawthorne's source.

3. Christina's appearance here is at odds with the nineteenth-century view of children with which Hawthorne was clearly familiar. Hawthorne's portrayals of children throughout all his fiction correspond closely to the nineteenth-century ideals of cherubic, flowerlike children. The child auditors featured in the frame tales of *The Whole History of Grandfather's Chair*, *Biographical Stories*, and *A Wonder-Book* fit this mold without exception. Hawthorne's inclination toward sentimentalism of childhood reaches its peak in *A Wonder-Book* where all the children have flower names (Primrose, Periwinkle, Sweet Fern, and Dandelion, for instance) that emphasize their decorative role as listeners and their innocent, natural condition. (See Mary Lynn Stevens Heininger for a discussion of the progression of the sentimentalism of the image of childhood.) Christina's plainness, then, violates the depiction of children that nineteenth-century Americans found necessary to their view of themselves and their world.

4. Christina's relationship with her mother was actually more complicated than Hawthorne probably knew. Georgina Masson, in her biography of Christina, recounts that midwives at Christina's birth, "buoyed up by the predictions of astrologers . . . believed her to be a boy . . . since Christina was born with a caul which enveloped her from her head to her knees, leaving only her face, arms and lower part of her legs free; moreover she was covered with hair." Maria Eleonora, Christina's mother, "was in no condition to be told the truth and they waited several days before breaking the news to her" (20–21).

5. The juxtaposition of the first-person narrator Miles Coverdale and his attraction for and description of the darkly beautiful Zenobia in *The Blithedale Romance* (1852) mimics to some extent the roles of Mr. Temple and Christina. Zenobia is presented as a powerful, strong, queenlike woman of untraditional beauty. The story of her life and death is explored, related, and judged by Miles Coverdale, dilettante writer. Coverdale's authority is undercut virtually from the beginning of the book, and Hawthorne differentiates so clearly between himself and his narrator that there is little chance for the reader to invest Coverdale with Hawthorne's authority.

Works Cited

Auerbach, Nina. *Woman and the Demon: The Life of a Victorian Myth*. Cambridge: Harvard UP, 1982.

Baym, Nina. *The Shape of Hawthorne's Career*. Ithaca: Cornell UP, 1976.

Christina, Queen of Sweden. *The Works of Christina, Queen of Sweden*. London: Wilson and Durham, 1753.

Cott, Jonathan. *Pipers at the Gate of Dawn*. New York: Random House, 1983.

Hart, Walter. *The History of Gustavus, King of Sweden*. London: n.p., 1767.

Hawthorne, Nathaniel. *The Centenary Edition of the Works of Nathaniel Hawthorne*, ed. William Charvat et al. Vol. I, *True Stories*. Columbus: Ohio State UP, 1972.

Heininger, Mary Lynn Stevens. "Children, Childhood, and Change in America, 1820–1920." In *A Century of Childhood, 1820–1920*, ed. Mary Lynn Stevens Heininger. Rochester, N.Y.: The Margaret Woodbury Strong Museum, 1984.

Kesselring, Marion. *Hawthorne's Reading, 1828–1850*. Folcroft, Penn.: Folcroft Library Editions, 1975.

Masson, Georgina. *Queen Christina*. New York: Farrar, Straus, and Giroux, 1969.

Sale, Roger. *Fairy Tales and After*. Cambridge: Harvard UP, 1978.

Struwwelpeter or Pretty Stories and Funny Pictures. Frankfurt am Main: Literarische Anstalt, n.d.

Varia

The Story of the Unhappy Willow

Claribel Alegría

Translated by Darwin J. Flakoll

Claribel Alegría was born in Esteli, Nicaragua, but spent most of her growing-up years in Santa Ana, El Salvador. She has traveled widely in Central America, gathering material for anthologies of contemporary literature and history. She has published ten volumes of poetry, three short novels, and a book of children's stories and has collaborated with her husband (and translator) on many other works.

"The Story of the Unhappy Willow" is published for the first time in this volume of *Children's Literature*.

I

Once upon a time, there were two large weeping willow trees who had grown up next to the river and had never moved from there. The two willows had a young son who was small and always seemed to be sad.

"Our son sighs all the time," the mother said one evening. "Each day that goes by he seems to be growing weaker and more nervous. Everything upsets him, even the wind."

"I've been noticing the same thing," the father answered, "and the way he is always trying to tip back his head and look at the sky. Who ever heard of such a thing? Something bad is happening to him, and it worries me. I don't like it at all. Those children are the only creatures who seem to make him happy. He loves to watch them coming and going and to listen to their chatter."

Children's Literature 17, ed. Francelia Butler, Margaret Higonnet, and Barbara Rosen (Yale University Press, © 1989 by The Children's Literature Foundation, Inc.).

"Why don't we tell the water nymph about him?" the mother whispered.

The nymph was their friend. Once when she was being pursued by an evil sea genie, they had hidden her in their branches, and since then she had told them to ask her whatever they wanted and she would grant them their wish.

A chill breeze was blowing and the two willows were shuddering with cold, but they beckoned to the nymph with their long, graceful arms, and she pirouetted toward them atop the water, spreading her fragrance about her. . . .

II

The boy awoke on the riverbank just as other children were arriving. He rubbed his eyes and stretched, and one of them came over and invited him to join in their games.

"What's your name?" he asked. The boy, who was sitting between the two willows, was startled at the question. He felt a lump in his throat and a stinging water sprang from his eyes.

"My name is Andres," the other continued, "and why in the world are you crying?"

But the boy didn't know what it meant to cry.

"Come along and let's play," Andres told him. The two willows pushed him gently with their branches.

It was fun getting his hands and feet wet and helping Andres build a dam across the little brook that ran into the river. But when the other children learned that he didn't have a name they all started laughing.

"What shall we call you?" they asked him. "Don't you have parents?"

The boy nodded, but he didn't know what to say.

He suddenly felt all alone, as if he didn't belong to the rest of the group. He didn't understand what was happening to him, and he didn't remember anything. He stood there motionless. The willow trees looked at each other helplessly and then back at the boy.

Suddenly one of the boys cried, "Let's call him Jose," and they all agreed.

"Jose, Jose, Jose!" they chorused, and everything was all right again.

At the end of the afternoon Andres invited him home.

"Come on," he said. "We're going to have chicken for dinner!"

They were the last to leave the riverbank, because they had been busily gathering smooth, shiny rocks in a small bucket, and they ran all the way.

III

The cook was plucking the chicken when they arrived. Jose stared at her wide-eyed.

"Why is she doing that, Andres?"

"That's the chicken we're going to eat tonight. Don't you like chicken?"

"No," Jose shuddered, "I could never eat a bite of that!"

Andres felt embarrassed, and he walked out of the kitchen whistling, with his hands in his pockets. Jose followed him thoughtfully. He liked his new friend a great deal and didn't want to say anything disagreeable, but the sight of the dead chicken had made him sick.

"Do you know how to play the drum?" Andres asked finally to break the silence.

"No," Jose said gratefully. "Please show me how."

The two boys ran up to Andres's bedroom, where a shiny new drum lay on the table. Andres picked up the drumsticks and, with a flourish, began beating out a rhythm. He felt proud and his smile widened when he saw Jose's look of admiration.

"At school they say I play very well," he said. "It's difficult, but I'll teach you, and perhaps someday you can play in the parades."

In the rest of the day, Jose learned how to beat out a simple rhythm on the drum, and then they went outside and Andres taught him how to play catch with a softball.

"Why don't you stay overnight?" Andres suggested, "and tomorrow we'll go to school together."

Jose agreed happily. After he had climbed into bed, he wanted to think about everything that had happened since the beginning of the day, but he was too tired, and he fell asleep.

IV

On the way to school, Jose took long steps to enjoy the feeling of being able to move his legs without anything holding them down.

"Let's run, Andres, and see who wins!"

They ran all the rest of the five blocks to school. The breeze stood still to watch them, and some of the houses along the way opened their windows to watch the two boys racing past. Andres won the race, while Jose, who was gasping for breath, felt happy and sweaty, and that was good, too.

Andres introduced him to his classmates. There was one boy in the class who didn't take his eyes off Jose during the whole hour. During recess, when Jose started playing with the others, he came up and said:

"Hey you, where do you come from?"

Jose didn't know what to say. Andres was nowhere in sight, and the other boy, who was bigger, started laughing at him. Then all the others around them laughed, too.

Jose was confused. He just wanted to make friends with everybody and run and play with them. He had thought all the others wanted to do the same thing, but now he felt as if something inside had been broken.

"I'm not going to stay at your house tonight, Andres," he shouted. "We'll see each other tomorrow."

He ran as hard as he could toward the river and hid between the two willow trees. He cried for a long time and dug his fingers into the earth, which gave him a strange sense of comfort. The two willows had been happy to see him, but now they grew worried, and they bent down to caress him with their long branches.

Jose began thinking.

"Who could my parents be?" Jose asked himself. "I'm sure I must have parents, but I don't remember them. And I must have a name, but I can't remember that either.

"What ever will I say when they start asking me questions again? I don't know—but Andres is clever and perhaps he will help me. What a shame that he likes to eat chicken."

He tilted his head back to gaze up at the sky, which was a deep blue, even bluer than the door of the schoolhouse, and he breathed in the fragrance of the willow trees. How peaceful it was here in their cool shade.

V

The next morning Andres came to the riverbank very early and asked him to go to school again. Jose didn't want to, and so the two of them stayed by the water's edge, watching a school of small black minnows. The boys tossed bits of leaves to them, and the fish swam to the surface to nibble the pieces and find out whether they were good to eat. At any sound they darted away rapidly, leaving circles in the water.

"Aren't you hungry?" Andres asked after a long time. "Let's go home, but don't let my parents know that I played hooky."

"You mean they make you go to school even if you don't want to?" Jose was amazed. Andres broke out laughing, and the two of them raced to his house.

Andres's father opened the door for them. He had a wide, kindly face, and Jose liked him from the very first. He didn't feel shy in front of him, even though he had gray hair.

When they were seated at the table, Andres's father asked him in a friendly tone:

"Where do you live, Jose, and who are your parents?"

Jose remained silent for a moment, and his lips began trembling. Finally he answered:

"I live by the river, and I don't know who my parents are, but I'm sure they are somewhere."

"Don't be afraid. We're only trying to help you. Why don't you tell me the truth?"

"I am telling the truth," Jose replied. "That's the way it is."

Andres's father smiled incredulously and said, "Maybe you'll tell me later on."

Jose felt tears welling up in his eyes once more, but he kept quiet. How could they not believe what he was saying? Particularly Andres's father. Did even Andres believe he was a liar? No, that was impossible. They knew each other too well. They were best friends.

VI

The following day during lunch, Andres's father continued questioning Jose.

"If you don't want to tell us where you have run away from, I'll have to report you to the police," he said. "Your parents will be very worried about you. Tell me why you ran away."

"I don't know who my parents are, and I live by the river's edge where Andres found me. Isn't that so, Andres?"

"Yes," the other replied, "and when I asked his name, he told me he didn't know and he started crying. We all decided to call him Jose, but we still don't know his last name."

"How very strange," the father said. "For everyone's sake, I'm going to have to report you, Jose."

"What's the police?" Jose asked Andres when his father had left the table.

"The police chase robbers," his friend told him. "They're very brave. Haven't you ever seen them dressed in their uniforms, with their caps and pistols and police whistles? They direct traffic, too.

"Don't you worry, Jose. When they find out you've told the truth, they won't know what to do with you. Maybe they'll let you stay with them, and you can become a policeman yourself when you grow up. Wouldn't you like that? They're terribly brave."

"No, Andres. I don't know any policemen, and you're my only friend. I want to stay here and live with you. Why don't we go down to the river where we can talk?"

The two boys sat down under the willow trees.

"Or you could run away and join the circus," Andres went on. "Have you ever been to the circus? There are lions and elephants and horses and men who train them to do tricks."

Jose looked at him silently. He didn't know what to think.

"Tonight it would be better if you stayed here until everything is arranged. I'll bring you a blanket and something to eat. I'll come and tell you what's happening, and if you don't want to go to the police, I'll help you escape. Nobody will know where you are except me."

Andres spoke as if to lend Jose courage.

"Who can my parents be?" Jose asked himself as he dug his fingers into the earth. "Where can I escape to? I don't want to become a policeman."

VII

About six o'clock that evening, when the sun was setting, the nymph rose out of the water. Seeing Jose alone, she drew near him. She realized that she had left her work unfinished.

"Why are you so sad, Jose? What's bothering you?" she asked in her watery voice.

Jose had never seen her before, but this didn't bother him. Her kind face and her words made him trust her.

"I don't know who my parents are, and because of that they want to take me to the police. Andres's father doesn't believe I'm telling the truth."

"I understand you, Jose. Human beings don't trust each other, and they're always inventing difficulties. I don't think they really want to live peacefully together with each other, without arguing and fighting.

"How would you like to become a tree—one of these willows, for example? See how peaceful they are; nothing bothers them. They enjoy themselves by looking at their reflections in the water, listening to the chatter of the children who come to play here, exchanging jokes with the wind, letting the birds sing in their branches. You can see what a happy life they lead."

The two willows trembled as they listened. They had made a terrible mistake when they asked the nymph to transform their son into a human child! They had thought it would be for his good and had never dreamed he would suffer so. But now everything would be put right, and surely he would choose to remain here with them forever.

"No," Jose answered. "All I want is to know who my parents are and to live in Andres's house and not to let the police get me."

At that moment they heard the voices of Andres and his father.

"I have to leave, Jose," the nymph told him. "Everything is going to work out for the best." She sank, twirling into the water, leaving circles behind her like the minnows.

"Jose, what are you doing here?" the father asked. "Your brother told me that you'd come down here to play. But it's time for dinner now, so let's go home."

"Papa," Jose pulled his hands out of the earth and rubbed his eyes with his forearm. "I was playing for a while, but then I fell asleep. I dreamed about a fairy, but I can't remember what she said. Let's go, Papa."

When the three humans left, the two willows stood silent and amazed. They would never understand what had happened, but they bowed their long branches in humble assent.

Reviews

Critical Apertures

Margaret R. Higonnet

Opening Texts: Psychoanalysis and the Culture of the Child (*Psychiatry and the Humanities*, volume 8), edited by Joseph H. Smith and William Kerrigan. Baltimore: Johns Hopkins University Press, 1985.

Narrative Theory and Children's Literature (*Studies in the Literary Imagination*, volume 18, no. 2, Fall 1985), edited by Hugh T. Keenan. Atlanta: Georgia State University, 1985.

Du jeu, des enfants et des livres, by Jean Perrot. Paris: Editions du Cercle de la Librairie, 1987.

Children's literature, so long understood as a closed world because of its archetypes and its narrative structure, now seems increasingly permeable and fluid. Our postmodern era has made children's literature into a touchstone for literary and social reflections and reassessments. The dizzying thought that we are signs using signs for other signs, which unsettles the stomachs of many hardy academics, becomes even more vertiginous if we add into the equation the insight developed by Philippe Ariès that the "child" too is a social construct, at once the "father" and the semiotic offspring of another sign. Certainly children's literature as a separate literary institution is a historical construct, much of its interest lying in the makers to whom it points. Mary Douglas's analysis of purity and pollution may help us recognize the multiple social functions of this genre: first, it preserves a realm of purity, dependence, and ignorance; in turn, it also preserves the system of "high" literature by fencing out the presocialized and subversive Other, marked by a subliterary verbal code and polluting didacticism; and it inscribes a myth of origins and integrity whose nostalgic appeal has, if anything, intensified in an age dominated by a philosophy of fragmentation

Children's Literature 17, ed. Francelia Butler, Margaret Higonnet, and Barbara Rosen (Yale University Press, © 1989 by The Children's Literature Foundation, Inc.).

and alienation. To steal a phrase from *A Room of One's Own*, the child and children's literature have the magical power of reflecting a narcissistically enhanced image of the spectator—in this case the adult maker, purchaser, and critic. As a genre on the margin of canonical literature, children's literature constantly tests our criteria of aesthetic value, yet its marginal status has obliterated attempts to explore its formal and thematic participation in the literary system from which, again and again, it has been excluded.

Opening Texts, a rather loose collection of pieces, attempts closure through a condensed meditation by William Kerrigan on the "formidable array of objects, rituals, and fictions" that we pass on to our young. In his thumbnail sketch of the "second culture," as it has developed through eighteenth-century allegories to twentieth-century realism, he stresses a certain antagonism between child and adult, a rivalry to catch the golden ring of life. Both anthologies repeatedly ponder this proleptic struggle of the present with the future: how do child readers interpret such inscribed tensions?

Kerrigan's thesis finds support in Nicholas Tucker's delightful essay on lullabies. Citing Leslie Daiken, Tucker notes that lullabies may not only blandish or bribe a baby but also threaten it. Indeed, his most interesting observation bears on the thematic freedom of the lullaby. Since a very small baby won't understand the words, the text may be anything at all—with the result that lullabies offer an unrivaled record of women's popular culture. The richness of endearments, the delicacy of details or promised treasures, the pathos of ordinary fears: all build an evocative picture of the world women have constructed and its limits.

Sam Pickering's informative survey shows how the allegorical mode of the *Pilgrim's Progress* shifted under the impetus of Lockean ideas and came to transmit the increasingly secular values of the middle classes in the eighteenth and early nineteenth centuries. To be sure, animal types for the vices and such personifications as Miss Patient continued to delineate and impose a moral hierarchy. But the goal of these more realistic pilgrimages, as Pickering's numerous examples richly demonstrate, was no longer heaven but happiness, material success, and social promotion, to be reached with the help of the educator, mentor of an ostensibly rationalist bourgeoisie. Scattered throughout the essay are insights into such matters as the importance of the justified fight as a test of moral character in stories for boys, in contrast to girls' stories, where competitiveness is unacceptable. By the end of the eighteenth century, then, the influence of *Emile* and *Robinson Crusoe* had unwritten much of the older moral message; writer-educators like Joachim Campe and Mary Wollstonecraft began to praise the value of experiences outside the ivory tower of the schoolroom.

Anne Scott MacLeod likewise traces a change in children's literature, in an essay that supports Kerrigan's thesis of antagonism. She starts from the seemingly immutable myths of a stable childhood world that structured American literature into the fifties: the stability of the family, the "natural" authority of parents, and the decency of society are all unquestioned premises. In the writing of the past thirty years she observes a trend toward writing about older children subject to self-doubt, sexual torments, and even suicide. Even more significant, the new image of adult society is drawn in dark outline, stressing the inadequacy of parents and the corruption of society. MacLeod's interpretation of this evidence is cautious; she points to an exchange of knowledge between adults and children mediated by this new realism as well as a blurring of lines between the two generations. She concludes pessimistically that today's authors are not only tormented by self-doubt themselves but, in their stress on solipsistic, negative protagonists and plots of betrayal and failure, are hostile toward "the very concept of childhood," "fundamentally anti-child" (115).

Other essays by Maria Tatar and Jack Zipes will be familiar to many readers. Zipes's preface to *Don't Bet on the Prince*, reviewed elsewhere in this issue, proposes a feminist rereading of fairy tales in the context of "power, violence, social conditions, child rearing, and sex roles." He argues (against Bettelheim) for the need to challenge the oedipal paradigm and other ostensibly ahistoric archetypes. If socially conditioned family arrangements reinforce arbitrary sex roles in the tales and in life, and if they reinforce the capitalist socioeconomic system to boot, then we must try to rearrange or "reutilize" fairy tales in order to follow Rilke's advice: "You must change yourself."

Taking a more traditionally Freudian approach, Maria Tatar argues that, for the Grimms, stepmothers (or more generally "mothers in their various incarnations as stepmother, witch and mother-in-law") embody premeditated evil, and she traces a doubled plot of suffering by daughters and granddaughters at the hands of hostile maternal figures. Her explanation for the plot is in part anthropological: the father has violated laws of endogamy. Similarly, she finds that the female plot of evil "dovetails" with the plot of a father's incestuous desire; the taboo situation in the second plot implicitly motivates the wrath of the stepmother in the first. Here and in her book *Hard Facts*, Tatar argues that passivity and victimization are not exclusively feminine plights in fairy tales. Female evil predominates, for whatever reason (Tatar points to the audience's own desires); the incest motif has virtually vanished from our modern retransmission of the tales.

Despite the delicate intimacy of Roger Sale's confession about his childhood in Ithaca, when *A Tree Grows in Brooklyn* was for him a landmark, and the serious scholarship of Steven Marcus on Wordsworth, these essays do little to enhance the unity of the collection. In general, the volume seems not to innovate but to sum up established thought by one profession for the amusement of a second.

Hugh Keenan's remarkable anthology on *Narrative Theory*, by contrast, through its taut focus on a particular set of questions makes a major contribution to our thinking about children's literature. He has organized the volume around the problem of repetitive narrative patterns. The book will be indispensable for critics of children's fiction, and it raises challenges that will interest students of narrative in general.

Perry Nodelman grapples with a central problem for critics of children's literature: its simple, archetypal, repetitious, formulaic nature. In short, he poses a challenge to conventional ideas about interpretation and value, especially as these depend upon irony and uniqueness. Taking modern time-fantasies (Alison Uttley, Philippa Pearce, Nancy Bond, Ruth Park, and Janet Lunn) for his material, he argues that successive writers elaborate the positive and negative psychological implications of their themes of escape, exile, and exchange across time. (One could add many other examples of his paradigm, from Nesbit to Lively.) Finally, the essay hesitates provocatively between identifying an obsessive, antithetical core of our ambivalence toward children (19) and arguing that structures of recurrence call for a less negative interpretative approach.

If Nodelman stresses simplicity, almost all the other essays in the volume help us to appreciate the structural complexities of works for children. The most deconstructive of these essays is one by Susan Gannon on the quest plot in Stevenson, whose obsession with doubles makes his narrative the perfect subject. Like

Nodelman, Gannon traces contradictory impulses in her materials, finding tensions between a plot of maturation and a process of self-repression, set against a historical background of political, religious, and familial divisions. The ambiguity of freedom, authority, and ambition for the adolescent make her findings pertinent to a psychoanalytic theory of the genre. But Gannon stresses more formal and epistemological features, drawing on Hillis Miller's and Peter Brooks's work on repetition and uncertainty in narrative structure.

Rod McGillis interprets *The Secret Garden* in light of secrets and puzzles. "Secrets are to be shared": they catalyze community by delineating insiders and outsiders. While a secret once revealed ends the plot, secrets and puzzling details also interrupt linear narrative and resist definitive dis-closure, the opening up that closes off other readings. McGillis beautifully connects this thesis to the theme of "queerness," that is, of the uncanny inseparability of the familiar and the unknowable, life and death.

Displacement figures too in Virginia Wolf's essay on the humanization and idealization of the island motif. Northrop Frye argues in the explanation of his cycle of modes that the increasing "displacement," from mythic to ironic, corresponds to a development in readers' own sophistication. Wolf's lever, which permits her to release the complexities in a series of robinsonnades like *Island of the Blue Dolphins*, leads her to conclude that the more mythic and less ironic a text, the better it is adapted to young readers.

Lois Kuznets's essay on narrative framing and serial structures focuses on Mary Norton's *Borrowers* series. She notes a shift from a complex double frame to a more distant ominiscient narrator in the later books, a transformation that she connects to the allegorical significance of the *Borrower* characters. After observing that the series forms a bildungsroman, she explores different effects of the frames, which give rhetorical plausibility, establish "semi-scientific" sources of evidence, invite comparison between inner and outer characters, and imply authorial self-reflexiveness, as well as readerly autonomy. At the same time that Kuznets sheds light on Norton, she enhances our understanding of frames and their interaction in serial fiction.

Reflexivity serves as the focus also of Anita Moss's dense and illuminating study of metafictions, stories concerned with "the narrative forms of ordinary life" as well as the very nature of narrative. She is interested in "how stories within stories interlace to form an overarching structure; how characters function as both tellers and listeners; how children's writers choose to end their stories; and how they conceive of the process of storytelling itself through their fictional child authors" (80).

The last two essays in the Keenan volume focus on the reader. Jon Stott reassesses his own cultural assumptions about narrative that led him initially to misread Highwater's *Anpao* through stereotypes of Native Americans, and he offers instead an ironic reading of a story about a failed hero. In "Necessary Misreadings," Peter Hunt forces us to rethink the angle of vision from which we examine narrative sequence and structure. Hunt, who has written earlier about "childist" criticism, unpacks "adultist" preconceptions about the valid units of narrative form and its effects on the reader. Whatever the relationship may be between children's culture(s) and adult culture(s), the differences between the two force us to concede the possibility of counter or "mis"-readings of such texts as *The Wind in the Willows*, whose parts have elicited such rival allegiances. He proposes attention to narrative "shape," a looser concept that corresponds to a synthetic and performative rather than analytic, purely textual view of structure. And again, he points to "associative semantic fields," especially the fluid relationships of verbal and visual codes in picture books.

If we look back from Hunt to Nodelman, we may be reminded of Kerrigan's hypothesis: perhaps overcodifications and simplifications as well as contradictions in children's literature flow from the ambivalence of adults toward the state of childhood for which they ostensibly write. Another question that reader-response criticism needs to address is whether the way children read texts written for them differs from the way they might read any other texts. Can this angle of analysis, in short, justify treating children's literature as a separate field? Is it completely irrelevant that certain authors "intend" their texts for children?

The Keenan volume suggests that children's literature is far more complex, ironic, and indeterminate than is generally thought, and that the best works in the future may go even further. Although he would probably not agree with Wolf's theory about children's growth toward understanding progressively more ironic archetypal modes, Hunt implies that fragmentation, or self-deconstructing texts, correspond to what we are learning of children's methods of interpretation from the work of developmental psychologists.

At the same time, these essays show that children's literature responds to current theories of narrative that one might have thought applicable only to adult texts.

Jean Perrot's study of children's literature in the context of play, *Du jeu, des enfants et des livres*, resembles the Keenan volume in its forceful application of contemporary theories to the close analysis of children's books. A kaleidoscope of *aperçus* into the ways texts work, this book serves as an excellent introduction to the range of experiments, verbal and visual, in contemporary French books, yet it also draws upon comparisons to other classics, from Defoe to Sendak and Busch to Anno. Perrot's erudition shows in his references to Bachelard, Barthes, Bergson, and Bettelheim (to take some of the B's in the index), but it rests lightly on his style, often tongue-in-cheek. He is a comparatist who has written on Russian folktales and on Henry James, a student of psychoanalysis and anthropology who applies these interests to a body of literature that is far vaster than any corpus a T. S. Eliot would have recognized. And it is just this ecumenism that makes him such a provocative interpreter of children's literature.

Perrot starts from the functions of surprise and foolishness (*bêtise*) in these playful texts. He takes the Christmas gift (echo of nineteenth-century gift books!) as a model for understanding the pleasure a child may gain from opening up and plunging into a book, as well as the more cynical linkage between imaginative gift and commercialized consumption. Whereas Roland Barthes represents the reader's pleasure as essentially sexual, Perrot stresses the manifold (literally polymorphous) cognitive and sensuous delights of reading, without ever losing sight of the precisely structured vehicles of our delight. Though Bakhtin does not figure in the index, the carnivalesque, ambulatory, performative drollery and slapstick features of children's texts draw out some of Perrot's most incisive observations about the relationship between children's and adults' culture. Play, after all, is about rules or limits and their testing, and this book explores such major themes as the quest for liberty and autonomy through fantastic play. Children's books are not only heterocosms but microcosms, games for learning how to play the larger and longer game of life, and the last part of Perrot's book focuses on this initiatory function.

This book, then, returns to the questions set up by the Smith and Kerrigan volume, but with a pleasurable difference. Skipping, leaping, and twisting through texts and issues, the lithe movement of Perrot's mind leads us to discover secret openings and unsuspected depths with a seductive ease that makes us eager to read those works with which we may not yet be familiar. Perhaps the impression this book gives of casting shafts of light derives from a different use of psychoanalysis: not to divide adult from child, but to unite them.

Adults and Children

Hugh T. Keenan

Poetics of Children's Literature, by Zohar Shavit. Athens: The University of Georgia Press, 1986.

The title of this book seems straightforward enough, but, as Alice might say, its contents get curiouser and curiouser as one reads on. Shavit proposes a large scope and purpose: to account for the literary quality of children's literature—hence the "poetics" of the title—and to relate children's literature to the mainstream of adult literature. For a book of two hundred pages, that is indeed a large double charge. But, with the aid of recent theories of semiotics, largely the work of colleagues at Tel Aviv University, the author feels confident in explaining the various influences that adult society has had on children's literature. Her thesis is that the forms and content of children's literature are signs of the concerns and beliefs of adult society.

Unfortunately, Shavit does not clarify what she means by poetics and semiotics and their relation to children's books until the conclusion of her work. Because of this, the preceding seven chapters often seem merely to offer observations that readers either already agree with or recall as truisms of contemporary scholarship on children's literature. Among these are the propositions that children's literature begins in the eighteenth century, that children's authors have to appeal to both adults and children, that children's books fall into two categories—those accepted by the establishment and those rejected by it but enthusiastically read by children. But the reader cannot so easily accept some other broad assertions and blanket judgments that Shavit makes in her early chapters.

Poetics of Children's Literature is divided into three sections: "State of the System," "Solutions," and "System and History." There is no apparent reason why the third section should not, as the reader expects, come first; furthermore, chapters within these sections are often as nonsequential as the sections themselves. "Translation of Children's Literature," for example, comes between chapters

Children's Literature 17, ed. Francelia Butler, Margaret Higonnet, and Barbara Rosen (Yale University Press, © 1989 by The Children's Literature Foundation, Inc.).

discussing noncanonized and canonized children's literature. Each chapter is based on a few "test cases"; in many cases, the selection of cases is open to question.

In the main, Shavit believes that the educational slant on children's books has led to the perception that they are inferior to adult literature, although she feels that evaluation is changing: "During the last ten years or so, new interest has arisen in the field of children's literature, and important work has been done, notably, in the compilation of national histories of children's literature"(x). Yet this interest is not that new: Bettina Hurlimann's book on European children's literature appeared in 1967, and the first edition of Harvey Darton's history of British children's books came out even earlier. M. F. Thwaite's history was published in 1963, and Cornelia Meigs's *Critical History* came out in 1953. As to the purpose of her own study, Shavit asserts quixotically: "In this study I relate this newly developed field to the latest achievements of poetics and semiotics, areas that are quite new to the English-speaking world. I believe that the time has arrived to extricate children's literature from the narrow boundaries of the past and to place it in the foreground of literary scholarship, facing the future"(x). Like an early-twentieth-century anthropologist, such as Margaret Mead, Shavit believes that children's literature follows the same pattern of development in every society; that is, school texts and didactic works precede imaginative writing and adversely affect its development.

These biases cause Shavit to accept uncritically Phillipe Ariès's *Centuries of Childhood* (1965) as the basis for her first chapter, "The Notion of Childhood and Texts for the Child." At the same time the study ignores the demographic corrections of Ariès made by Lawrence Stone's *Family, Sex and Marriage in England, 1500–1800* (1977). In this chapter Shavit's test case is a comparison of five versions of "Little Red Riding Hood"—Perrault's, the Grimms', and three modern, mass-market American editions. But, curiously, in a study based on semiotic theory, Shavit fails to provide an explanation for the vogue for fairy tales among adults in seventeenth-century aristocratic French society. In short, she fails to ask how this literature is significant for its adult audience. The sophistication and satire of the Perrault version is obvious in contrast to the naïveté and didacticism of the Grimms', but no one would accuse the Grimms of being unsophisticated. Shavit also notes that the American versions are highly censored. Yet Jack Zipes's *Trials and*

Tribulations of Little Red Riding Hood (1983) has made most of this information redundant.

Shavit's second chapter, "The Self-Image of Children's Literature," really concerns the poor self-image of children's writers and their methods of compensating for it. It is easy to demonstrate the inferior cultural status of children's literature: its awards are minor, its scholarly studies relatively few, and it is usually taught in departments of education. Few would dispute the fact that awards are often based more on societal agendas or educational value than on the literary merits of the books themselves. All would agree that, if they are to be successful, writers have to appeal to a dual audience of adults and children. But is it a sense of inferiority that leads children's writers to direct their works primarily to one group rather than the other? According to Shavit, the writers who appeal mainly to adults find their material accepted into the canon, while those who appeal mainly to children remain uncanonized.

The test case for this chapter is provided by the two versions of Roald Dahl's *Danny the Champion of the World*, written first as a story for adults and later turned into a book for children. Shavit's comparison of the two versions shows how constraints on language, subject, narrator, character relationships, and narrative structure result from rewriting for children. But these points hardly need demonstration; any one familiar with both types of literature recognizes the differences. Furthermore, Shavit's choice of this example betrays an ignorance of many children's writers of the nineteenth and twentieth centuries who have written "unconstrained" works for children—that is, works that could be read equally by children and adults. Shavit says such a test case was hard to find because "not many writers write for both children and adults" (44). Yet one need only reflect briefly on the statement to come up with numerous examples she could have examined in the works of such writers as Rudyard Kipling, Mark Twain, and, in our own time, E. B. White, Randall Jarrell, and Judy Blume.

Shavit's consideration of "The Ambivalent Status of Texts" draws on a favorite tenet of current reader-response critics—that children prefer uncomplicated, single-vision texts. But, one might add, so do many adults. Shavit's test case here comprises three versions of Carroll's *Alice in Wonderland*. Unfortunately, this comparison ignores the fact that *The Nursery Alice* was planned and marketed for a much younger child than Carroll's original draft or its published revision.

Shavit notes that the story is simplified in three modern American versions intended for the mass market—the kinds of books often found in grocery store display racks; it is hardly surprising that these have been simplified. But Shavit does not explain this phenomenon of simplification within the context of reader-response theory. Instead, she asserts that "almost any reliable information is lacking on how children do indeed realize texts and in what way it is different from that of adults" (70). Such information is readily come by in scholarly journals, though, and there are recent books by Arthur W. Applebee (1978) and Suzanne Romaine (1984) on the subject. Shavit dismisses such studies as "too speculative" and as having "no sound scientific basis." Evidently, this chapter was heavily cut, because the bibliography lists Hebrew translations of *Alice* as well, but the text makes no comparison between them and the English versions.

There are similar problems in other chapters. In "Translation of Children's Literature," for example, she employs the mainly Hebrew translations of *Gulliver's Travels* and *Robinson Crusoe* to show that, on the one hand, the translations of children's books are generally freer and less literal than those of adult books and, on the other, that adult matters, such as political satire, sex, and scatology, are often omitted from such works as *Gulliver's Travels* when they are translated for children. Since adults translate these books for a market of adults buying books for children, the surprise would be if these adult elements were left in. Shavit's observation about this form of censorship is mixed with pseudo-scientific jargon, as in this assertion about translation: "Hence, the final product of the act of translation is the result of the relationship between a source system and a target system, a relationship that is itself determined by a hierarchy of semiotic constraints . . ." (111).

In "The Model of Development of Canonized Children's Literature," Shavit provides the reader with a survey of English children's literature from the seventeenth through the nineteenth century. She insists, though, that "the very same stages of development reappear in all children's literatures"—that is, that didactic children's literature gives way to imaginative writing. It would be difficult to accept this point without a great deal of proof. None is given. According to Shavit, canonized children's literature grew out of the books promoted by the educational/religious establishment. But such books as *Alice in Wonderland*, the Robin Hood stories, and the Grimms' fairy tales prove the opposite.

In her final chapter, "Stratification of a System," Shavit advances some interesting hypotheses, chief among them that the chapbooks of the eighteenth century led to the development of today's non-canonized and commercial literature. The popularity of the chap-books did not go unnoticed by the educational/religious establish-ment; and to meet this competition, writers of canonized works began to imitate the format and subject matter of the chapbooks. Thus, Shavit argues, children's literature, whether canonized or not, grows either directly or indirectly out of the chapbook tradi-tion, and this origin accounts, in large part, for the inferior status that still is accorded to children's literature. These intriguing ob-servations are hurried in at the end of her study, but they lead one to wonder whether, if *Poetics of Children's Literature* had attempted less and limited itself to the rigorous examination of one facet of children's literature, such as the chapbooks, it might not have ac-complished more.

Feminist Revisions: Frauds on the Fairies?

Elizabeth Keyser

Fairy Tales and Society: Illusion, Allusion, and Paradigm, edited by Ruth B. Bottigheimer. Philadelphia: University of Pennsylvania Press, 1986.

Don't Bet on the Prince: Contemporary Feminist Fairy Tales in North America and England, edited by Jack Zipes. New York: Methuen, 1986.

Disenchantments: An Anthology of Modern Fairy Tale Poetry, edited by Wolfgang Mieder. Hanover: University of New England Press, 1985.

The Kiss of the Snow Queen: Hans Christian Andersen and Man's Redemption by Woman, by Wolfgang Lederer. Berkeley and Los Angeles: University of California Press, 1986.

> *The realm of fairy-story is wide and deep and high and filled with many things. . . . In that realm a man may, perhaps, count himself fortunate to have wandered, but its very richness and strangeness tie the tongue of a traveller who would report them. And while he is there it is dangerous for him to ask too many questions, lest the gates should be shut and the keys be lost.*
>
> —J. R. R. Tolkien, "On Fairy-Stories"

Despite Tolkien's warning about the perils of exploring and reporting on the "realm of fairy-story," men—and, increasingly, women—persist in doing so. Certainly, if we judge from the essays in *Fairy Tales and Society*, *Don't Bet on the Prince*, and from Wolfgang Lederer's book-length study of "The Snow Queen," many questions are being asked, and the tongues, or pens, of the reporters are hardly becoming tied. In fact, in the case of women reporters, tongues once bound are now being loosed, and the tales themselves are being freed to speak in unprecedented ways. And although Tolkien goes on to condemn the "analytic study of fairy-stories . . . [as]

Children's Literature 17, ed. Francelia Butler, Margaret Higonnet, and Barbara Rosen (Yale University Press, © 1989 by The Children's Literature Foundation, Inc.).

preparation for the enjoying or the writing of them," contemporary writers, especially women writers, appear to have based their revisions of familiar tales, as well as their creations of new ones, on just such analysis. Almost every poem in *Disenchantments*, according to Wolfgang Mieder, contains within it "a critical discussion" of a familiar tale; together, as his title suggests, they offer a sustained critique of the illusion that we can all "live happily ever after," at least as society is now constituted. While the poems in Mieder's collection serve primarily to expose what their writers believe to be the lies and, more dangerous, half-truths of the best-loved fairy tales, the selections in Jack Zipes's anthology, according to his introduction, provide an alternative vision. As the title, *Don't Bet on the Prince*, indicates, the writers of feminist fairy tales reject not only the "happily ever after" ending but also the recommended means of obtaining it. Nonetheless, these writers recognize the "uses of enchantment," its revolutionary potential. Although the most polemical and thesis-ridden of these new tales do perpetrate what Charles Dickens called a "fraud on the fairies," the best, like the best fairy-tale criticism, open gates to new realms, admit those previously excluded, and entice the disenchanted to reenter.

In his introduction to *Fairy Tales and Society*, Lutz Röhrich seems to recognize how feminist explorations of the realm of fairy story can both break new ground and endanger the old. On the one hand, he pays tribute to feminist fairy-tale scholarship: "In the past decade the women's movement in particular has sharpened our view of the role of the feminine in fairy tales. Completely new perspectives have resulted" (4). On the other, he wonders whether some tales, viewed from these new perspectives, are not beyond the borders of modern fairyland: "As feminist commentators contend, there are, indeed, astonishing relics and role constraints in connection with gender from the patriarchal realm. . . . Can tales which pass on such material continue to lay claim to a legitimate place in the modern world?" (5). Röhrich temporizes that especially in "fairy tale 'renewals' and reformulations of well-known traditional material, one has to ask whether there is not a lot of ballast in the form of motifs that should be tossed overboard"; but as feminist essays included in both *Fairy Tales and Society* and *Don't Bet on the Prince* convincingly demonstrate, many of these motifs are an integral part of the tale, not only in popular versions but in those we have come to think of as classics of children's literature.

According to the four essays in *Don't Bet on the Prince,* written over a period of nearly fifteen years, fairy tales provide models of female development based on patriarchal assumptions. Marcia Lieberman, in "Some Day My Prince Will Come," first published fifteen years ago in *College English,* takes issue with Alison Lurie, who had argued that fairy tales portray women as "competent and active" (185). Although Lieberman admits that this is true of some little-known fairy-tale heroines, she examines Andrew Lang's *Blue Fairy Book* to show that the most familiar ones combine beauty with passivity. Active female characters are either evil or nonhuman. In "Feminism and Fairy Tales," Karen Rowe agrees with Lieberman that fairy tales encourage "conformity to those predestined roles of wife and mother" (214), "yoke sexual awakening and surrender to the prince with social elevation and materialistic gain" (217), and "transmit clear warnings to rebellious females" (217). Rowe, however, does acknowledge the ways in which fairy tales can aid "a female's rite of passage" (214) and raises the question that *Don't Bet on the Prince* attempts to answer: "Do we have the courageous vision and energy to cultivate a newly fertile ground of psychic and cultural experience from which to grow fairy tales for human beings in the future?" (223). A brief excerpt from Sandra Gilbert and Susan Gubar's *Madwoman in the Attic,* first published, like Rowe's essay, in 1979, analyzes just one pair of fairy-tale antagonists—the angelic Snow White and the diabolic queen. But Gilbert and Gubar, by interpreting the queen as a demonic female artist whose "plots" against Snow White represent attempts to escape imprisonment in male texts, represented by Snow White's coffin, go well beyond the identification of sexist stereotypes. Jack Zipes's own essay, the only one written expressly for this volume, deals not with the texts of the tales but with the illustrations of a single text—"Little Red Riding Hood." After summarizing his previous argument that Perrault and the Grimms, in revising the old tale, rationalized male domination by placing the blame for male violence on the victim, Zipes shows how illustrators from Doré to the present have contrived to suggest complicity between girl and wolf. While not everyone will, like Zipes, find a sexual innuendo in every illustration, his essay does provide still another example of the way in which fairy tales present women not as they are but as they appear to desirous and fearful males.

Unlike most of the selections in *Don't Bet on the Prince,* the essays in *Fairy Tales and Society* were written for a specific occasion, and they approach fairy tales from a wide variety of perspectives. Still, as Röhrich writes in his introduction, "the role of the feminine in fairy tales" is a theme this "volume repeatedly addresses" (4). Maria Tatar's essay, "Born Yesterday: Heroines in the Grimms' Fairy Tales," is in a similar vein to Lieberman and Rowe's analyses and, at first glance, adds little to them. Yet Tatar, like Ruth Bottigheimer in "Silenced Women in Grimms' Tales," demonstrates that sexism in fairy tales can be subtle as well as blatant. At first Tatar would seem to be exonerating the tales by showing that the male hero is typically rewarded for the feminine virtues of compassion and humility, but she goes on to argue that, while the hero exercises these virtues voluntarily, the heroine is forced to endure humiliation.

Bottigheimer presents a thesis similar to Tatar's—"men could be silent, but women were silenced" (118)—but as her subtitle, "The 'Fit' Between Fairy Tales and Society in Their Historical Context," indicates, she connects the silenced women in the Grimms' tales with the nineteenth-century German ideal of the silent woman, an ideal that cut across social classes. Bottigheimer identifies three strategies used by the Grimms or their informants to reinforce the cultural ideal of the silent woman: silence is often imposed on female characters as prohibition or punishment; the editors, where women were concerned, reversed their usual practice of substituting direct for indirect speech; and finally, women are often described as answering or crying out but seldom as questioning or commanding. Thus Bottigheimer's essay, like Zipes's in *Don't Bet on the Prince*, makes us question whether the sexism is inherent in the oral tales or has been brought to them by the male writer, illustrator, or scholar.

Rainer Wehse writes in "Past and Present Folkloristic Narrator Research" that "for the earliest researchers, the center of interest was *content*, then came the *teller*, and currently the *telling* in terms of performance, situation, and relationship to vital processes" (250). This shift is reflected in many of the essays in *Fairy Tales and Society* and becomes especially obvious when one compares Karen Rowe's "To Spin a Yarn: The Female Voice in Folklore and Fairy Tale" with her earlier essay in *Don't Bet on the Prince*. The latter, while still useful, represents a point of view that, as Kay Stone points out in "Feminist Approaches to the Interpretation of Fairy Tales," has become itself a stereotype. According to Stone, contemporary feminist scholars, instead of condemning fairy-tale heroines, are adopting a mythic approach, one sensitive to "the subtle inner strength of heroines" (231) and attuned to the "feminine voice" wherever it may be found. In her more recent essay, Rowe examines the role of the female tale-teller in such male texts as Ovid's *Metamorphoses*, *The Arabian Nights*, and Perrault's and Grimms' tales as well as in the French *veillée* and German *Spinnstube*. Such an examination suggests that men have long recognized and paid tribute to women as repositories of profound wisdom and tellers of truths but, after giving them their say as narrators, "having attributed this transformative artistic intelligence and voice to a woman," have claimed "the controlling power of retelling, of literary recasting, and of dissemination to the folk—a folk that includes the female community of tale tellers from which the stories would seem to originate" (61). Rowe's discussion of the story-telling situation in *The Arabian Nights* (a situation which, as Rowe points out, the revised title obscures) is especially impressive. She not only deals with Scheherazade's talking cure but with her sister's role in it and Shariyar's appropriation of it. Rowe concludes that we may "wish to reconceptualize Madame d'Aulnoy, Mlle. L'Héritier, and Madame de Beaumont, not as pseudo-masculine appropriators of folkloric tradition, but as the reappropriators of a female art of tale-telling" (71).

Although Kay Stone's "Oral Narration in Contemporary North America" does not center on the female voice, her observations tend to confirm Rowe's. Stone discusses the telling of traditional tales in rural areas, the telling of nontraditional stories in urban settings, and neotraditional tale-telling, a movement that grew out of the 1960s counterculture and gained momentum in the 1970s. Of traditional tale-tellers Stone writes, "Within the intimate family or small gatherings of friends, women were active narrators, but in larger and more public settings, male narrators predominated. . . . Women tend to be seen (and often see themselves) as preservers rather than as creators of expressive forms, and thus they assume the role of passing on material to others, notably children, rather than taking on the role of public performer" (18). She concludes that in the rural setting men perform primarily for adults, women for children. In the more sophisticated urban setting "the great majority of performers are—and have been from the early days of organized storytelling—women," but only because in this setting the "public at large no longer regards storytelling as a significant literary expression" (19–20). In the urban setting, as in the rural, women perform primarily for children, though in schools and libraries rather than in the home. Only with "the reevaluation of *Märchen* as adult entertainment" have men "reentered the scene as important performers" (23). Thus Stone's research on contemporary tale telling, like Rowe's historical study, suggests that once tales enter the realm of art or command an audience that contains adult males, the tellers become male and the female voice is muted. Stone's essay also confirms what we have long known about children's literature: that its association with women and the institutions they have dominated—the home, the public library, the school—has prevented it from gaining more than a marginal place in male-dominated academia.

Both of Rowe's essays urge women to become "reappropriators of a female art of tale-telling," and Stone suggests that this is indeed happening among neotraditional tale-tellers. Further evidence of this phenomenon can be found in both *Don't Bet on the Prince* and *Disenchantments*, though I would not agree on the evidence of these collections alone with Zipes's contention that the feminist criticism of fairy tales "has failed to keep pace with the contemporary feminist fairy tales" (32). In fact, of the dozen stories in *Don't Bet on the Prince* only a few actually fit Zipes's description of a feminist tale—one that marks "a shift away from the male-centered society" (31) and points "toward new possibilities for individual development and social interaction" (32). Of the stories designated for young readers, only Angela Carter's "Donkey Prince," Jane Yolen's "Moon Ribbon," and perhaps the Merseyside Fairy Story Collective's version of "Snow White" meet these criteria. Jeanne Desy's "Princess Who Stood on Her Own Two Feet," a version of the animal groom story, is a witty satire on sexist social conditioning but, as such, is more likely to appeal to grown women than to children. Further, the tale begins with and continues to center on the princess's longing for a mate. Left to her own devices, she is bored and lonely, and we never see her, as we do, say, George MacDonald's Princess Irene, learn to cope with ennui by developing inner resources. The heroine of Jay Williams's "Petronella" is more active, but the object of her quest is a prince ("I'll find a prince if I have to rescue one from something myself"), and she is willing to settle for the first one she finds ("You're not much of a prince. . . . But you're the best

I can do"). Tanith Lee's "Prince Amilec," featuring what Lederer calls "the riddle princess" and Stith Thompson, the "suitor test," is a charming tale, but it too contains flaws when exposed to critical scrutiny. One of these is that Prince Amilec realizes that he loves the young witch rather than the princess only when she models the latter's wedding dress. Then he sees her as "the most beautiful girl I have ever met" and summarily rejects his nasty-tempered fiancée. The witch's ready acceptance of her belated suitor confirms the reader's growing suspicion that, though we are not to *bet* on the prince, we are still somehow to obtain one.

In contrast, the message of three out of four feminist fairy tales "for old (and young) readers" seems to be not only "don't bet on the prince" but beware him. "Wolfland," also by Tanith Lee, is an exciting gothic tale that young adults would probably enjoy. In a sinister turn of the "Little Red Riding Hood" screw, the heroine, Lisel, discovers that Anna, her mysterious grandmère, can change into a werewolf and that she has bequeathed that power, along with her estate, to Lisel. But though "Wolfland" features active, independent, and resourceful women, and suggests an intergenerational bond between them, it portrays men as extraordinarily violent and sadistic and suggests that, in order to resist them, women must become the same. In Michael de Larrabeiti's "Malagan and the Lady of Rascas" a jealous husband, who fears that his beautiful wife will betray him while he is away fighting in the Holy Land, orders the court magician to give her the head of a horse. The horse-faced lady proves a better manager than her husband, and he returns to find his estate in admirable order. But in this tale, unlike the traditional tale of enchantment, love does not serve to break the spell. Instead, the knight returns and repudiates his faithful but horse-faced wife. Only when the vengeful magician gives him too the face of a horse does he come to appreciate her. The knight's cruelty and his wife's meek endurance of it surely place this tale in the "Patient Griselda" rather than the feminist fairy-tale category.

Perhaps the most startling selection for this anthology is Margaret Atwood's "Bluebeard's Egg," the title story of an acclaimed collection. One of the longest selections, "Bluebeard's Egg" is, despite its title, a realistic story of contemporary bourgeois life and is feminist in the manner of Doris Lessing's "To Room Nineteen" or *The Golden Notebook*; that is, it features a heroine who is almost wholly dependent for her identity upon her husband and her marriage, and it exposes the horrors of such dependence. Because we are largely restricted to the heroine's unreliable point of view, it is hard to know whether her husband, a highly successful cardiologist, is the Bluebeard of the title. He has had two previous wives about whom his present wife knows little, and she is intensely curious about what she takes to be his carefully guarded inner life. But all we really learn to his detriment is that he slips an extra syllable into feminism ("femininism"), refers to the cleaning lady as "the woman" (something his wife doesn't think to resent), and may have touched, deliberately or inadvertently, his wife's best friend at a party. On the other hand, his wife becomes pathetic in her desperate attempts to assure herself of her superiority to him and even sinister in her prying and spying. Thus we tend to sympathize with the doctor when, in answer to her question "Don't you ever wonder what I think?", he patiently replies that he always knows—because she always tells him. "Bluebeard's Egg" is fine psychological detective fiction—late Henry James in a contemporary setting—but feminist fairy tale it is not, for either children or adults.

Three stories for young and one for older readers seem deserving of the name feminist fairy tale. Angela Carter's "The Donkey Prince" is not one of the more striking stories in the collection; in fact, one wonders why one of her wolf tales—"The Werewolf," "The Company of Wolves," or "Wolf-Alice"—was not selected instead of "Wolfland." Still, "The Donkey Prince" is a charming tale in which a courageous girl's love and devotion to the donkey Bruno not only breaks the spell that has afflicted his people but tames the Wild Men of Savage Mountain. True, she marries the disenchanted Bruno, but marriage is not her object in aiding him; it is but an episode in her adventurous "working girl" life. In "The Moon Ribbon" Jane Yolen rewrites "Cinderella," elaborating on the mystical bond between mother and daughter hinted at in the Grimms' version of the tale. The way in which Sylva follows her mother's moon ribbon to discover the "tall woman dressed all in white" also reminds us of the way in which MacDonald's Irene discovers and later returns to her grandmother. Sylva needs no prince to vanquish her stepmother and stepsisters, whom we take to be inner, not outer, obstacles to her passage into adult womanhood. In the Merseyside Collective's rendition of "Snow White," the working class heroine is both an artist and a champion of social justice. As the queen's jeweller, she is offered the opportunity to become a princess, but she insists instead on better conditions for her people. And, as in "The Moon Ribbon," there is no suggestion of a prince. Still the figure of the queen is somewhat disturbing. To be sure, she is less obsessed with beauty than she is with power, which her magic mirror enables her to wield. And she seems attracted to rather than repelled by Snow White. But the feminist objection to traditional tales still holds as the powerful and commanding woman is "hurtled screaming" to her death and her body "shattered into fragments."

Of the tales designated for older readers, only Meghan Collins's "Green Woman" approaches the cutting edge of modern feminism. Like "Bluebeard's Egg," Collins's tale is realistic rather than fantastic, but it is set in colonial times and narrated by its heroine, who is regarded by most of her community as a witch. What the reader quickly discovers, however, is a wonderfully strong, wise, independent, but convincingly vulnerable woman. Living on the outskirts of her community, she ministers at great risk to herself to the physical and psychic ills of its inhabitants. She is the respected confidante of the village parson as well as the mistress of the village sawyer. But though she thoroughly enjoys the latter's moonlight visits, her first commitment is to the craft, inherited from her mother, which she hopes to pass on to their unborn daughter. One of the finest stories in the collection, "The Green Woman," unlike "Wolfland" and "Malagan and the Lady of Rascas," seems more likely to be appreciated by mature readers. So too, I think, does Joanna Russ's "Russalka or the Seacoast of Bohemia," though it is placed with the tales more suitable for children. "Russalka" rings ironic changes on both "The Little Mermaid" and "The Frog Prince," for this mermaid, after undergoing a transformation, succeeds in winning *her* prince only to find herself entrapped in what, to the mature reader, appears to be a stereotypical modern marriage. Like the king in "Malagan and the Lady of Rascas," the prince calls on the court wizard, in this case to undo what he thinks to be a spell but what is in fact the true identity his wife has tried in vain totally to efface. The wizard, a thinly disguised psychiatrist, determines that Russalka is suffering from "compulsive graphomania" among other things and takes away all her writing materials. At this point the mature reader begins not only to detect parallels with Charlotte Perkins Gilman's "The Yellow Wallpaper" but to suspect that Russalka's story is actually that of Russ herself. "Russalka," like "Wolfland" and "Bluebeard's Egg," is a haunting tale, but all three, as well as "Malagan and the Lady of Rascas," do more to document women's oppression than they do to celebrate their resistance to it.

The selections in *Don't Bet on the Prince*, then, are closer in spirit to the poems in *Disenchantments* than the introductions to the two volumes would indicate. Zipes stresses a utopian, visionary quality that many of the selections lack; Mieder chooses to emphasize the poets' pessimism, even cynicism, about fairy-tale resolutions. Yet, as he concedes, "many of the pessimistic statements conceal a quiet hope for a better world where these anti-fairy tales will once again become fairy tales" (xiv). Also, though Mieder dwells on the generalized dissatisfaction with the fairy-tale view of reality, he mentions in passing that many poems "deal specifically with women's concerns and do not shy away from homosexual issues" (xiv). In fact, about two-thirds of the 101 fairy tale poems, arranged according to the tale they retell or comment on, are written by women. Few of the poems are suitable for children (Eleanor Farjeon's "Coach" and those by Roald Dahl are exceptions), but many would prompt stimulating discussion in the children's literature classroom. Among these are poems, like Alfred Corn's "Dreambooks," that recall childhood responses to fairy tales or, like Lisel Mueller's "Reading the Brothers Grimm to Jenny," that express a parent's ambivalence.

Among the most fascinating poems in *Disenchantments* are those in which the poets retell a tale from an unlikely vantage point or reveal unexpected thoughts on the part of a protagonist. Male poets often betray their dis-ease in a sexist society: tales from the perspective of the frog prince reveal him resisting disenchantment or longing to regain his frog life; in male versions of "Sleeping Beauty," the prince, after gazing on Sleeping Beauty, either leaves her undisturbed or joins her in her sleep—in either case, he seems to fear his inability to arouse her. Other male fears are expressed in Guy Wetmore Carryl's doggerel version of "Little Red Riding Hood," which makes explicit what the illustrators analyzed by Zipes left implicit: "And yet it was better, I fear, he should get her:— / Just think what she might have become! / . . . A woman of awful renown, / Who carried on fights for her feminine rights / As the Mayor of an Arkansas town" (101). Still other male poems, like William Hathaway's, in which Rumplestiltskin resolves to "buy beauty young, / Raise her dumb, and fuck stars in her lovely eyes" (176), and Gerald Locklin's, in which a dwarf regrets the loss of Snow White to one "who'll never know the pleasure wrested / from a woman willing yet unwilling" (151), suggest why so many female poets celebrate lesbian love or at least strong bonds between women. The loss of such bonds is deplored by Louise Gluck's Gretel: "Now, far from women's arms / and memory of women, in our father's hut / we sleep, are never hungry. / Why do I not forget?" (68) and by Olga Broumas' Cinderella, who, after marriage to the prince, regrets being "Apart from my sisters, / estranged from my mother . . . a woman alone / in a house of men" (85). Such bonds are affirmed by Robin Morgan's two Gretels, who reject Hansel's bread crumbs for the gingerbread house of the "Great Good Mother Goddess" (69) and by Broumas' Rapunzel, who joyfully welcomes the lover who "might have been, though you're not / my mother" (55). Finally, regeneration for both sexes is suggested in Phyllis Thompson's version of "The Frog Prince." In a stunning reversal of the enchantment theme, it is the frog who disenchants the princess: "I feel a spell / Dissolve, and I come green to your hands again" (28).

Wolfgang Lederer in *The Kiss of the Snow Queen* is, as his subtitle indicates, also concerned with redemption in the sense of healing or wholeness. In his preface Lederer tells how the book grew out of a series of case conferences he led at a California mental hospital, and he goes on to treat Andersen's protagonists, as well as Andersen himself, like patients and the reader like a less experienced colleague. In the first part of the book, Lederer summarizes and analyzes each chapter of the tale, beginning with Andersen's opening promise, "When the story is done you shall know a great deal more than you do now." Lederer could have made the same claim, for his commentary is, for the most part, wonderfully illuminating. A summary can hardly do it justice, but, in short, Lederer reads the puzzling tale as a paradigm of adolescent development. Kay, the male protagonist, performs the tasks enjoined upon prepubertal boys in Western society: "differentiation from women and girls" and achievement in "masculine" pursuits, such as sports and science. "The effect of the splinters, therefore, appears to be that they bring about the onset of a perfectly normal, if disagreeable, adolescent phase" (27). Kay's abduction by the Snow Queen represents "the defensive-protective hibernation of the emotions during adolescence" (30). Most of the story, however, is devoted to the quest of Gerda, the female protagonist; and the number of trials, developmental stages she must undergo, is consistent with what Nancy Chodorow and others have enabled us to understand about the greater complexity of female development. Gerda is detained first by an old woman, whose garden represents withdrawal "to the safety of self-absorbed, narcissistic isolation" after the first stirrings of sex (43), then by the "riddle princess," "who yearns for but fears womanhood and who therefore sets impossible tasks and obstacles for the men who woo her" (51), and finally by the little robber girl, still another "refuge from anxieties about eventual heterosexual involvement, but this time by means of a detour into homosexuality" (57). The animals who aid Gerda represent her own animal instincts; that the reindeer must leave Gerda short of her goal and that she must rely instead upon a miracle to direct her to it signify, for Lederer, Andersen's failure of nerve as does his final insistence upon the protagonists' childlike innocence.

To explain Andersen's failure, Lederer in the second half of the book examines the author's life, especially his relationship with his parents and grandmother as well as his unhappy romantic attachments to both women and men, and certain of his other writings, most notably "The Red Shoes," "The Little Mermaid," and "The Girl Who Trod on the Loaf." He concludes that Andersen was hopelessly alienated from his instinctual self and that Karen in "The Red Shoes," like his illegitimate half-sister by the same name, represents all that he abhored in his mother—illegitimate and the mother of illegitimate offspring—and himself. As a result, Andersen became like his little mermaid, incapable of "delivering the loving thrust that would draw blood but make her *real*" (172, his emphasis). Lederer is particularly brilliant on the significance of shoes for Andersen and argues persuasively that they always represent the ego, the self. Thus Inger, in "The Girl Who Trod on the Loaf," is the person Andersen in his flight from the specter of Karen eventually became—the one who, in an effort to keep shoes clean, trod on the loaf of life. Finally, Lederer returns to the Andersen symbol with which he began his discussion—the shattered mirror of "The Snow Queen"—and sees reflected in its fragments the tragedy of Andersen's life: "True integration of his personality not only would have required the union of Gerda (anima) with Kay (logos), but would have had to include also, as in a new trinity, Karen (the shadow). Such integration, such 'at-one-ment,' he never conceived of, much less reached" (177).

One is reluctant to quibble with a book that throws so much light on an important children's classic and does so in such an engaging and conversational style. I can think of no better support than Lederer's book for Simon Grolnick's claim that "psychoanalysis itself stands within the folkloristic tradition. The patient and the analyst tell and retell, interpret and reinterpret the story of the patient. Oral tradition prevails until, in the fashion of Perrault or Grimm, the decision is made to write up and publish a case report" (Bottigheimer 212). Yet from the book's subtitle, "The Redemption of Man by Woman," to its epilogue, there is much to disturb a feminist critic. First, the various "temptations" withstood by Gerda look different from a feminist perspective. After reading Olga Broumas's version of "Rapunzel," for example, we are likely to interpret differently Gerda's "seduction" by the old woman and to question her identity as the "goddess of organic death" (41). And after reading Torborg Lundell's essay we are likely to see the riddle princess not as desperately seeking "a man strong enough, courageous enough . . . to help her conquer her fear of her own sexuality" (49) but as an independent heroine with the "capacity to make decisions about her own life" (155). Finally, after reading Lederer's own analysis of "The Little Mermaid," we are likely to admire the knife-wielding robber girl as one capable of "delivering the loving thrust" that would make both her and Gerda real. Even more disturbing, however, are the assumptions about the essential nature of woman underlying Lederer's interpretations. In analyzing the episode in the Snow Queen's palace, Lederer concludes that Kay, in attempting to spell the word "Eternity" from the fragments of ice, has succumbed to the hankering for immortality that besets mankind. But not, according to Lederer, womankind. "Woman, by virtue of her ability to give birth, and to nurture, and to nurse, and to make grow—by virtue of her attachment to the vital and organic processes of nature altogether, has also always understood and lived with the fact of death" (66). In Lederer's view, woman does not aspire, like Kay, to direct her own destiny; she merely acquiesces in it.

According to Lederer, "The Snow Queen" is not only "the story of adolescent moratoria, but it is, above all, *the story of the redemption of a lonely, inhibited intellectual by the love of a woman*" (155, his emphasis). After a brief survey of this theme in myth and literature, Lederer acknowledges that "the opposite—the redemption of woman by man—also exists. . . . But a woman redeems through love . . . the woman does not need to pass tests, she does not need to become a hero, and she does not need to become more than she has been. She proceeds with the unswerving purpose of a sleepwalker, and in the process only becomes more—what she already is" (157). Lederer's assumption that woman need not become a hero perhaps explains the gender-related bias Lundell discovered in the type and motif indexes—how the compilers, even when confronted with instances of female heroism, failed to recognize agency and self-determination. In his epilogue Lederer, in order to impress upon the reader the need of contemporary man for woman's healing power, reverts to the image of the shattered mirror: "Division is everywhere, society has fallen into ever smaller factions. . . . One of these partisan struggles being waged in the Western world today is the struggle for the liberation of woman. It is a cause of such undoubted merit that one must wish it well. And yet—one cannot help but fear that all this concern with independence will submerge a truth basic to human nature: that men, at any rate, cannot get on without women." We are reminded here of those who would argue that women constitute a special interest group. Lederer, by regarding women as a mere splinter of the mirror of society, contributes to the very fragmentation he deplores. He concludes his otherwise admirable study on this regressive note: "Without the validating love of woman, without the love of *his* woman, *for whom* he works and hunts and fights and *to whom* he brings his victories and his wounds—man in himself would be an empty shell. . . . [Gerda and Kay] remind us how lonely we are or have been; how, if we are men, we need the validating, the confirmation, the redemption by woman; and if we are women, how the redemption of such a lonely man is one of the magic feats, one of the miracles a woman can perform" (183, his emphasis). Lederer's belief in such magic and miracles places him in the fairy-tale tradition rejected by the poets of *Disenchantments* and demonstrates no less than some of the male poems in that volume the need, not for man's redemption by woman, but for further feminist research, criticism, and fairy tales.

Jack Zipes's own fairy tale in *Don't Bet on the Prince*, "A Fairy Tale for Our Time," portrays a little girl in search of the kidnapped fairy tale. In vain Steffie searches the endangered forest and the equally endangered city until, about to give up, she meets an old lady resembling Madeleine L'Engle's Mrs. Whatsit. Steffie "knows" she should not speak to the old woman but does so anyway and learns that she too is endangered—by the "boss people," who are about to cart her off. Only when Steffie tells a story, a story that is both her own and the old woman's, does the latter literally take flight, leaving her oppressors far behind and leaving Steffie in possession of the fairy tale. Ironically, Zipes is guilty of the kind of overt moralizing that Dickens, in "Frauds on the Fairies," deplored. Yet "A Fairy Tale for Our Time," apart from its none-too-subtle allusions to such modern ills as pollution, pornography, and even young women in business suits, does succeed in suggesting that, if neither women nor fairy tales are to be silenced, women must become conversant with the female voices of the fairy-tale past, amplify and record them for future generations, and, empowered by them, raise their own. But they must not break off where Steffie does—with the old woman's inability to make herself heard. They must get beyond, as only a few of the writers in *Don't Bet on the Prince* succeed in doing, the image of women as victims—their stories untold, ignored, or interrupted. To perpetuate such an image would indeed be a fraud on the fairies, since, as Karen Rowe has shown, "the origin of fairy" is "closely related to female arts of birthing, nursing, prophesying, and spinning." If *contes de fées* are "not simply tales told about fairies" but "implicitly tales told by women" (63), then women need not tread cautiously or report timidly on the "realm of fairy-story," for it is they who can ransom the kidnapped fairy tale and liberate, rather than pollute, the fairy ground.

Child Readers and Renaissance Writers

Juliet Dusinberre

Children's Literature of the English Renaissance, by Warren W. Wooden. Edited and with an introduction by Jeanie Watson. Lexington, Kentucky: The University Press of Kentucky, 1986.

Warren W. Wooden's essays on childhood and children's reading in the sixteenth and seventeenth centuries were projected as part of a comprehensive study which would have included work on drama and the oral tradition, and which would, no doubt, have dealt comprehensively with theoretical problems raised in several different places in this book. The collection ranges from investigations of Caxton's *Fables of Aesop* (1483), the Childermass sermons presented by the Boy Bishops, John Skelton's presentation of childhood and death in *Philip Sparrow*, and attitudes to childhood in Marian England, to John Bunyan's *Country Rhimes for Children* (1686). Between these boundaries lie two essays on fairy literature, the first dealing with Michael Drayton's *Nymphidia* and the second more generally with the treatment of sprites in Renaissance writing. In another chapter, Wooden develops further the work on John Foxe's *Book of Martyrs* touched on in the first essay in this collection. His best work—sadly, his last piece before his early death—is on John Taylor (1580–1653), known in his own time as the Water-Poet. The volume is compulsive reading for its lucid and unpretentious style, careful scholarship, and infectious enthusiasm for a subject that is still, in the crowded area of Renaissance studies, largely unworked: a *must* for hopeful graduate students, but distinguished by a freshness of approach that makes it accessible to a much wider readership.

The Water-Poet essay encounters head-on the question of literacy, publishing, and marketing, stressing that John Taylor reached out for new readers with the invention of the thumb Bible. The concept of the child reader is problematic in a period when many children listened rather than read, but Wooden gives a real sense of a subculture of books passing from hand to hand, of oral traditions written down for beginning readers, of Bible stories trans-

Children's Literature 17, ed. Francelia Butler, Margaret Higonnet, and Barbara Rosen (Yale University Press, © 1989 by The Children's Literature Foundation, Inc.).

formed into rhymed versions easily learned for reciting, and of the book as a living thing whose pages are eagerly turned—not many adults around, peering and preaching. Rightly, Wooden questions the category of children's literature, eschewing the easy assumption that Taylor's audience was confined to children. One feels that Wooden might later have revised the earlier essay on Bunyan's *Country Rhimes* in the light of his discussion of Taylor, commenting on the mnemonic and popular character of Bunyan's verses and tracing their roots to the secular and itinerant world to which both Bunyan and Taylor originally belonged. The vitality of Bunyan's poems, despite the author's moralizing, lies in an evocation of everyday sights and sounds, which seems more in the tradition of Comenius's *Orbis Pictus*, with its Baconian emphasis on things observed (beautifully discussed and splendidly illustrated in Wooden's first essay), than in the pious tradition of Foxe. Indeed, Wooden's convincing argument for Drayton's *Nymphidia* as a work intended for wide readership and suitable for reading aloud suggests continuity between Drayton and Taylor as well as between Taylor and Bunyan. Both Taylor and Bunyan look forward as well as back. Wooden connects Taylor's *Sir Gregory Nonsence His Newes from No Place* with the satiric writings of both More and Erasmus, but he might perhaps have made specific connections with *Utopia*, strongly suggested by the passage he quotes. Both the Utopian echo and Taylor's travel pamphlets based on his own journeys (anticipating Cobbett) make the reader long for an essay on Elizabethan travel literature, which must have been as fascinating to young readers then as it was later to the fifteen-year-old Virginia Woolf.

If Taylor's *Nonsence* looks forward to Edward Lear, Bunyan's *Country Rhimes*, with their joyous comic evocations—as, for instance, of the Hog which the poet revels in for its own sake before he recalls that it is supposed to represent a man—belong in spirit to the world of Hilaire Belloc. Bunyan's imagination was constrained as well as inspired by his Puritan vision, as was Milton's, and the latent secularity of these poems recalls a less austere Bunyan, dominated by his love of music and his youthful passion for bell ringing: a figure who slips unwittingly out of his own allegory both in these *Country Rhimes* and in the second part of *The Pilgrim's Progress*, and who provides reading aids to help children to read his verses. Wooden might have inferred the growth of child readers from the difference between Foxe's method of integrating pictures and text and Bunyan's deliberate forcing of young readers to read the text by refusing pictures, which were later inserted by adults who misunderstood his intentions and spoiled the impact of the plain text.

The work on Foxe remains the most problematic in the book. *The Book of Martyrs* emerges here as a horrific narrative demonstrating the savagery of adults in the name of religion, the violence and intolerance of the age in which it was written (see the section on the Jews and the Turks), the sadism of its author in his relish for describing torture both in the text and in the woodcuts (one of which is reproduced here), and the total ignorance of psychology evident in a culture which could have conceived of presenting this kind of reading matter to children. Wooden points out that the horrific figures come across as "caricatures or cartoon villains in the comic book vein" but does not ask the questions, which might have been inescapable in the projected study, of how this kind of childhood reading might have contributed to the fanaticism and violence of the adults responsible for witch-hunting as well as for the English civil war, and whether the mild secular discourses of Comenius discussed in the same chapter might not be seen as the reaction of a generation heartily sick of Foxe. Wooden gives a vivid survey of Foxe's treatment of children, but perhaps he might have asked more about the fantasy elements in the narrative, not least those surrounding the creation of good children. It is evident from other essays in the book that this period did not, in the main, regard children as pure and innocent but as depraved through original sin (Calvin's doctrine). The analysis of Foxe's fantasies of childish piety —often, one suspects, formulated for the reproof of adults more than for the edification of child readers—might have been related in the completed work to the fascinating essays in this collection on the Childermass sermons and on childhood or, as Wooden calls it, "childship" in the Marian period.

Marian Catholics cultivated the idea of childhood as a symbolic state and as a way of recalling wayward believers to a united church, stressing the mother-and-child bond and using Christ's call to little children to underline the obedience and simple faith which the church required of its members. The essay is full of wonderful material, notably the quotation about the real child of whom "yow wold think that butter wold not melt in his mouth" but who, alas, proved to be less innocent than he looked (*there,* John Foxe!). But the essay is a little cautious in the questions it asks. Childhood does seem to be used in this period to reinforce hierarchy, but Henry VIII in suppressing the Childermass ceremonies claimed that the children created a "mockery" of authority, and a quotation from one of the Childermass sermons in the earlier essay conjures up a lively vision of boys behaving just as wildly in church in the medieval period as they have done in later times. Wooden suggests that Udall's *Respublica* about Obedience and Faith, was suitable for performance by faithful and obedient children, but he would no doubt have considered in his projected study of the drama whether in some plays of the period children become the means through which authority is challenged—as it is by the simple shepherd-poet in the pastoral world and again (as Empson argued) in the much later world of Lewis Carroll's Alice. Both this essay and the equally fascinating one on Childermass sermons are full, as the whole book is, of the excitement of a new field. The quotation from Erasmus's Childermass sermon about how there is in every child "a certayne natyve and naturall goodnes / and as it were a certayne shadowe and ymage of innocencye or a hope rather and dysposition of a goodnes to come" seems an extraordinary anticipation of Schiller in an age generally much more committed to Calvin's attitude toward children. The interest of the sermons Wooden quotes here, together with his suggestion of possible Childermass sermons moldering unsought in old cathedral libraries, almost had me flying over to Ely to have a quick look for further riches.

The loss of the possibility of reading Professor Wooden at more length on the drama of this period makes itself strongly felt in the paper on Elizabethan fairy literature entitled "A Child's Garden of Sprites," which in its consideration, among other things, of the appeal of *A Midsummer Night's Dream* to children, raises the question of why children read at all. One answer is provided by the example of Francis Kirkman, unaccountably consigned to a footnote, who recounts his fantasies of *becoming* the powerful knights whose stories he read. It would be illuminating here to have more discussion of the boy actor and indeed of the phenomenon of the children's companies and the plays specifically written for them. Did Lyly have in mind the enjoyment of the boys who had to perform his parts? Even in Wooden's discussion of the masques Jonson wrote for Prince Henry one longs to know whether he saw any differences, from the child participant's point of view, between *The Entertainment at Althorpe*, written for the nine-year-old boy, and *Oberon, The Fairy*

Prince, written for the teenage Henry. One feels again that a political question might have been asked about the fairy topos as a place of power for children, as it undoubtedly was for Kirkman and as that very different garden is for Stevenson's child in *A Child's Garden of Verses*. The essay, which opens with a quotation from *The Tempest*, suggests to the reader Shakespeare's known source of Golding's translation of Ovid's *Metamorphoses*, thereby uncovering the whole area of translations of the classics and their possible appropriation by children in the Renaissance.

Some of the assumptions in this stimulating essay also deserve further probing. I doubt very much that a child would be riveted by the changeling myth in *A Midsummer Night's Dream*, a story which explains for parents why the symbolic child of the Marian vision is so different from the urchin who won't behave in church. I also feel that the consigning of fairy tales to the nursery once they become too dreadful for adult consumption is presented somewhat uncritically here, raising the ghost of Charlotte Yonge and many later writers who have complained that the definition of children's literature is that it consists of books that are too feeble for adults to read—a view by no means totally dead, either in or out of the academy.

Professor Wooden never quite escapes the problem of defining children's literature raised by the essay on Skelton's *Philip Sparrow*, which suggests difficult questions about the use of children in adult rituals which the projected study would doubtless have explored more fully. But this essay, as with all the others in the book, made me eager to read the originals again and to think of them within the new context of childhood reading which the whole book invokes. That, together with the sheer enjoyment of reading such lucid writing, is the greatest service any writer can perform for any reader, adult or child.

German Children's Literature

Ruth B. Bottigheimer

Handbuch zur Kinder- und Jugendliteratur: Vom Beginn des Buchdrucks bis 1570, edited by Theodor Brüggemann and Otto Brunken. Stuttgart: J. B. Metzler, 1987.

Handbuch zur Kinder- und Jugendliteratur: Von 1750 bis 1800, edited by Theodor Brüggemann and Hans-Heino Ewers. Stuttgart: J. B. Metzler, 1982.

Kinder- und Jugendliteratur der Romantik, edited by Hans-Heino Ewers. Stuttgart: Reclam, 1984.

Kinder- und Jugendliteratur der Aufklärung, edited by Hans-Heino Ewers. Stuttgart: Reclam, 1980.

Moore, Cornelia Niekus. *The Maiden's Mirror: Reading Material for German Girls in the Sixteenth and Seventeenth Centuries* (Wolfenbütteler Forschungen 36). Wiesbaden: Harrassowitz, 1987.

These books, as a group, exemplify new developments in the scholarship of children's literature—developments applicable to analyses in all areas of the subject, not merely those defined by the political and linguistic boundaries of Germany from the fifteenth to the nineteenth century. Taken together, they cover German children's literature from Humanism and the Reformation through the Enlightenment to Romanticism. One of them, Metzler's handsome *Handbuch zur Kinder- und Jugendliteratur: Vom Beginn des Buchdrucks bis 1570*, has both founded and facilitated a new area of study, early modern German children's literature. Both the handbook and Cornelia Niekus Moore's more specifically focused volume on girls' literature offer intensive discussions of German children's literature before 1570, a subject which, until recently, nearly everyone agreed did not exist. Taken together, the Metzler handbooks represent an extraordinary set of research tools.

The format of each of the Metzler volumes is similar: introductory remarks are followed, in the "Historical Section," by discussion

Children's Literature 17, ed. Francelia Butler, Margaret Higonnet, and Barbara Rosen (Yale University Press, © 1989 by The Children's Literature Foundation, Inc.).

of individual books and then by a bibliography that describes each of the works in bibliophilic terms, the bookbinder's craft keeping company with the illustrator's art. Each volume also includes several other listings that offer alternative means of locating, identifying, or assessing any given book: by chronology, genre, printer or publisher, and present library or archival location. All these listings are united by a clear system of numerical cross-referencing which is wonderfully error-free. Finally, an extensive bibliography of secondary literature is divided into two indexes in standard German fashion, one for people (*Personenregister*) and one for places and things (*Sachregister*).

In both Metzler volumes the editors have adopted a relatively unified approach to diverse literary forms by including in their discussions categories that reflect a variety of critical and scholarly concerns: reader-response; readership (age, sex, social class, educational prerequisites); means of mediating (reading aloud, reading alone, being read to); intentions of the author/editor/publisher (amusement, instruction, circumstances of use); content and structure; and subsequent influence. Though these questions are not uniformly applicable, simply setting up the categories and trying to provide information within them introduces a wealth of new socio-historically based data and immeasurably enriches the study of children's literature.

The historical section of the first volume (circa 1470 to 1570) is divided into four areas: religion, grammar and rhetoric, moral education, and didactic entertainment. The editors' inclusion of these categories clearly expresses an expansion of the genre. Comportment books and religious guides, until now considered only marginally a part of children's literature, join those literary forms which correspond to children's literature as it came to be known in the nineteenth and twentieth centuries, for the editors perceive an affinity and continuity between genres with behavioristically utilitarian intentions and modern literary forms.

Otto Brunken's informed remarks, supplemented by those of Cornelia Niekus Moore on literature for girls and Wilfried Dörstel's on illustrations, constitute an enlightening outline and definition of children's literature in this early period. Brunken's discussion begins with an excursus into the earliest work known in the German language for children, Bishop Arbeo's 760 A.D. German-Latin dictionary. Its inclusion demonstrates Brunken's cautious attempt to expand the boundaries of children's literature. If the genre is to encompass everything written for children's use, then instructional and catechetical books must join those produced for children's amusement; this is especially important to the Humanist period, when some of the greatest minds of the day—Erasmus, Calvin, Zwingli, Reuchlin, Melanchthon, and Luther himself—wrote books specifically intended for young readers.

In his introductory article, "Zum Bildegebrauch in der frühen Kinder- und Jugendliteratur," Wilfried Dörstel defines illustrations in children's literature in terms of their function and purpose: as visual messages with specific duties—orientation, specification, and emphasis. For children and unschooled adults pictures might serve as alternatives to the written word. Considered a didactic aid, pictures generally illuminate text, but sometimes the relationship reverses, so that text comments on illustration, as it does in children's picture Bibles and in children's encyclopedias like the *Orbis Pictus*.

The 1750–1800 volume opens with a set of excellent essays by Hans-Heino Ewers. Initially planned as the only volume, it appeared in 1982; in it, Ewers makes his crucial redefinition of children's literature. On the one hand, he expands the canon to include everything written specifically for children and adolescents, whether it be adult literature rewritten for a younger readership, informational handbooks, inspirational reading, instructional manuals, or belles lettres. And on the other hand, he evinces a broad concern for the process and scope of children's reading which shifts scholarly perspective to the reader and her (or his) milieu, anchoring both in place, time, social class, and educational level.

In addition to this remarkable and welcome broadening of the discipline, the history of children's literature was extended far into the past because of the amount of new material that turned up in the course of preparing the 1750–1800 volume. It became clear that the theory of children's literature as a phenomenon of the eighteenth century was not only out-of-date but basically incorrect. Hence, the subsequent volumes address an earlier period but are the offspring of this pivotal 1750–1800 volume.

Ewers discusses how the growing institutionalization of school in the eighteenth century promoted the process of segregating the instructional from the fictional. But despite this separation, Ewers points out, children's fiction continued to be characterized by contents in which precept and example far outweighed formal esthetic requirements, an emphasis perfectly in step with prevailing theories of child rearing and pedagogy. John Locke's *Thoughts on Education* permeated German child-rearing and educational principles for much of the eighteenth century and offered the viewpoint that intelligent discourse with children would effectively overcome instinct and accustom the child to virtuous patterns of conduct. Although Locke advocated introducing the young child to reading as soon as it could speak, he urged a gentle regard for the child's own interests, specifying that novel and engaging readings would excite the child's curiosity and desire to learn.

Parental zeal to perfect childish intelligence must have laid heavy burdens on youthful spirits and elicited rebellious responses, for when Jean-Jacques Rousseau published *Emile* in 1762, the pendulum began to swing in the other direction. Emile hardly saw a book before his twelfth birthday, learning instead from observation and ingenuity. His natural text would have been *Robinson Crusoe*, and, indeed, adherence to Rousseauian ideas and an outpouring of novels based on *Robinson Crusoe* continued together into the nineteenth century.

The final introductory essay in this volume treats literature for girls. Its author, Dagmar Grenz, is familiar to Germanists for her fine study *Mädchenliteratur*, which describes and defines the gender-specific norms of reading material produced for girls in the eighteenth and nineteenth centuries. Authors already well known in the realm of German-language children's literature (like J. H. Campe) are discussed here and, as in the earlier volume, some of the weightiest authors of the day—Lessing, Herder, Gottsched, and Lavater—make their appearance in this unfamiliar context.

To a certain extent one may view the handbooks' dramatic extension of the field of children's literature as a natural outgrowth of two decades of research and publishing in the field of social history. Numerous studies, such as those by Philippe Ariès and Lloyd de Mause, have deepened contemporary knowledge about the history of childhood and the family and have provided the sort of historical context in which the documents considered here can be understood as genuine children's literature, even though they differ vastly from the contemporary canon.

Only two problems in the Metzler volumes are apparent to me. The first is that neither handbook touches on *Schundliteratur*, the blood-and-gore, sex-and-violence readings which the publishers of every age provide for a surprisingly broad public and which other segments of the public routinely—and vainly—try to censor and to suppress. The second is the contributors' lack of detailed distinctions between works created according to different religious faiths in their essays. The religious landscape in Germany in the sixteenth, seventeenth, and eighteenth centuries was a highly differentiated one. Set against a relatively monolithic Catholicism, the various sects of a splintered Protestantism advocated quite different and sometimes opposing approaches to the selection of reading material appropriate for young eyes. Taking these differences into consideration would have enhanced the interpretations and readings of the sources, which are sensitive and enlightening in every other respect.

At prices that have become prohibitive for Americans since the radical shift in foreign currency exchange rates, these reference books can be bought only by institutions. But any college or university which hopes to offer children's literature or German social history should make a point of obtaining the complete set.

Hans-Heino Ewers's two text collections, *Kinder- und Jugendliteratur der Aufklärung* (Reclam 1980) and *Kinder- und Jugendliteratur der Romantik* (Reclam 1984), make admirable companions for Metzler's 1750–1800 volume, offering long and worthwhile introductory essays together with many of the actual texts: riddles, verse, fairy tales, and excerpts from children's almanacs. One hopes that additional Reclam text collections for the earlier period will soon follow.

Gender determines the subject of Cornelia Niekus Moore's study, *The Maiden's Mirror*, an unusually broad and rich source of information about and analysis of sixteenth- and seventeenth-century literature for girls. Moore has virtually created and defined this area of scholarship, which did not exist before she mined the holdings of the Herzog August Library in Wolfenbüttel. In these pages we see girls viewed both as potential wives and mothers (in courtship and cosmetics manuals) and as possible spinsters. Literature for girls' amusement per se does not emerge until the end of the seventeenth century, and then only under a cloud of dark suspicion that it might subvert virtue's development. Catechisms, Bibles, and prayer books join novels, books of manners, and cooking manuals in a flood of books that presuppose a broadly literate readership.

And, indeed, the seventeenth century was a period in which Protestant schools expanded and new Catholic teaching orders were initiated (the Augustinians, Ursulines, and Salesians, for example). Moore's *Maiden's Mirror* along with Dagmar Grenz's *Mädchenliteratur* (1981) opens the doors to four centuries of gender-specific children's literature.

Together with such historical studies as Steven Ozment's *When Fathers Ruled: Family Life in Reformation Europe* and socio-historically oriented literary studies like Rudolf Schenda's recent articles on reading, the Metzler reference books, Reclam's text collections, and Moore's and Grenz's gender studies chart new ways to approach children's literature in general as well as in Germany.

Grimm Translation and Scholarship

J. D. Stahl

The Complete Fairy Tales of the Brothers Grimm. Translated by Jack Zipes. New York: Bantam, 1987.

Grimms' Bad Girls and Bold Boys: The Moral and Social Vision of the Tales, by Ruth B. Bottigheimer. New Haven: Yale University Press, 1987.

The Hard Facts of the Grimms' Fairy Tales, by Maria Tatar. Princeton, N. J.: Princeton University Press, 1987.

This entirely new translation is based on the seventh edition of the *Kinder- und Hausmärchen* (*Children's and Household Tales*); however, it contains not only the 210 tales available in other English editions,but 32 tales not previously translated into English. These are tales that the Grimm brothers published in various other editions of their collections but eventually omitted for different reasons. Jack Zipes's translation is a valuable, timely, and accomplished achievement, both for scholars and for the general reader. He himself addresses in his "Note on the Translation" a question that may occur to many: "Why publish another translation?" His answer is that most available translations are either too antiquated or too trendy. His goal is "to respect the historical character and idioms of each tale and to retain a nineteenth-century flavor while introducing contemporary vocabulary and terms when . . . apropos." For the most part, he succeeds admirably. Zipes follows the language of the original tales in detail and with great accuracy, yet he avoids (with only rare lapses) bookish or forced constructions. A significant part of his achievement is to have created a plain, unobtrusively idiomatic American English style that is, in many respects, equivalent to the direct prose of the German originals. It is startling at times to come across distinctly American idiom here, such as the description of the central character of "The Brave Little Tailor" (no. 20), in which Zipes informs us that "the little tailor was no slouch." Yet it is important to remember that many of these tales were collected

Children's Literature 17, ed. Francelia Butler, Margaret Higonnet, and Barbara Rosen

in various German dialects that would seem equally as vernacular to a speaker of High German as American slang to an educated speaker of American English.

In particular, Zipes captures the often wry, sardonic, subtle humor of the German, not necessarily in the same sentences where it is most visible in the originals, but often adeptly in expressions that help re-create the spirit of the German stories. This humor often arises from a laconic statement of the mundane or the grotesque. In "The Knapsack, the Hat, and the Horn" (no. 54), we read: "'One day's just like the next,' responded the charcoal burner, 'and every night, potatoes.'" At such moments, Zipes actually seems to be improving on the original. On the other hand, there are inevitably passages where the English seems flat in comparison to the German. It is an inescapable *quid pro quo,* because the vividness of idiom is often not directly translatable. The mastery of this translation is visible as much in its total effect as in any of the particular details.

Zipes succeeds less well with the rhymes, which often seem unidiomatic and forced for the sake of rhyme, while the German seems precisely the opposite: all the more idiomatic for rhyming. The rhyme in "Help us, help us, little duck! / It's Hansel and Gretel, and we're really stuck!" is not worth the departure from accuracy and elegance that it forces. A few times the effort to find a rhyme seems to have led to unnecessary inaccuracy, the most egregious example being the translation "There's blood all over, and her foot's too small. / She's not the bride you met at the ball" in "Cinderella" for "Der Schuck ist zu klein, / Die rechte Braut sitzt noch daheim" (The *shoe* is too small, the true bride still sits at home—my emphasis). A child—who knows that the shoe is the important element—will be quick to spot the illogic of the change. In general, the freer the verse translations (in terms of rhyme scheme), the more apt they seem.

Zipes's perhaps a little misleadingly titled introduction, "Once There Were Two Brothers Named Grimm," (misleading because its cuteness belies its scholarly thoroughness) is a concise, valuable survey of the life and work of the Grimm brothers. He also gives a brief history of the reception of the tales and sketches the major critical approaches and controversies, with succinct critical assessments. He does not advocate any particular approach here, merely pointing out in conclusion that the tales keep alive "our utopian longing for a better world that can be created out of our dreams and actions" (xxxi). Of special value in his survey of the evolution of different schools of criticism is his emphasis on their interaction and his inclusion of frequently neglected critics. Zipes conscientiously follows the order and numbering of the German tales and also helpfully lists the reasons (when known) for the omission of the tales the Grimm brothers decided to excise. The notes, very useful for scholars, list the oral contributors of each story when possible and the date of the tale's first publication in German. The list of contributors of oral and literary tales serves to reinforce the point that most of the tellers from whom the Grimms gleaned their stories were from the middle class and the aristocracy, not, as is often assumed, the peasantry.

The collection is timely for several reasons. It appears at a time when educators are beginning to rebel against the mental pablum of the "basal readers," sometimes urging, as Diane Ravitch has done (see *American Scholar*, Summer 1987), the introduction of "fairy tales, myths, legends, folklore, heroic adventures," and the like in the place of "vapid textbooks." Bruno Bettelheim's *On Reading* was one of the early works influential in leading this revolt. Zipes's collection presents the entire opus of the Grimm brothers in readable, vivid prose to an audience that has been prepared, through the debate initiated by Bettelheim and carried on with fervor by other scholarly and popular critics, to recognize the importance of the tales, even while their interpretation and function remain controversial.

Presenting the best-known half dozen or so tales ("Cinderella," "Snow White," "Hansel and Gretel," "Brier Rose" [better known as "Sleeping Beauty"], "Rapunzel," "The Frog King," and a few others) in the context of the complete collection will help both to sharpen our perceptions of the individual tales and to show how typical they are in some respects of the collection as a whole. It will also enlarge our understanding of how wide-ranging and varied the tales are, from didactic to sardonic, from etiological to cumulative or moral, and of how far some of the tales depart from our preconceptions of what the Grimms' fairy tales say and how they say it. For example, the Grimms' often-praised simple (if not simplistic) morality sometimes appears in the context of tales like "The Companionship of the Cat and the Mouse" that are obviously cynical and worldly-minded about how power operates in the world. Yet other tales (and not only the ten explicitly labeled as such) are overtly religious, "The Virgin Mary's Child" (no. 3) and "The Singing, Springing Lark" (no. 88), for example. Also noteworthy is the presence of a narrator in some of the tales, evident through asides, direct addresses to the reader, and formulaic beginnings and endings.

Many generalizations about the tales simply do not hold up to scrutiny when the whole collection is considered. The good do not always win out in the Grimms' fairy tales, as Bottigheimer's and Maria Tatar's books emphasize. Nor, as Alison Lurie and other feminists have pointed out, are good females always passive—contrary to mainstream feminist interpretations. Some of the tales, such as "The Three Spinners," which might be interpreted as a fantasy about escaping the social role of women as household slaves, appear to have been told from a female perspective; however, others unquestioningly reinforce patriarchal authority. Some of the tales, "The Jew in the Thornbush" (no. 110) and "The Good Bargain" (no. 8) in particular, are disturbingly and explicitly anti-Semitic. Both of these tales, as Ruth Bottigheimer points out, were included in the "Small Edition, where they would and did get maximum exposure among particularly impressionable young readers" (Bottigheimer 140). At times in the lesser-known tales, the feudal world from which the tales emerged leaps out in startingly brutal details: witches are burned at the stake, stepmothers are rolled downhill in barrels spiked inside with nails—the Inquisition lives again. Yet many of the tales teach compassion, often for unlikely creatures. Some stories, such as "The Master Thief," clearly represent the urges of the peasantry as an oppressed class; others seem curiously subservient to authority and the status quo. Yet the tales in their cumulative effect serve as witness to the wisdom and endurance as well as the prejudices of the folk. The collection displays a remarkable range of attitudes, as themes and motifs appear and reappear in various permutations.

The tales finally omitted by the Grimm brothers are a particularly odd and incongruous mixture of stories. Some, such as "The Carpenter and the Turner" (no. 226) and "The Stepmother" (no. 229), are extremely brief or fragmentary; some are typical *pourquoi* tales; others, notably "Puss in Boots" (no. 216), are stories familiar to us from Perrault and other sources. Some, such as "The Children of Famine" (no. 238), seem almost pointless, while others, such as "The Three Sisters" (no. 228), are complex and fascinating. The

Grimm brothers excluded these stories because they originated outside the German tradition (the French or the Dutch, for example), because they duplicated other tales, because they were fragmentary or confused, because they were exceptionally brutal, or because they appeared to be literary fairy tales.

The illustrations by Johnny Gruelle, well known for his Raggedy Ann and Raggedy Andy books, represent a pastiche of popular styles. They present an often pleasing combination of the cartoon-like and the romantic, though they sometimes verge too close on caricature, as in the grotesque portrayals of old women, who contrast a bit too stereotypically with the virginal innocence of his idealistically portrayed young girls. Gruelle's illustrations represent yet another of the many forms of interpretation that have made it difficult to see the reality of the original tales through our cultural preconceptions and our ignorance of the context in which the tales came into being.

Jack Zipes's translation makes the complete texts accessible to a broad English-speaking readership; Ruth Bottigheimer's scholarly study examines the texts themselves in context and detail. Her work represents a new level of thoroughness and precision in American scholarship about the Grimms' fairy tales. Bottigheimer synthesizes historical and textual approaches to illuminate the diverse meanings of the entire collection of the *Kinder- und Hausmärchen* (*KHM*), not in one edition only, but in the transformations from the 1812 to the 1857 editions as well. Especially important is Bottigheimer's painstaking attention to the literary qualities of the text, qualities often ignored by such critics as Bruno Bettelheim or Alan Dundes. Her reading of the tales is informed by a healthy scepticism about the validity of psychological approaches that claim to find "universals" in tales that are actually historically and ideologically conditioned. She begins with the basic premise that "any consideration of the content of the *KHM* must include an appreciation of the extent and nature of Wilhelm Grimm's reformulation of the text" (7). By establishing the political, social, and cultural context of the Grimm brothers' endeavors, she is able to demonstrate in detail the historical relativity of the values and attitudes revealed in the tales. She illuminates Wilhelm Grimm's methods by a telling comparison: "Chaucer's method [in the *Canterbury Tales*] individualizes tales that were already well-known and presents them as they would be told by a specific narrator, who is, in turn, also Chaucer's literary creation. Wilhelm Grimm worked in the opposite direction: he collated individual versions of stories to return to what he imagined to be the tale's core" (11). That imaginary core was at least as much the expression of nineteenth-century bourgeois, romantic German ideas about gender, class, nature, morality, and society as of enduring concerns of humanity.

Bottigheimer demonstrates through careful textual analysis that the morality of the *KHM* is not universal but is, instead, distinctly determined by certain ideas about society and about gender in particular. "Wilhelm Grimm's social purpose emerges from the additions and substitutions made in the collection as it grew toward the canonical two hundred tales. Diligent work, gender-specific roles, a generally punitive stance toward girls and women, and a coherent world view conducing to stability in the social fabric take shape over his years of editing and expanding the collection" (19). Men and women, boys and girls, are not treated equally in the *KHM*. This perhaps self-evident assertion is explored in new detail here, through examination of a comprehensive range of tales. So, for example, Bottigheimer analyzes the fire and water imagery of the tales and finds, inter alia, that "the composite image of fire which emerges . . . shows that in their collection it belongs peculiarly to male figures and is closely associated with gender antagonism" (25). Women's natural or supernatural powers, in the pre-Christian tradition of a "peculiarly female ability to control, direct or affect natural powers," a tradition reaching back to the *Merseburger Zaubersprüche* (*Merseburg Spells*), are reflected in the ability of young females to cast spells—an ability not only not limited to witches, but explicitly granted to young and beautiful women, an indication of a "latent belief in the natural powers of women, especially of virgins" (50).

However, Bottigheimer also draws attention to the pervasive silencing of female voices through Wilhelm Grimm's editorial changes in progressive editions. Through systematic investigation of the frequency of the use of such verbs as *sprechen* (speak) and *sagen* (say) to introduce male and female utterances, she shows how females are increasingly deprived of their voices in patterns that Bottigheimer regards as "unconscious expressions of Wilhelm Grimm's deeply held convictions" (55). Thus, some of the tales' contradictory features emerge into sharp focus. "A great gulf separates the mentality producing the tales in which women lay spells in order to direct natural forces from one that insistently condemns women to a silence during which they are often exposed to mortal danger" (71). Punishment, enforced silence, and social isolation fall much more heavily on women than on men in *Grimms' Tales*.

The evidence of this gender-skewed vision, much of it ignored or overlooked by earlier critics, is meticulously marshaled. Bottigheimer employs various methods, including comparative analysis of different versions of a tale in successive editions, charts presenting speech patterns, the examination of such place imagery as towers, forests, and trees, and the consideration of illustrations, social conditions, and religious dimensions. In light of the thoroughness and comprehensiveness of this study, certain small omissions and distortions seem uncharacteristic, such as the claim that the "odious women" in "The Lazy Spinner" (no. 128) is "the only female who lights a fire in *Grimms' Tales*" (29), which ignores "Hansel and Gretel," where "Gretel had to go out, hang up a kettle full of water, and light the fire" (Zipes 63). What may seem to be a trivial detail nonetheless casts a slight shadow of doubt upon other claims about general patterns, claims that at times seem in danger of being overextended, especially in light of the well-acknowledged diversity of the tales. For example, the conclusion that "water (or at least certain kinds of water), appertains exclusively to women" (29) does not seem to reckon with "The Fisherman and His Wife" (no. 19), where the fisherman has access to the powers of the sea, personified in the fish. That tale also seems to present an example of "a male who successfully lays a spell" (50) which Bottigheimer implies is not to be found in the tales. The fisherman's address to the flounder, "Flounder, flounder, in the sea, if you're a man, then speak to me" (Zipes 72), contains the imperative form required for Bottigheimer's definition of a true spell, though it might be argued that the flounder, like the horse in "Ferdinand the Faithful and Ferdinand the Unfaithful" (no. 126) is in actuality a prince, and that the spell casting, though performed by the husband, is ultimately controlled by his greedy wife. These examples are quibbles, however. Paradoxically, it is Bottigheimer's exceptional care to avoid dubious generalizations about the tales that makes minor exceptions to her claims all the more visible.

Particularly valuable in *Grimms' Bad Girls and Bold Boys* are the lucid, objective discussions of eroticism, the work ethic, and anti-

Semitism in the *KHM*. Bottigheimer discusses elements of eroticism in the European tradition, in the texts, and in the illustrations of the *Grimms' Tales*, showing how, despite the efforts of Wilhelm Grimm to tone down or eliminate sexual suggestions, erotic implications remain. Concerning the work ethic, Bottigheimer makes the intriguing point that "in tale after tale, honest physical labor, a generally acknowledged virtue, is a demonstrably unproductive route to financial reward" (123). The emphasis on wealth as a mark of grace rather than as the reward for labor and virtue is a sign that "the ideas about wealth that inhere in tales concerning work belong to the experience of the laboring poor, for whom the Calvinist system of values was both alien and irrelevant" (129). Bottigheimer indicts Wilhelm Grimm's contribution to anti-Semitism in the historical context of the "collective resentment of the poor" against outsiders, once the monks, then the Jews, as an expression of "nationalistic resentment against a French conqueror who had enfranchised Germany's Jewish population" (142).

The "moral and social vision" of *Grimms' Tales* is, as this book convincingly demonstrates, a circumscribed and sometimes contradictory one. The drama of Bottigheimer's investigation is the mystery of cultural selectivity: how and why the folktales collected by the Grimm brothers changed in editorial revision and how those changes altered the meanings of texts that became central to a society's definition of itself, as well as influential in many other societies. Bottigheimer's hard, clear look at the tales refuses to treat them as having vatic authority, but neither does it underestimate their power. Both Bottigheimer's careful analysis and Zipes's capable translation will better enable us to see the *Grimms' Tales* for what they are, in their entirety, in relation to each other and in relation to the culture and time that produced them: no more and no less.

In a field in which well-defined—not to say dogmatic—critical approaches are the rule, Maria Tatar's *Hard Facts of the Grimms' Fairy Tales* is the exception. Whereas most critics, especially critics of the fairy tale, are bent on establishing their own viewpoints to the exclusion of others, Tatar's aim seems almost diametrically opposite—to give all viewpoints a fair hearing, even to the exclusion of her own. If there is a slight preference for one approach over the others here, it is an inclination to see the fairy tales as indicative of psychological realities—still a far cry from a dogmatically psychological approach. So Tatar asserts: "That fairy tales translate (however roughly) psychic realities into concrete images, characters, and events has come to serve as one cornerstone of my own understanding of the texts in the Grimms' *Nursery and Household Tales*" (xv). Even the phrase "*one* cornerstone" is characteristic here: Tatar's method is inclusive, not exclusive. She applies common sense and perspicuity to some of the most heated controversies in the field, skillfully synthesizing the most arcane and complex discussions in the fields of folktale and fairy tale criticism, history, anthropology, and sociology. Few scholars will be so well versed in all of the areas she addresses as to find nothing new or valuable in her summaries. If at times the book seems to lack focus and direction, it nonetheless provides a great deal of insight into the tales.

Apart from bringing the insights of critics from many different disciplines to bear on the tales, Tatar offers close readings of selected tales from the Grimms' collection. She also pursues general themes and issues, such as the classification of the tales as children's literature, the nature of the family as portrayed in the tales, and the different representation of the male and female heroic characters, or male and female villains. The most interesting parts of these readings contradict widely held preconceptions of what the tales contain. For example, "the conventional wisdom [concerning the male hero of the fairy tales] . . . proves to be a fairy tale so far as German folklore is concerned. 'Innocent,' 'silly,' 'useless,' 'foolish,' 'simple,' and 'guileless': these are the adjectives applied repeatedly to fairy-tale heroes in the Grimms' collection" (86). Further, "the heroes of the *Nursery and Household Tales* may, for the most part, be unlikely to win prizes for intelligence and good behavior, but they are even less likely to garner awards for courage . . . they often remain both cowardly and passive" (88). However, "for all their shortcomings, the simpletons in the Grimms' fairy tales possess one character trait that sets them apart from their fraternal rivals: compassion" (88).

This correction of widespread misconceptions about male heroes in the folktales is complemented by Tatar's attention to the distortion of virtues affirmed in heroines. "If male protagonists must routinely submit to character tests and demonstrate compassion, their female counterparts are subjected to tests of their competence in the domestic arena—tests that are usually carried out without the aid of helpers" (116). Along these lines, Tatar criticizes "psychoanalytically oriented critics [who] have admired the deft way in which these stories split mother images into two components: the good (and usually absent) mother and the evil stepmother," (144) countering that "what is especially remarkable about fairy tales is the extent to which they inflate maternal evil" (145). She points out that even fathers who offend against fundamental rules of morality are portrayed as noble, whereas stepmothers are represented as innately villainous. She explores the ways in which the tales penalize female curiosity, gloss over male brutality, and valorize male curiosity as "gateways to the world of high adventure" (168). Tatar also interestingly demonstrates that Wilhelm Grimm intensified violence and deleted sexual innuendos in the tales.

Tatar adds to her discussion of individual tales an awareness of the Grimms' financial and publishing history, knowledge of reviews and of competing books by contemporaries (such as Ludwig Bechstein's *Neues Deutsches Märchenbuch*), and familiarity with the social history of the movement from folktale traditions to literary culture. She places a valuable emphasis on the influence of the nature of the listener on the transmission of an oral tale, and on the fluidity of the "narrative spectrum that leads from folklore to literature" (32). On that spectrum, she places the Grimms' tales "somewhere near the midpoint," which, understood in context, is not as vague as it may sound. Tatar unravels the knotty problem of definition by calling the "entire class of traditional oral narratives *folktales*" and "its naturalistic subset *folk tales*" (33). The term *fairy tale,* on the other hand, is used by Tatar to designate "narrative set in a fictional world where preternatural events and supernatural intervention are taken wholly for granted" (33). In contrast to the fairy tale, the "folk tale" is "sharply biased in favor of earthy realism," she writes. Another element of Tatar's inclusiveness is her interest in illustrations, which she rightly views as a major interpretive influence; it is axiomatic for her that "the simplicity of fairy-tale plots invites multiple readings and allows interpretive pluralism to reign supreme" (51).

Throughout, Tatar offers succinct and informative summaries of the many specialized approaches to these fairy tales. She summarizes the main arguments of Vladimir Propp, Eleazar Meletinsky, and other Soviet structuralists; Freud, Jung, Bettelheim, Marthe Robert, and less well-known psychological critics; Kurt Ranke, Antti Aarne, Stith Thompson, and similar exponents of the Finnish school; Linda Dégh, Alan Dundes, and other folklorists; social/historical critics Jack Zipes, Robert Darnton, and many more. It is characteristic of her approach that many of its most memorable ideas are paraphrases or quotations; Tatar has an eye for catchy aphorisms, such as Wallace Stevens's " 'Reality is a cliché from which we escape by metaphor' " (79–80) or "Nietzsche once observed that fear is an index of intelligence" (96). Therein lies the weakness as well as the strength of Tatar's book.

These three Grimm books are indicative of an interesting and valuable international phenomenon: the study of children's literature across national boundaries. Not only are Jack Zipes, Ruth Bottigheimer, and Maria Tatar thoroughly steeped in the study of German literature and literary history, thus enabling them to make the Grimms' oeuvre accessible to a broader scholarly audience that may not be well versed in German, but their work in turn (Zipes's work in other volumes included) represents scholarly advances that should become indispensable to German scholars as well. In fact, it seems entirely appropriate to find American scholars of German children's literature addressing an international audience. Folktales, after all, though often expressed in regional and local forms, have always transcended narrowly defined national boundaries.

Traditions and Modernity: A Rediscovery of India

Meena Khorana

Seasons of Splendour: Tales, Myths and Legends of India, by Madhur Jaffrey, illustrated by Michael Foreman. New York: Atheneum, 1985.

The Story of Prince Rama, by Brian Thompson, illustrated by original paintings and by Jeroo Roy. New York: Viking Kestrel, 1980.

Indira Gandhi, by Francelia Butler. World Leaders Past and Present. New York: Chelsea House Publishers, 1986.

The Village by the Sea, by Anita Desai. Harmondsworth: Penguin Books, 1985. William Heinemann, 1982.

Sumitra's Story, by Rukshana Smith. New York: Coward-McCann, 1982.

A Hindu Primer: Yaksha Prashna, translated and retold by A. V. Srinivasan, illustrated by Kamla Srinivasan. Glastonbury, Conn.: IND–US, 1984.

In recent years, India has once again been discovered through literature, motion pictures like *Gandhi* and *A Passage to India*, and a series of television programs like *The Jewel in the Crown* and *Mountbatten of India*. After four decades of freedom, India is also presenting a new image of itself to the Western world—a pride in its artistic and cultural heritage *and* its achievements in science and technology—in such exhibitions as the *Festival of India* held in various American cities in 1986. In the wake of this widespread media exposure, contemporary literature for Western children also reflects a resurgence of interest in India. But the split public image of India as either a land of traditions and steadfast values or a newly independent nation with aspirations for progress in industry, medicine, and education, has generated new stereotypes in children's literature. Recent biographies of well-known Indians, retelling of

Children's Literature 17, ed. Francelia Butler, Margaret Higonnet, and Barbara Rosen (Yale University Press, © 1989 by The Children's Literature Foundation, Inc.).

folktales, and new fictional works similarly either celebrate the folklore of India or focus on its impatience for technological progress.

All six books selected for this review, published in England or the United States in the past seven years, reflect this dichotomy between modern aspirations and traditional values. Madhur Jaffrey in *Seasons of Splendour* initially sets out to illustrate how Indian rituals and folklore lend constancy and meaning to life in India's current environment of rapid progress and shifting values. Using her childhood experiences and extended family as the subject, she gives Western readers a glimpse of India's oral tradition as it is transmitted to the younger generation. A vast variety of folktales are organized into eleven sections according to theme and their corresponding lunar phases. Beginning with "The Day of the Banyan Tree" on a moonless day in May, she narrates myths and stories as they might be told at religious celebrations during the course of a Hindu calendar year. Complementing this structure are Michael Foreman's illustrations of the various phases of the moon and the stories associated with each season, in which he uses black-and-white drawings for details from the author's life and color illustrations for the lively action of the folktales.

The author's autobiographical accounts that open each section of the book paint a fascinating picture of how Western and Indian traditions merge in an extended family of over forty members, with Jaffrey's barrister grandfather at the head. The book focuses on the harmony rather than the inevitable conflicts of a dual culture. While the menfolk sipped whiskey sodas and played bridge, the women of the household "reinforced ties with the hindu past" by tending to the deities in the "puja-room." Through rituals and entertaining stories, they handed down ethical values and the rules of conduct for respectful daughters-in-law, faithful wives, and devoted brothers and sisters. The stories were created anew with each retelling, and the children made sure that their favorite details were retained. The author seems conscious of no discord between Hindu heritage and Western education at Catholic and Anglican schools. While the elders rest indoors on the hot summer afternoons of Delhi, Jaffrey and her cousins sneak to the shade of the tamarind and mango trees to prepare scripts for theatrical performances to be staged under grandfather's rolltop desk. In one such venture, in order to accommodate the bow-and-arrow skills of a cousin, they make the exiled Rama and Sita meet Robin Hood and his Merry Men.

The folktales in this collection stress the universal themes of domestic happiness, good triumphing over evil, and the meek and virtuous being rewarded while the proud and arrogant are punished. The rhythmic waxing and waning of the moon, a recurring symbol of the passage of time, creates a sense of wholeness amidst the duality of old and new, past and present, sorrow at the death of the children's grandfather and joy at the memories he has left behind. There is also a continuity to the structure of the book when it returns full circle to summer; the hot winds blow, and ripe mangoes chilled in a tub of ice water are enjoyed once again. The charm of *Seasons of Splendour* can be attributed to Jaffrey's skillful arrangement of various levels of meaning as Indian traditions are handed down from mother to daughter through rituals and play.

Brian Thompson's *Story of Prince Rama* is a traditional retelling of the epic *Ramayana*, which is kept alive, as we see from Jaffrey's account, through prayers, storytelling, and theatrical performances during the yearly Dussehra-Diwali festivities. Compared to Jaffrey's lively prose, Thompson's version is simplistic; it lacks the richness of poetic detail, the polish and economy of oral tradition. In introducing Ravan, the demon king of Sri Lanka, Thompson writes, "Rama knew that Ravana would be a terrible enemy. He was strong and cunning and he had ten heads and twenty arms" (10). Jaffrey's description is much more visual and specific: "Ravan could smile a ten-mouthed smile, twirl ten moustaches at once, and let loose a rainfall of arrows from ten golden bows" (48).

In an effort to be simple and direct, Thompson does not go beyond the key elements in the story. Many legends, specific names of characters, places, and details of feasts are omitted in order not to overwhelm the reader; yet Thompson's style also suffers from wordiness, unnecessary details, and colloquialisms. For example, "Rama's teacher explained to Rama that he and Lakshmana were going to have to kill this terrible creature. He said that they could take only bows and arrows and that they would need all the courage they could find in their hearts" (10). Clichés from Western folklore are lavishly employed, while the author ignores essential details, as well as Indian imagery and figurative language. We are told that Ravan threatened Sita by saying: "And if you don't change your mind and marry me, I will chop you up into little pieces and cook you for my breakfast" (44). Here Ravan, misusing the powers he had gained through ascetic discipline, sounds more like the ogres of Western fairy tales than the intelligent ruler of a highly advanced and prosperous kingdom. Thompson is also insensitive to the subtle nuances of Indian thought and culture. When Sita insists on accompanying Rama into exile, he has her say: "I have sold all our household goods" (24). The division and sale of property in an extended household has materialistic and selfish overtones not appropriate here; moreover, Sita was the future queen and had no need to sell her property. In addition, Rama, Sita, and Lakshmana are constantly referred to as "three friends." The nature of their family relationships is important to Hindu culture; they were not in exile as friends, but because they had accepted their social obligations. Rama, as ideal son, fulfilled his father's promise to Kaikeyi and went into exile; Sita, as ideal wife, followed her husband; and Lakshmana, as ideal younger brother, accompanied Rama and Sita into the forest to serve them.

Although every storyteller is free to add details and adapt a text, Thompson's *Story of Prince Rama* lacks the rich texture and depth of the original story and robs the epic of its cultural identity. This version is a mere retelling of the *Ramayana* in the idiom of Western folklore. The book's only claim to recognition lies in the paintings by Jeroo Roy and the original Rajput paintings commissioned three hundred years ago by Jagat Singh, King of Udaipur, to illustrate a manuscript of *Ramayana*.

Francelia Butler's well-documented biography of Indira Gandhi presents Indian history and culture with imagination, truthfulness, and understanding through the experiences and achievements of one individual. The sense of *dynasty,* the idea that a single family can shape the destiny of a nation, is the established theme of the biography. Butler traces the history of India through the Nehrus from Mughal times to the struggle against British domination and, finally, to the leadership of free India. *Indira Gandhi* is as much the story of India's struggle for freedom as it is the personal story of Indira Gandhi and her legacy of social responsibility and national commitment.

The vast material of the biography is organized into fourteen chapters. The text is graphically arranged on each page in a wide column; numerous black-and-white photographs and quotations by

Indian leaders, historians and friends and critics of Indira Gandhi complement the text to give additional insight into the private life and personal warmth of Indira Gandhi. The extensive research is well integrated into the narrative, and Butler's prose style retains its freshness and sense of discovery.

Although the biography focuses on the public life of Indira Gandhi, Butler sensitively and economically establishes the inner person so that the subject emerges as a real human being with strengths and weaknesses. We see the shy, lonely adolescent pained by constant separations from family members as they serve prison terms; we see the makings of the political activist who, at the age of twelve, formed the Monkey Brigade, a children's organization within the independence movement, because she was too young to join the Congress Party; we see the independent woman who defied the Indian tradition of arranged marriages by falling in love with and marrying Feroze Gandhi, who was neither of her religion nor of her social standing; and we see the idealist who helped victims of World War II in London when, ironically, her own father was in a British prison in India for his acts of civil disobedience. While hinting at the conflicting demands of national commitment, family, and personal goals, Butler never sentimentalizes this struggle, nor does she descend to idle speculation over Gandhi's marital problems and disputes with her daughter-in-law, Maneka. Butler also avoids exploiting the subject of women's rights and feminism; instead, she assumes the stance that Gandhi herself did—she had risen above such narrow definitions of herself, and she wanted to be judged not as a woman but as a human being and leader.

Indira Gandhi is a valuable biography for young adults that promotes understanding by providing information on Indian history, culture, and social conditions. Its most outstanding quality is Butler's insight into the political perspective of India; her objective analyses of Indian politics and foreign policy is not biased by the usual American condemnation of India's treaties with the Soviet Union. Through Gandhi's life and accomplishments, the biography suggests that India has endured the vicissitudes of history because of its dynamic leadership and its ability to blend the old and traditional with the modern and democratic.

In marked contrast to this approach, Indian novelist Anita Desai perpetuates the neocolonial stereotype of India as an ancient land burdened by its traditions and its unwillingness to progress. *The Vil-*

lage by the Sea is a sociological investigation of change as effected by the adolescent hero in a backward village in India, a theme common to numerous realistic novels set in postindependence India. Desai weaves together several themes, locales, and characters to point out the inevitable choice that villagers have to make in modern India. The natural harmony of Thul, a fishing village near Bombay, is more apparent than real, we learn, when the author shows us the villagers' perennial hunger and poverty and the lives regularly claimed by storms. Conflict is introduced to Thul when industry invades in the form of a tractor loaded with steel pipes for the construction of a fertilizer factory. The older fishermen resist change because the sea will be polluted, because they will lose dignity by becoming menial laborers, and because the lush green fields and coconut trees will be bulldozed to make room for shops, railway lines, and roads. Only the protagonist, Hari, symbolizes progress by accepting and training for change. Alone and burdened by responsibilities, Hari goes to Bombay in search of a better life only to find a different type of human misery and degradation—overpopulation and filth, pavement dwellers, crime and violence, and beggary. He is lucky to find a job in a third-rate restaurant for Bombay's coolies.

Mr. Panwallah, who trains Hari to repair watches, becomes the expression of a Darwinian theory of "survival of the fittest." Youth and adolescence become the metaphor for change and progress. Desai likens Hari's search for an identity to Thul's search for a new economy in modern India. Thul, though generations old, must become young and invigorated; it must adapt in order to survive. The burden of hope is placed on a younger generation already disenchanted with the vagaries of fishing life and the lack of ready cash and jobs, and full of impatience for a better life. "'You are young,'" says Mr. Panwallah. "'You can change, and learn, and grow. Old people cannot, but you can.'" Hari returns to the beauty and peace of Thul as a mature young adult with a vocation and enough money to start a poultry farm. Hari's return from his archetypal journey on the festival of *Diwali*—the day Rama, the hero of the *Ramayana*, returned to his kingdom after fourteen years in exile and destroyed all evil forces—symbolizes hope, prosperity, and domestic happiness.

Desai's intricate plot, poetic prose, and sensitive vision transform every detail in the microcosmic world of Thul, and the novel raises some important questions. Does industrial progress mean that an entire way of life has to end? Cannot the wisdom and beauty of traditional ways be assimilated in the new, industrialized India? Ironically, the environmentalist, Sayyad Ali, comes to Thul to study the near-extinct Baya birds before their habitat is despoiled by industry; is there nothing else worth preserving in Thul? The novel's message is clear: the uneducated older generation is unable to survive, and the village youths should train themselves vocationally for industry. Written to be read only by an English-speaking elite, the novel reinforces the image of India as an overpopulated, poverty-stricken country whose problems must be solved by technology.

Another novel that examines traditional Indian values and finds them inadequate in a modern context is *Sumitra's Story*, by the British author Rukshana Smith. Eleven-year-old Sumitra Patel and her family flee to the welfare state of England after Idi Amin enforces his "Africanization" plan to expel Asians from Uganda and appropriate their lucrative businesses. In England, they become victims of a more blatant form of social and racial prejudice; they are no longer part of the privileged class as they were in Uganda, where they were "beneath the British but above the natives" (25). The British see them as a threat, and the Patels, on their part, find English culture repulsive and withdraw into the Indian community. We are given a brief glimpse of the parents' trauma—Bap's loss of dignity in working as a factory hand and Mai's sense of alienation at having lost her home—but they appear to be one-dimensional in their adherence to Indian traditions.

It is the issue of adolescents and the double burden of their assimilation into adult society that the author forces us to face. We share Sumitra's poignant search for an identity: "In the street she felt Indian, at home she felt English. Nowhere, nowhere did she feel like Sumitra. But who was Sumitra, and what did she feel like?" (90). Which community did she belong to? Sumitra and her friends reject Indian values which would relegate them to a *samsara* of prescribed duties, an arranged marriage, and the perpetual childhood of financial dependence. They have fantasies of running away from home and brood over newspaper accounts of Asian girls who have committed suicide because the strain of living two lives was unbearable.

Failing in her efforts to combine the best of both cultures, Sumitra devises her own symbolic rites of initiation into British society and separation from her community and family. She finds a permanent job with a travel agency, shares an apartment with English friends, and rejects her Hindu ethics of duty to family. In isolation she grapples with her loss of childhood and the anxiety at what is to come. She finds an answer to her personal and racial problem in a nightmare: she dreams that the only ones to whom race, occupation, and language matter are the stunted ones, the dwarfs. This defining of herself as a superior person who has risen above narrow prejudices gives Sumitra the courage to break barriers and the strength to face her family's ostracism and the prejudice of British society.

Sumitra's Story, which received the Garavi Gujarat Annual Book Award for Racial Harmony, is a sociological investigation of national, racial, cultural and generational barriers in England. The author takes the stance that all ethnic groups in England are committed to keeping their traditions alive by exerting emotional, social, and financial pressures on their children through family dictatorships. Indian parents, secure in their cultural roots, face no conflicts; but their daughters, while being raised and educated in western society, are expected to isolate themselves from it, to shut it off until the next school day. Although Smith's ironic vision presents both sides of the racial problem in England fairly, her tone and solution to Sumitra's dilemma suggest that Indian traditions are too orthodox and inflexible to adapt to a western, more individualistic environment, and that immigrant groups should conform to British values at the expense of their separate cultural identities.

A. V. Srinivasan's *Hindu Primer: Yaksha Prashna* is an attempt to instill the pride in Indian cultural roots that is missing in *Sumitra's Story*. A translation from the Sanskrit of a group of riddles from the *Aranya Parva* (Book of the Forest), one of the eighteen books that comprise the epic *Mahabharata*, the book is part of a larger movement on behalf of the Indian community in North America to resolve the inevitable tensions of a heritage propagated in a social vacuum.

The philosophical questions of the *Yaksha Prashna* were posed to Yudhishthira by his divine father, Yama Dharma, as an initiation rite to ensure that Yudhishthira had developed the leadership skills needed to win the conflict between the Pandavas and Kauravas, symbolizing the victory of good over evil. The analogy of the exiled Pandavas (the heroes of the *Mahabharata*) is apt, as Srinivasan intends *Yaksha Prashna* to serve as an instructional tool to encourage children to place Hindu thought and values in the context of their lives in the United States.

In the twenty-two sets of questions, Yudhishthira is questioned on various aspects of *dharma* (duty) and how to fulfill one's social, familial, ethical, and spiritual roles. Acquiring a skill, whether of a *brahmin* (priest) or a *kshtriya* (warrior), is equated with duty. The *Yaksha Prashna* does not preach self-denial or rejection of material comforts but suggests a reconciliation of the conflicting demands of *dharma* (right conduct), *artha* (material wealth), and *kama* (desire). Through moderation and a recognition of one's duties, one can participate fully in the affairs of society, raise a family, and achieve *moksha,* or release from rebirth and the wheel of time. The book provides modern youth with valuable guidelines for righteous conduct, but we do not see them being tested against the cultural conflicts that Indian teenagers face in North America.

Limited by its scope and genre, each book reviewed above touches on only a single aspect of life in India. The constant opposition between India as a land of steadfast beliefs and India as a land of progress gives western children the limited message that India has to get past its traditions in order to achieve technological advancement. We need authors who show greater variety in their choice of genres and treatment of subject matter. Instead of the serious and instructional tone of the "novel of progress," we need more humor and expressions of joy and wonder at being alive. We need more analysis of the conflicts between parents and children over dating, arranged marriages, and career choices; the cultural impact of rapid technology on villagers; the colonial past and issues of race relations; and friendship between children of various Indian communities. In essence, instead of books with an extra-literary agenda, we need literature that is reflective of the inner child.

Bloomsbury and Wonderland

Regina Barreca

Julia Duckworth Stephen: Stories for Children, Essays for Adults, edited by Diane F. Gillespie and Elizabeth Steele. Syracuse: Syracuse University Press, 1987.

Alice to the Lighthouse: Children's Books and Radical Experimentalism in Art, by Juliet Dusinberre. New York: St. Martin's Press, 1987.

The editors of Julia Stephen's previously unpublished stories for children recognize that the chief interest in these brief works must arise from the fact that they are written by the mother of Virginia Woolf. The stories—nine in all—represent a curious mix of the unconvincingly didactic and the eccentrically ingenious. We seem to meet endless numbers of indistinguishable little boys (several are named Tommy, and this doesn't help) who long for adventure but are horrified when their wishes come true. There is, for example, the little rich boy in "Emlycaunt" (a name which remains mysterious) who wants to "live where there were only animals" and gets his wish only to find out that he prefers to live with his safe and pleasant family. This is not a surprise. What *is* surprising is the unresolved tension between the imaginative and real worlds presented in these stories, so that the tale about this particular Tommy and his vision of the world of animals ends with Tommy's sister (a bitter disbeliever who undoubtedly will come to no good) saying " 'I'm sick of Emlycaunt,' " followed by the narrator's "And so perhaps are you?"

This may be the best way to end a story if its purpose is to send the child to sleep; if, however its aim is to spark the imagination or delight the senses, then these stories cannot be judged successful. It is wonderful when a tale ends with a sense of the intertwining of the real and the imaginary, or a reframing of what is everyday into what is delightfully absurd. Unfortunately, we have here only a sense of the narrator wanting to escape the story as much as the children want to escape the confines of their worlds.

Children's Literature 17, ed. Francelia Butler, Margaret Higonnet, and Barbara Rosen (Yale University Press, © 1989 by The Children's Literature Foundation, Inc.).

Of course Julia Stephen's stories are important documents, regardless of their merit as tales for children. It is interesting to see that Woolf's mother can be rightly charged with the criticism so often, and so often wrongly, applied to her daughter's books: an uneasy flirtation with the issues of caste and economics results in the tentative equation of the good with the conventional. "Dinner at Baron Bruin's" presents the nicely middle-class Pig family, who learn that they do not fit in with the elegant and dangerous upper class, populated as it is with the likes of Colonel Isegrim, the Wolf. (Wolf is a flesh-hungry charmer who wants to call on the daughter of the family.) This tale ends with the Pig family burying their noses in "such a mess as pigs love . . . quite forgetting their elegant manners and resolving never to dine with the aristocracy again."

In "The Duke's Coal Cellar" we meet poor little Jim Brown, whose mother is a fierce washerwoman, locking him out of the house when she goes to work. Jim is forced to "feed himself during the day and to have some coppers over for his mother at night." But Jim has an unshakable desire to enter one of the biggest houses in Brunswick Square, the home of the duke of Brunswick himself. This tale interestingly inverts the traditional theme of a child's desire to run away from home, because Jim seems to have as little right to enter his own house as he has to enter the duke's. He does slip through open doors into the duke's house and ends up in the cellar; the story closes "happily" when Jim is restored to a mother who did truly miss him, despite her inability to offer him an affectionate welcome: "No sooner did she see that he was really back than she began to scold him." As the policeman comments, "That's the way with 'em. They kicks up no end of row, whichever way things come out." What else, it is implied, can we expect from a washerwoman?

There is a great deal of "us" and "not-us" in these stories, creating barriers that are difficult for the modern reader to rise above. However, some of the stories are richer than others and offer the critical reader, at least, a provocatively complex response to a difficult problem. In "The Mysterious Voice" Jem learns that he can be as naughty as he likes without incurring punishment. Eventually he kills a pet monkey by accident and is heartbroken by the result of his own insensitivity. Then his rich aunt, newly arrived from India with her "treasures" (including a native woman to work as a servant), gives him another pet monkey, saying: "Every time you see him it will remind you of the worst punishment you have had, which was causing the death of that poor little monkey." In its examination of the rights and responsibilities of the owner to the owned, the story does at least present us with the uncomfortable, unstated, but inevitable comparison between Auntie's "black servant . . . with gold bracelets on her hands and feet" and Jem's pet. Julia Stephen's writings for adults, also included in this volume, allow us to see the sensitive and thoughtful way she approached the conventions of her society; but the stories she wrote for children translate convention into unconvincing prescription.

How should we approach the interaction between the mother's and the daughter's texts? Juliet Dusinberre, in her wonderfully skillful and insightful study, clearly formulates "the interaction between children's books and adult's books, between children and adults, between theories and images." In her chapter on "Virginia Woolf and the Irreverent Generation," she argues, for example, that Lewis Carroll's work in the Alice books "set a precedent in challenging authority which released the energies of many writers toward a new secular fiction." Dusinberre's case is strong. She lucidly presents the sociological, psychological, and critical framework for her arguments, and, if we occasionally wonder whether she can support the theory that locates significant sources of artistic complexity in children's texts, overall she is nevertheless convincing. She deals with Virginia Woolf throughout her study, focusing on Woolf's relationship to her mother—especially on the impact of the latter's death on her daughter—though there is no mention of Julia Stephen's own writings or of the recently discovered child's story by Woolf herself.

In contrast to the edition of Stephen's tales, however, Dusinberre's book might directly benefit scholars of children's literature. Dusinberre connects the subversive nature of the modernist work of art with the subversive nature of children's literature, indicating that the willingness and ability of modernist writers to be unconventional can be traced to the texts of their childhood. *Alice to the Lighthouse* argues that "Carroll's looking-glass, superimposed on older mirror images, helped to shape the mental landscape of these [modernist] writers." She believes that many characteristically "modernist" elements, such as the "speeding up and fracturing of narrative sequence" can be compared to—and often traced back to

—Carroll's *Through the Looking-Glass*. "Carroll's words," she writes, "echoed in the minds of Woolf's and Eliot's generation."

But Carroll was not the only influential author, according to Dusinberre; so were Stevenson, Twain, Nesbit and a number of less prominent writers. She can find example after example to illustrate her points, as when she asserts that "the oscillation between adult and child consciousness which critics found so disconcerting in Kenneth Grahame . . . represented a transitional movement between the writer as authority figure and the repudiation of that authority which is so marked in Virginia Woolf's novels." She states clearly the psychological underpinning to her arguments: "Freud writes that 'every child at play behaves like a creative writer, in that he creates a world of his own, or rather, rearranges the things of his world in a new way which pleases him.'" Dusinberre deals as ably with Willa Cather as she does with Virginia Woolf, with Mark Twain as well as Lewis Carroll. *Alice to the Lighthouse* is an extraordinary book, learned and provocative.

Writing for Children about the Unthinkable

Hamida Bosmajian

The Children We Remember, by Chana Byer Abells. Photographs from the Archives of Yad Vashem, The Holocaust Martyrs' and Heroes' Remembrance Authority, Jerusalem, Israel. New York: Greenwillow Books, 1983, 1986.

The Cage, by Ruth Minsky Sender. New York: MacMillan Publishing Company, 1986.

Children of the Dust, by Louise Lawrence. New York: Harper & Row, 1985.

The touchstones of children's literature are shaped by the needs of their creators to write, paint, or draw a work that does not necessarily have the child reader in mind from the outset but later becomes meaningful to children. However, an awareness of audience seems more urgent when the writer or artist creates a work for children that deals with such extreme situations as the Holocaust and nuclear war, as do the three works here. One sign of such awareness in Holocaust literature for the young is the self-censorship and careful selection of details in these narratives. Yet the very presence of this selectivity, conscious and unconscious, may well lead the reader to ask if these subjects are ultimately appropriate for the young reader and if works about them do not, in fact, serve to undermine the young person's trust and confidence in the future.

Children's literature helps to prepare young readers for the more complex narrative forms that convey cultural traditions. This holds true not only for the personal socialization processes as fairy tales reveal them, but also for narratives based on historical events. For example, *Little House on the Prairie* is part of the mythos of "manifest destiny" realized in American history, politics, and literature. The Ingalls family lights out for the territory beyond the western horizon and thereby unintentionally supports the notion that one can always move. Holocaust and nuclear war narratives, however, introduce an important difference by insisting that the historical

Children's Literature 17, ed. Francelia Butler, Margaret Higonnet, and Barbara Rosen (Yale University Press, © 1989 by The Children's Literature Foundation, Inc.).

or imaginary patterns on which the narrative is based must never again be repeated, or should never be allowed to occur. This affirmation of the future is, almost by definition, a primary intention of the writer whose audience is young people. A more personal motive, especially for a writer who has survived the Holocaust, is to share some of the trauma of the past with a new generation, to record the experiences of a generation that has been lost, and to shape empathy and historical awareness in the reader who is exposed to the narcissistic privatism so frequent in "literature for young adults."

The greatest challenge is, no doubt, to create a book about the Holocaust or nuclear war for the preschool child. The archivist Chana Byer Abells attempts such a work in her photo book *The Children We Remember*, which she dedicates to "all of today's children." Abells, whose forty-two page text contains a mere 201 words, arranges the thirty-eight photographs into a general story pattern that begins with life before the Nazis in a small town, at school and synagogue, and on the playground. Life changes after the Nazis arrive—children have to wear the Star of David; shops are closed and synagogues burned; people are homeless and starving in the streets, though they do assist each other as best they can. Abells shows the intensification of this extreme situation through three statements, each accompanied by a photograph that visually expands the text: "The Nazis hated the children because they were Jews" (photo of a goose-stepping SS parade); "sometimes they took them away from their families and sent them far from home" (photo of two boys separated from adults, possibly their relatives, by a fence); "sometimes they put children to death" (photo of a soldier aiming his gun at a woman and child). She follows the last statement with nine portraits of named and unnamed children, introducing them simply: "These children were killed by the Nazis." The final section, about survivor children, is arranged in the following order: children who escaped to Israel, were rescued by Christian families, hid in the forest, or "pretended to be non-Jews." The last photograph is of a priest surrounded by altar boys, one of whom is Jewish.

The last image is disturbing to the adult reader who knows about the conversion pressures exerted by well-meaning Christians and who understands how such a picture may subtly communicate the message that denial of Jewish identity is the way to survive. The question of authorial and editorial care in the choice and placement of images becomes more puzzling when we compare the 1986 and 1983 editions. Although both editions end with a toddler walking down a street in a deserted village, the later edition makes this a full page, rather than the small, snapshot-sized image that appears in the first. The last full-page photo in the first edition shows two smiling children who survived, an image that leaves quite a different impression with the reader than the photo of the priest and altar boys that closes the later edition. All of this highlights the need for more than usual editorial care in arranging books of documentary images about historically traumatic situations.

There are no intimate pictures of Jewish family life in Abells's book, an interesting omission, since young adult literature about the Holocaust generally celebrates the warmth and love experienced by the child before the Holocaust. But Abells does select photos of destitute and starving children supporting each other as an indifferent world passes them by. These images, especially that of a girl with knowing eyes who holds a younger, still unaware sibling, haunt the viewer. Documentary images of concentration camps are understandably excluded, a censoring also characteristic of most young adult Holocaust literature.

Abells also omits any geographical or historical contexts in her description of the Nazi persecution of the Jews. This vagueness implies, albeit unintentionally, that there was no end to this persecution and that a continuous threat remains. While such unresolved tension may be appropriate in a work for adults, it is doubtful whether it is suitable for small children. By way of contrast, in Toshi Maruki's *Hiroshima No Pika*, the continuing threat of a nuclear holocaust is also implied, but the author makes it very clear that Hiroshima's destruction will not repeat itself "if no one drops the bomb."

In the end, Abells's photo images are shards, painfully gathered memory points. While the tone of the book and the range of its text suggest a preschool reader, it is perhaps a mistake to assume such a clearly identifiable audience. Her volume may simply be her well-intentioned, life-affirming tribute to the children who no longer exist; but as a book for children, it has limitations. Nonetheless, *The Children We Remember* is not only a touching book but a tentative yet important step *toward* the kind of touchstone work that Toshi Maruki's treatment of the dropping of the first atomic bomb in *Hiroshima No Pika* has become.

In another act of remembering, Riva, Ruth Minsky Sender's autobiographical self in *The Cage*, begins her story with a note of release and relief: "It is good to be alive. I feel calm and happy this morning. I had no nightmares last night—I slept well. No screams, no moans, no cries for help. Restful sleep. It happens so very, very seldom." This muted optimism frames her daughter's questions and leads Riva to raise the traumatic past into consciousness so that "suddenly it is 1939 again."

The Holocaust is always in the present tense in Sender's memoir as she narrates, in the voice of an intelligent and sensitive teenager talking to a younger sister, the chronology typical of so many survivor accounts: intimate, ahistorical family life before the trauma; the arrival of the Germans and the upsurge of anti-Semitism; the Nazi-enforced ghetto; ghetto life and its deterioration through poverty, starvation, and raids; the terrible train journey to the camp; camp life with its horror, brutality, and tedium; liberation and possibilities for a new life.

However, the depth of *The Cage* is not to be found in the graphic details of the concentrationary universe, but rather in the reality and symbol of the "good mother" trapped in the trauma of history. Riva's mother had wisdom and love, but she could not prevent the horrors of the Lodz ghetto nor avoid her deportation; Riva, the surrogate good mother, could not prevent the eventual deaths of her younger brothers. Now her own daughter pleads for assurance that it "will not happen here." At the end of the novel, Riva can only repeat that "as long as there is life there is hope," a profound platitude that was her own murdered mother's futile assurance to her. This key phrase expresses the narrator's personal need rather than her pedagogical impulse to alert her daughter to the need for heightened critical and historical awareness to preserve her world. It is self-censorship of a different kind.

This need for critical consciousness of the next step, to change individuals and society, is explicitly communicated in Louise Lawrence's *Children of the Dust*. Lawrence sees that we will not survive as a species unless we alter our modes of thinking and thereby prevent a nuclear war. However, her novel for young adults relays this message through such a well-told and exciting tale that the reader may be too immersed in the story to absorb the message.

The three parts of *Children of the Dust* move the reader from the hour of the nuclear holocaust to two alternative worlds: the bunker existence of the military-technological power structure that seeks to perpetuate prenuclear paradigms of war and the agrarian communities that develop in relatively protected areas on our radiation-ravaged earth. Those who are part of the military-technological order will become as extinct as the dinosaurs, for they cannot adjust physically, psychologically, or morally to a postnuclear holocaust earth. They are replaced by mutants whose fur-covered skin and eyes with pinprick pupils protect them from the heat of a sun no longer tempered by the ozone layer. Their highly developed intuitive and psychic powers, as well as their profound communal values, allow them to shape a new way of life. The reader follows Catherine, who embodies the qualities and powers needed for survival, from a self-preserving child to a blind old woman, scarred by radiation, but nevertheless a *magna mater* of a new species.

Ultimately, Lawrence's proleptic story is allegorical and visionary. The radical and quick mutations that make possible the survival of intelligent life on earth move the narrative into the mode of fantasy romance with its instant fulfillment of desire. But this mode is ironically checked through the insistence that Homo sapiens will become extinct. The novel raises many challenging questions and issues for the young reader, among them the problem of the "otherness"of both mutants and Homo sapiens.

Yet Lawrence succumbs to one of our culture's favorite mythic paradigms: new life through apocalypse. At the end of the book, the human Simon realizes that the mutant Laura is *Homo superior,* "not a genetic throwback . . . an evolutionary consequence. . . . She maintained the continuity of creation and bestowed meaning in everything. . . . He would give them as much as he could, for they were better than he was . . . *Homo superior,* the children of the dust." The evolution of an improved species implies a kind of "blessed assurance" in spite of the nuclear holocaust, and it thus obscures the author's message that we have to change our ways of thinking and perceiving to prevent a totally devastating apocalypse.

Children of the Dust should not be the only story about nuclear war that young people read. The flash-forward through fiction needs to include a range of modes; the visionary hope for a better and integrated world needs to be balanced by the kind of realism found in Whitley Strieber's *Wolf of Shadows* (1985) or in Gudrun Pausewang's *Die letzten Kinder von Schewenborn* (*The Last Children of Schewenborn,* 1983, which has not yet been translated).

Some of the difficulties of writing for children and young adults about past and future holocausts are illustrated in the three examples reviewed here. Nevertheless, the effort needs to continue. In *The Uses of Enchantment* Bruno Bettelheim, himself a survivor, points out how Scheherezade told stories for a thousand and one nights to save her life and liberate the king from his obsession and depression. We, too, must recollect and imagine many more tales to help free our civilization from its consuming obsessions and death-bringing powers.

Dissertations of Note

Compiled by Rachel Fordyce

Ambanasom, Shadrach Ateke. "The Adolescent Protagonist in the African Novel: An Analysis of Five African Novels." Ph.D. diss. Ohio University, 1985. 288 pp. DAI 47:1320A.

"The purpose of this study was to find out if the five novels analyzed and their protagonists had any endearing qualities that would recommend them to African secondary school readers." The novels are *Weep Not Child, Houseboy, A Son of the Soil, The Dark Child*, and *Without a Home*. Ambanasom concludes that the "African novelists examined in this study generally view their protagonists as devices for the articulation of certain perspectives on social, cultural and political issues, placing much less emphasis on purely adolescent concerns."

Anderson, Celia Catlett. "Style in Children's Literature: A Comparison of Passages from Books for Adults and for Children." Ph.D. diss. University of Rhode Island, 1984. 173 pp. DAI 45:3337A.

This dissertation in linguistics, using "a computer program and syntactic code based on those used by York University in Toronto" analyzes the basic dictional differences between literature composed for children and literature written for adults, using the writing of authors who wrote for both audiences: Nathaniel Hawthorne, George MacDonald, Oscar Wilde, and John Gardner. Anderson found that the differences "in the children's passages reflect a stronger tendency towards everyday speech, that children's authors borrow more conventions from conversation and from oral traditions when writing for a child audience," but that the differences were slighter than had been anticipated. Moreover, "Coordination was only marginally more frequent in the children's passages, and subordination nearly equal in both sets. The reduction of prepositions in the juvenile samples seems of more significance syntactically [and] in the children's passages there are larger increases in the amount of dialogue and in the use of Germanic based words."

Appleman, Deborah Ann. "The Effect of Heuristically-Based Assignments on Adolescent Response to Literature." Ph.D. diss. University of Minnesota, 1986. 105 pp. DAI 47:3957–58A.

Based on the 1981 National Assessment of Educational Progress Reading/Literature Assessment indicating that "students do not seem to possess interpretive skills necessary to compose critical responses to literature," Appleman examines the effect of guided prewriting on five heuristically based lessons. The results indicate that reading ability and genre (prose versus poetry) significantly affected test results and that the heuristically based lessons had a salutary effect on learning.

Baeshen, Lamia Mohamed Saleh. "*Robinson Crusoe* and *Hayy Bin Yaqzan*: A Comparative Study." Ph.D. diss. University of Arizona, 1986. 241 pp. DAI 47:4087A.

Baeshen analyzes the reputed influence of *Hayy Bin Yaqzan*, by the twelfth-century philosopher Abu Bakr Ibn Tufail, on Daniel Defoe's *Robinson Crusoe* and concludes that "the question of indebtedness, which may never be resolved, is less significant than the broader similarities in cultural, political, and religious circumstances." She points out the commonality of concern in the authors' approach to the issues of man's isolation from, and place in, society, of "the providential pres-

Children's Literature 17, ed. Francelia Butler, Margaret Higonnet, and Barbara Rosen (Yale University Press, © 1989 by The Children's Literature Foundation, Inc.).

ence behind natural forces," and of the relationship of man to nature. "Whereas Hayy prefers his solitary state to immersion in human society and remains on his island accompanied only by one faithful apostle, Crusoe eagerly sails back to the world of men, although he too adjusts poorly to the spirit of society and spends the rest of his life roaming the globe."

Binkney, Richard Harold. "A Study of the Criteria Adolescents Use in the Selection of Novels for a Recommended Reading 'Best' List versus the Criteria Adults Use in the Selection of Novels for a Recommended Reading 'Best' List." Ph.D. diss. Georgia State University, 1986. 344 pp. DAI 47:1167A.

Binkney's study "revealed that the standards of evaluation in critical appraisals of novels by competent adults are not the same as the standards of appraisal by adolescents. The study concludes that there is no substantial correlation between what children like to read and what adults approve." He suggests that it might be appropriate for adults to reappraise their criteria for evaluating young adult literature and account for the audience's interests in order to "foster a meaningful experience for the reader."

Charles, James P. "A Content Analysis of American Indian Literature as Presented in North Carolina High School Textbooks." Ph.D. diss. University of North Carolina at Chapel Hill, 1986. 117 pp. DAI 47:1634–35A.

Charles is concerned with selections by and about American Indians in North Carolina textbooks. He concludes that selections were not representative in terms of "tribal and regional diversity," nor do they represent "the range of genre being produced by American Indian authors." Moreover, the literature reinforced the idea of a savage savage, of the "living fossil and particularly the generic Indian stereotypes. It was also determined that the texts did not reinforce the noble savage stereotype."

Chew, Laureen. "Chinese American Images in Selected Children's Fiction for Kindergarten through Sixth Grade." Ed.D. diss. University of Pennsylvania, 1986. 151 pp. DAI 48:558A.

Chew's dissertation supports the conclusions of the Council on Interracial Books for Children that Chinese Americans in books are "one-dimensional" and stereotyped as to "environment, food, utensils, physical attributes, cultural celebrations, occupations, and recreation." Moreover, when portrayed in a cross-cultural manner, they are viewed as emulating western characteristics. "This tendency was especially prevalent in upper elementary grade fiction. A more integrative or multi-dimensional view of Chinese Americans appreciating, and able to function well in, both cultural contexts is disconcertingly absent." She hopes that in the future fictional writers will develop multi-dimensional characters, possibly based on the checklist of characteristics developed in her dissertation.

Comuntzis, Georgette Michelle. "Young Children's Understanding of Changing Viewpoints in a Televised Scene." Ph.D. diss. University of Utah, 1987. 200 pp. DAI 48:771A.

Comuntzis deals with children aged three to six and observes that "changes in visual perspectives created by different camera positions can be confusing to young viewers, dependent upon their age and perspective-taking ability." She is concerned with the manner in which young children develop the skill to change perspective.

Cox, Judith Hannings. "The Female Adolescent in East German Literature." Ph.D. diss. University of Texas at Austin, 1986. 196 pp. DAI 47:4400A.

Cox indicates that East German literature for children has changed significantly since 1960 and that it should be viewed in terms of recent "social developments and literary politics." She observes that "GDR adolescent literature has been a leading voice in calling for understanding of young people and their special problems and in calling for change in society." This has been accompanied by a shift away from idealistic characters and has produced greater respect for East German literature in the West. She concludes that the "female adolescent characters now attain comparison with well-known girls of other literatures. The question remains whether the GDR will continue to allow a literature that serves as a voice of frustration and change and one that young people can relate to." Works by Helga Schultz and Beate Morgenstern are discussed at length.

Cramer, Kerry John. "The Effects of Various Televised Adaptations of Children's Books on the Long Term Reading Interests and Recall of Fifth Grade Students." Ph.D. diss. Ohio State University, 1986. 80 pp. DAI 47:3687A.

Cramer's "findings support the belief that viewing a televised adaption of a book does enhance interest in reading the book, and that a short excerpt is more effective in producing sustained interest than a full-length presentation." Interestingly, he found that children "tend to recall descriptive details concerning physical appearance or setting significantly more often from the book than either of the televised adaptations." Also, their interest was captured much more readily by a fifteen-minute summarized version of *Tuck Everlasting* than by the full-length film.

Crandell, George William. "Ogden Nash: A Descriptive Bibliography." Ph.D. diss. University of Texas at Austin, 1986. 875 pp. DAI 47:3426A.

Crandell's work is "a comprehensive account of the printing and publishing history of all works by Nash published during his lifetime, 1902–1971." He attempts to be all-inclusive, listing the sixty-two separately published monographs, 1200 poems, letters, interviews, verse on dust jackets, greeting cards, translations, recordings, lyrics, and poetry set to music. A list of screenplay collaborations is appended.

Dagavarian, Debra A. "A Descriptive Analysis of Baseball Fiction in Children's Periodicals, 1880–1950." Ed.D. diss. Rutgers, The State University of New Jersey at New Brunswick, 1986. 258 pp. DAI 48:69A.

Dagavarian views baseball fiction in children's periodicals as "a cultural artifact of our society" and as such analyzes its historical, social, and literary origins and impact on a child audience. Based on the assumptions that "children's literature . . . plays a role in the socializing process" and that "the basis for structured behavior is a normative orientation to a situated activity system," in this case baseball, she analyzes thirty-five stories written between 1880 and 1950 and concludes that there is no particular trend among them. Five major themes do emerge, though: "interpersonal support, individual responsibility, sacrifice, modesty, and fair play."

Drakeford, Vere Noeline. "Play Wishes Manifested in Children's Theatre." Ph.D. diss. New York University, 1986. 415 pp. DAI 47:3243–44A.

"This study establishes that the six universal wishes which motivate play—new experience, security, response, recognition, participation, and the aesthetic, are extensively manifested in children's theatre in three distinct forms in differing degrees—in plays written for children's theatre; in audience identification during performance; and in individual audience identification with character." Although he acknowledges that children's responses to plays differ widely by age (based here on written responses of 1501 children), Drakeford shows that this overt link between play themes and dramatic plays has considerable implications for the playwright and director of plays for children. The study is based on performances of Aurand Harris's *Androcles and the Lion* and five other plays for children.

Dressel, Janice Hartwick. "Listening to Children's Literature Read Aloud: Its Effect on Selected Aspects of the Narrative Writing of Fifth-Grade Students." Ph.D. diss. Michigan State University, 1986. 281 pp. DAI 47:3307A.

Dressel fashioned a structured writing program to assess factors that affect narrative writing. She concludes that "since children identified as low readers appear able to control language when they are producing it, educators need to seriously consider using productive in addition to receptive language modes when evaluating language competence."

Elsholz, Carol F. "A Content Analysis of Reading Incidents in Selected Award-Winning Children's Books." Ed.D. diss. East Texas State University, 1987. 77 pp. DAI 48:616A.

Elsholz uses the twenty-seven books that have been awarded the Sequoyah Children's Book Award from 1959 through 1985 "to determine if the reading incidents in these books include characters who are possible role models of reading for children." While the type of material the characters in these books read is widely varied, characters in all but one of the books exhibit tendencies to read, and the reading is "almost always portrayed as being meaningful and important to the characters." Naturally, the authors' biases about reading are also frequently apparent.

Emerson, Sheila. "Ruskin: The Genesis of Invention." Ph.D. diss. Rutgers University, The State University of New Jersey at New Brunswick, 1986. 222 pp. DAI 47:4088A.

Emerson examines Ruskin's "fascination with the animation and interrelations he locates in the world outside himself" and his sense "that writing is both an audible and visible medium, one that signifies ideas while being itself a physical act and object." Although she is concerned primarily with his major works of criticism, it is possible to generalize her analysis to his work for children.

Fisher, Ruth Newton. "A Comparison of Tenth Grade Students' Small Group Discussions to Adults' Small Group Discussions in Response to Literature." Ed.D. diss. Virginia Polytechnic Institute and State University, 1985. 354 pp. DAI 47:2062A.

Fisher concludes that free discussions of literature "may help students offer resonses that are more like the responses of adults in free discussions," although she does not explain why this is more desirable.

Funk, Gary Dean. "An Axiological Analysis of the Predominant Values in Contemporary Children's Literature." Ed.D. diss. Oklahoma State University, 1986. 133 pp. DAI 47:2927A.

Funk applied ten social standards to twenty-eight works of fiction published over the past twenty-five years to emphasize a heightened awareness of social values as exhibited in contemporary children's literature. He believes that "the content of children's literature has historically been influenced by political, religious, and societal factors" and finds education "value-laden." He further believes that "an awareness of books' value content demonstrates to educators the importance of children's literature and aids them in promoting quality literature programs."

Glospie, Walter Wallace. "A Comparison of the Aged Portrayed in Contemporary Realistic Fiction for Children with United States Census Data." Ed.D. diss. Lehigh University, 1986. 102 pp. DAI 47:2971–72A.

Glospie's comparison includes "103 children's fiction books published between 1970–1986." Findings indicated that the books reflected society in terms of the sex and race of the aged, the "labor force participation by the aged," and "educational attainment." Major differences were indicated in the living arrangements of characters portrayed, in their marital status, in "activity limitation . . . due to chronic condition," and in "incidence of death." Her study suggests that there is a need for books that "portray the aged who are married" and who live with their spouses, and that they should portray "a more accurate representation of the aged male to female incidence of death."

Golden, Catherine Jean. "The Victorian Illustrated Book: Authors Who Composed with Graphic Images and Words." Ph.D. diss. University of Michigan, 1986. 290 pp. DAI 47:1333A.

Golden focuses on Charles Dickens, George Cruikshank, William Thackeray, Lewis Carroll, Dante Gabriel Rossetti, and Beatrix Potter to show "the benefits of illustrated texts designed by a single individual." Basically she finds Carroll's illustrations, although naive and anatomically incorrect when compared with Sir John Tenniel's, to be arranged on the page in such a way as "to develop themes essential to the text." She also discusses *Vanity Fair, The Rose and the Ring, Proserpine, The Tale of Peter Rabbit, The Tale of Benjamin Bunny*, and others. "This study aims not to suggest that pictures regularly be grafted onto literary forms other than children's literature and poetry, which today alone continue the Victorian illustrated tradition. Rather, this examination of self-illustrated fiction demonstrates the importance of keeping alive visual possibilities for contemporary texts."

Harris, Violet Joyce. "*The Brownies' Book*: Challenge to the Selective Tradition in Children's Literature." Ph.D. diss. University of Georgia, 1986. 300 pp. DAI 47:2972A.

The Brownies' Book, founded by E. B. DuBois and published between 1920 and 1921, was "the first children's periodical created by Blacks for Black children." Obviously, the intent of the periodical was to entertain as well as educate, to set standards for literature for blacks, and to mitigate negative stereotypes. Harris surveys the literary, educational, political, moral, historical, and cultural goals of the magazine and emphasizes its endeavor "to make colored children realize that being 'colored' is a normal beautiful thing."

Harrison, Tommy R. "Adolescents' and Teachers' Views of the Adolescent in Western Society as Portrayed in Selected Popular Novels of Adolescence: An Ethnographic Study." Ph.D. diss. University of Alabama, 1986. 202 pp. DAI 48:603A.

Harrison questions the generally held view that adolescence is a time of great emotional turmoil. He is also skeptical of the relevance of popular novels to adolescent life. Using an ethnographic approach and focusing on psycho-social development, self-reliance, and family and church ties, he concludes that "although life in Western society is . . . filled with storm and stress, adolescent life in the rural, Southern setting is less difficult."

Hathcock, James Nelson. "The Implied Aesthetic: The Criticism and Poetry of Randall Jarrell." Ph.D. diss. Pennsylvania State University, 1986. 243 pp. DAI 47:4084A.

Hathcock applies the literary standards Jarrell developed as a reviewer and critic to Jarrell's poetic works and concludes that his "attention to form, language, stance, and subjects . . . shifts" during his lifetime and that, in terms of his aesthetic opinions, some of Jarrell's lesser-known works are "more successful than some of his more famous poems."

Herb, Steven Lee. "The Effects of a Storyhour and Book Borrowing Strategy on Emergent Reading Behavior in First-Grade Children." Ph.D. diss. Pennsylvania State University, 1987. 95 pp. DAI 48:886A.

Herb found that a situation in which young children could borrow the book featured in a story hour was "markedly successful in influencing children's reading skills."

Hildebrand, Ann Eloise Meinzen. "A Portrait of Schooling Drawn from Award-Winning Fiction for Children, 1960–1980." Ph.D. diss. Kent State University, 1986. 340 pp. DAI 47:4241A.

Hildebrand's study is based on an appraisal of "the portrait of school as place [and] as a process." Her conclusions "reveal the generation's tacit message that schooling is (1) multi-faceted and embraces more than what occurs within the school's space or time; (2) a desirable, though far-from-perfect, educating and socializing agency; (3) an individual matter rather than a group or team experience; (4) a decidedly human enterprise, best accomplished in an atmosphere of intelligent nurturing; (5) a moral enterprise; (6) only one in an ecology of educating agencies."

Hornby, Melinda Cross. "The Influence of Television and Family on Children's Leisure Time Reading." Ph.D. diss. Stanford University, 1986. 155 pp. DAI 47: 1102A.

This dissertation in mass communications "concludes that the ongoing contact between parent and child is a stronger influence on reading than the parental values stressed through the family communication patterns. A finding characterized by the phrase: 'do as I do, not as I say.'"

Horton, Nancy Spence. "Young Adult Literature and Censorship: A Content Analysis of Seventy-Eight Young Adult Books." Ph.D. diss. Northern Texas State University, 1986. 125 pp. DAI 47:4038A.

The dissertation treats seventy-eight young adult novels to determine patterns of sex, violence, parental conflict, drugs, and condoned bad behavior. Horton concludes that even though these books may contain material that is objectionable to some, they are nonetheless chosen by teachers for their students to read; that they contain material of interest to teenage readers; that "young adult literature serves an important function in providing quality reading material of interest to teenagers"; and that "these reading experiences help broaden the learning environment for young adults."

Jackson, Susan McEnally. "The History of the Junior Novel in the United States, 1870–1980." Ph.D. diss. University of North Carolina at Chapel Hill, 1986. 510 pp. DAI 47:2780A.

Jackson's historical survey of the junior novel is divided into four major periods: 1870–1890, a period of family stories for girls, boys having entered the work force too young to be a viable audience; 1891–1930, a time when both male and female adolescents were identified as an audience "and the junior novel for boys appeared in the form of the school sports story"; 1931–1960, "when thematic emphasis shifted from providing models of proper conduct to fostering the social and personal adjustments associated with adolescence" precipitated by "developments in education and psychology"; and 1961–1980, when "a radical transformation . . . took place that significantly altered the parameters within which junior fiction was allowed to develop. . . . The result has been a pluralistic contemporary view of what is acceptable content, allowing a pessimistic tone, the inclusion of explicit sexual incidents, and the use of the ironic mode."

Jones, Beverly Walker. "A Study of the Recreational Reading of Third-Grade, Fourth-Grade, and Fifth-Grade Children." Ed.D. diss. State University of New York at Buffalo, 1986. 142 pp. DAI 47:3658–59A.

Jones tested 901 students to determine whether there were any major differences in children's reading interests by sex and age and to identify popular titles and the reasons for their popularity. Of the twenty-seven titles that emerged as most popular, "six were classified as realistic fiction, four as science and technology, four as mystery, three as sports, three as authored fantasy-make believe, two as humorous fiction, two as poetry, one as biography, one as historical and one as information."

Kinnard, Frankie Hendrixson. "The Effects of Two Young Adult Novels on the Cognitive Development of Moral Reasoning." Ed.D. diss. George Peabody College for Teachers of Vanderbilt University, 1986. 100 pp. DAI 48:887A.

Based on the results of oral and written discussion of two books, *The Pigman* and *Killing Mr. Griffin,* Kinnard concludes that "it is possible to modify moral reasoning through the use of selected young adult literature and subsequent writing or discussion."

Knight, K. Fawn. "A Study of the Revision Process as It Is Revealed in the Mansucripts of Katherine Paterson's *The Great Gilly Hopkins*." Ph.D. diss. Oakland University, 1985. 226 pp. DAI 47:2062–63A.

Using Paterson's working drafts, editorial notes, and her own description of the writing process, Knight analyzes the revisions of an established writer of children's fiction. "The study supported Nold's (1978) hypothesis that the skilled writer deals with the complex network of demands on his or her attention by attending selectively to only one or two aspects of what has been written [and that] the professional editor serves to affirm the effectiveness of what has been written and to increase the writer's awareness of reader needs."

Latrobe, Kathy Howard. "The Portrayal of Environmental Stress in Young Adult Novels." Ph.D. diss. University of Oklahoma, 1986. 132 pp. DAI 47:2489–90A.

This study deals with protagonists, excluding ethnic minorities, in fifty-seven young adult novels to determine "the types and intensities" of the problems they encounter. The assumption that novels in the 1980s "have moved away from the chaotic turbulency and exaggerated realism of the seventies and toward a more conservative portrayal of the adolescent protagonist" seems to be borne out. She also found that by restricting the ethnic background and ages of the main characters she minimalized the appearance of gender stereotyping; thus it was "possible to select and recommend novels" that do not perpetuate stereotypical characters, situations, and environments.

Leddy, Annette Cecile. "Swift, Carroll, Borges: A History of the Subject in Dystopia." Ph.D. diss. University of California, Los Angeles, 1986. 201 pp. DAI 48:644–45A.

Based on Horkheimer and Adorno's *Dialectic of Enlightenment*, Foucault's *Discipline and Punishment*, and Baudrillard's *Simulations*, Leddy's dissertation analyzes the major works of Swift, Carroll, and Borges "in terms of the social logic they share and expose" as opposed to similarities in genre. For the purpose of this study utopia emerges as "a hierarchical culture organized on the principle of binary opposition and the suppression of differences." In other words, utopia mirrors Western culture. "Finally we learn that the search for utopia so characteristic of Western narrative continues because the subject, represented in these works as both protagonist and reader, needs to believe in a metaphysical order that justifies the very social organization that has crippled him or her."

Levine, Myrna Epand. "Problem Solving Strategies 10 and 13 Year Olds Use to Comprehend Mystery Stories." Ph.D. diss. Fordham University, 1986. 233 pp. DAI 47:2524A.

Levine distinguishes between the inductive and deductive methods employed by adolescents to reach an explainable conclusion about the plots of two different mystery stories.

Lieberman, Debra A. "Reading, Television, and Computers: Children's Patterns of Media Use and Academic Achievement." Ph.D. diss. Stanford University, 1986. 152 pp. DAI 47:3225A.

Lieberman found that adolescent computer use was gender-linked to males (although "girls and boys rated their computer programming skill equally), and that having a computer at home and/or school was linked with high socioeconomic status but infrequent social activity. Use of video and arcade games were also tied to low social economic status, males, low reading enjoyment, low use of imagination and, in the case of arcade games, "frequent television viewing, and frequent social activity."

McKee, Nancy Carol. "The Depiction of the Physically Disabled in Preadolescent Contemporary Realistic Fiction: Content Analysis." Ph.D. diss. Florida State University, 1987. 167 pp. DAI 48:240–41A.

In a dissertation that analyzes the literary treatment of disabled children, McKee analyzes ninety-seven books published between 1965 and 1974 and compares them to works that appeared between 1975 and 1984. Typical characters in the earlier books are orthopedically impaired males and visually impaired female; in the later books, males were portrayed similarly, and females were health-impaired. She notes that most books are set in the northeastern United States, that stereotyping has decreased somewhat, "that types of stereotypes are less negative," and that character types have shifted from the "Super Crip" to the "Own Best Enemy."

McMillan, Laura Smith. "Censorship by Librarians in Public Senior High Schools in Virginia." Ed.D. diss. The College of William and Mary, 1987. 164 pp. DAI 48:356A.

McMillan cites fairly wide-spread censorship by Virginia public school librarians: "at least 8.7 percent and as much eighty-six percent" censorship in all the categories she tested. Interestingly, "there was no relationship between characteristics associated with the librarians or the communities to schools in which they worked and the extent to which these individuals were restrictive," because censorship was based on personal convictions rather than school or community policy or pressure. She concludes that school-librarian training should emphasize the principle of intellectual freedom as a major component of American education.

Master, Doris Leff. "A Literature Based Writing Curriculum for Intellectually Able Elementary Students." Ed.D. diss. Columbia University Teachers College, 1986. 321 pp. DAI 47:3974A.

Master's notes that, while "reading experience is closely related to writing ability, the review of the literature concerning language arts curricula for gifted children reveal[s] that few programs have been designed to nurture their writing ability by combining reading literature and structured writing activities." In effect, her dissertation is an exploration of strategies, employing poetry as well as folk and fairy tales, to nurture both activities. She found that students flourished in direct proportion to a teacher's knowledge of literature and ability to work with writing activities.

Maxwell, Rhoda Jean. "Images of Mothers in Adolescent Literature." Ph.D. diss. Michigan State University, 1986. 162 pp. DAI 47:3428A.

Maxwell selected books for her study from the ALA's "Best Books for Young Adults" in *Booklist*. Observing that roles of mothers, like opportunities for women, have changed dramatically over the past twenty years, Maxwell wonders if images of mothers in children's literature published since 1975 reflect these changes. She analyzes four types of literary mothers: those in transition, those "who are passive and/or unable to cope," those who are characterized exclusively from an adult perspective, and those who are empathetic and independent. She found that mothers are now more realistically portrayed than in the past, that most were trying to achieve some level of independence, and that "a few books portrayed mothers who were loving and supportive."

Meadows, Rita Emily. "The Portrayal of Older Adults in Basal Reading Textbooks of the Sixties and Eighties." Ph.D. diss. University of Florida, 1986. 146 pp. DAI 47:1673–74A.

As might be expected, Meadows observed significant differences in the treatment of older adults between the 1960s and the 1980s. Specifically, in the 1980s there were more female characters; "more blacks and fewer 'other groups' such as imaginary characters were presented . . . more illustrations were cartoonlike, rather than realistic"; and the characters were more wrinkled and appeared older.

Mino, Itsuko. "Fairy Tales and the Beginnings of Moral Stage Development in Children between Three and Four Years of Age: An Exploratory Study." Ed.D. diss. Harvard University, 1986. 236 pp. DAI 47:2015–16A.

Mino is convinced "that the relevant period for the study of moral growth begins earlier than has been indicated by recent general practice among investigators in the Piagetian-Kohlbergian stage development tradition." After telling children, between thirty-six and forty-eight months of age, a traditional fairy tale and assessing their reactions, he concludes that his "theoretical expectations [should] provide directions for future research."

Mosher, Linda Joy. "Using Children's Literature to Develop Thinking Skills in Young Children." Ed.D. diss. University of Massachusetts, 1986. 153 pp. DAI 47:2439A.

This dissertation, directed by Masha Rudman, is based on definitions of reflective thinking developed by John Dewey and B. F. Skinner and on "the psychological and aesthetic implications . . . in the works of Mornei Chukovsky and Arthur Applebee." Working with first and second graders and the stories of Arnold Lobel, Mosher concludes that it is possible to increase children's ability to think critically based on their reading of literature.

Mullarkey, Susan F. "The Adjunctive Use of the Developmental Role of Bibliotherapy in the Classroom: A Study of the Effectiveness of Selected Adolescent Novels in Facilitating Self-Discovery in Tenth Graders." Ed.D. diss. Ball State University, 1987. 280 pp. DAI 48:857A.

"The purpose of this study was to determine whether tenth grade adolescents can exhibit the three goals of bibliotherapy, identification, catharsis, and insight, thus achieving self-discovery, through reading contemporary adolescent novels and discussing them with their English teacher on an individualistic basis." Mullarkey tested specifically in terms of responses to female characters and "Literary Transfer and Interest in Reading Literature." Books read were Paul Zindel's *Confessions of a Teenage Baboon* and *My Darling, My Hamburger*, Richard Peck's *Don't Look and It Won't Hurt*, Katharine Paterson's *Great Gilly Hopkins*, Paula Danziger's *Pistachio Prescription*, and S. E. Hingon's *That Was Then, This is Now*. Mullarkey's conclusions include "Emotional maturity and self-discovery can occur if education is individualized and humanized" as well as other time-honored educational principles.

Nissel, Marva J. Goldstein. "The Oral Responses of Three Fourth Graders to Realistic Fiction and Fantasy." Ph.D. diss. Fordham University, 1987. 211 pp. DAI 48:857A.

Nissel found, among other things, that "story type (realistic fiction or fantasy) does not influence the way in which stories are interpreted." She suggests that further research into oral responses to literature is merited.

Norton, Terry L. "The Changing Image of Childhood: A Content Analysis of Caldecott Award Books." Ph.D. diss. University of South Carolina, 1987. 193 pp. DAI 48:857–58A.

Norton's dissertation is a content analysis of forty-eight Caldecott Medal books published between 1938 and 1985, "to investigate whether these highly-acclaimed and widely-shelved picture books reflect the idea that the social perception of childhood has altered since the early 1960s so that children and childhood innocence have diminished in importance." Dealing with current research in history, literature, psychology, biology, sociology, and communications, Norton concludes that "Caldecott winners have mirrored social attitudes toward children. However, content analyses of other categories of children's books are needed to confirm the results tentatively charted in this study."

Oksas, Joan K. "First-, Second-, and Third-Grade Children's Picture Preference of Caldecott Award Winners and Runners-Up, 1972–1984 in Selected Schools." Ed.D. diss. Loyola University of Chicago, 1986. 150 pp. DAI 47:1520A.

Oksas found that children did not always select Caldecott winners as their most preferred books and that preference often was related to age, social background, reading ability, school system, and sex. But, interestingly, "there was not a statistically significant relationship between race and the books selected."

Orman, Dale G. "The Development of a Curriculum on Death for the Elementary School Emphasizing the Unique Aspects of Children's Literature." Ed.D. diss. Temple University, 1987. 126 pp. DAI 48:297A.

Orman relies on music, art, and social studies to develop a curriculum "that concerns the affective and cognitive domains" and involves "various modalities" in dealing with death. Recommendations for future research in death education are offered.

Plackis, Anashia Poulos. "Alice: Carroll's Subversive Message of Christian Hope and Love." Ph.D. diss. State University of New York at Stony Brook, 1986. 264 pp. DAI 47:3049–50A.

Plackis's dissertation demonstrates the "underlying unity which links *Alice's Adventures in Wonderland* and *Through the Looking Glass and What Alice Found There* to Lewis Carroll's fundamental rejection of priestly organizations which persecute and disinherit dissenters who do not conform to their standards." She believes that Dodgson "viewed himself a spiritually independent, egalitarian layman, not a priest." She also links the works to *Paradise Lost* and the Bible.

Poe, Elizabeth Ann. "Reader-Responses of Pregnant Adolescents and Teenage Mothers to Young Adult Novels Portraying Protagonists with Problems Similar and Dissimilar to the Readers'." Ph.D. diss. University of Colorado at Boulder, 1986. 235 pp. DAI 47:2063A.

Poe explores the reaction of "pregnant adolescents and teenage mothers" to Linnea Due's *High and Outside* (about adolescent alcoholism) and Harriett Lugar's *Lauren* (about early pregnancy). While the readers sympathized with an alcoholic teenager and viewed the writing about her as realistic—even though they had not experienced similar circumstances—readers "were generally more intensely involved with the pregnant protagonist . . . finding comfort and support in the familiarity of her situation."

Prentice, Abbie Shuford. "Stereotyping in Text and Illustrations in the Caldecott Award Books for Children." Ph.D. diss. Claremont Graduate School, 1986. 204 pp. DAI 47:2929A.

Prentice observes that "children read pictures before they read print. They read gestures, and facial expressions, and body language—all before they read printed words. Reading images, then, is a way of knowing. This study examined the stimuli presented to children in picture books. It asked the question: What do children read in picture books?" For the most part she concludes that they read typical and stereotypical actions that portray the world as "clean and bright and white." Few of the Caldecott books that she examined illustrated ethnic minorities; when they did, stereotyping was rife.

Rahn, Suzanne. "The Expression of Religious and Political Concepts in Fantasy for Children." Ph.D. diss. University of Washington, 1986. 672 pp. DAI 47:3050A.

Rahn believes that one reason for fantasy's domination of children's literature is its "ability to present abstract and complex concepts" and make them accessible to children. Religious concepts that she explores are the Fall of Man, Redemption, and the "encounter with God." Works analyzed are by Hans Christian Andersen, Nathaniel Hawthorne, Rudyard Kipling, Lucy Clifford, and E. Nesbit, with specific attention to C. S. Lewis's *Magician's Nephew* and *The Voyage of the "Dawn Treader,"* Eleanor Farjeon's "Leaving Paradise," Kenneth Grahame's *Wind in the Willows*, and *Three Mulla-Mulgars*. Political concepts that she deals with are utopian structures and "a contemporary concern [for] the need to co-exist with other races, species, and ideologies." Works discussed are E. Nesbit's "Socialist fantasy" *The Story of the Amulet*, Beatrix Potter's *Tale of Two Bad Mice*, as well as the "non-human protagonists hobgoblins in *Hobberdy Dick*, elves and water spirits in *Power of Three*, and Bogeyman in *Fungus the Bogeyman*."

Ray, Rebecca Anne. "Children's Response to War Literature." Ph.D. diss. University of Utah, 1986. 173 pp. DAI 47:3689A.

Based on students' individual and group responses to juvenile war literature, Ray tries to determine what aspects of the texts' form produced comment. She concludes that "the specific features of the text which created these patterns were dialogue, emotional emphasis, plot characterization, and conflict."

Rittenbach, Gail Sylvia. "Authority Portrayal in Young Adult Fiction from 1974 to 1983." Ph.D. diss. University of Washington, 1986. 115 pp. DAI 47:4345A.

Rittenbach studied seventy-four young adult novels, half from the ALA's "Best Books for Young Adults" list, half from preference lists of young adult readers. She observed very little difference between the treatment of authority figures in the two groups and concludes that "ALA novels do not differ from YA novels in regard to positive authority portrayal, but YA negative portrayal exceeds ALA negative portrayal."

Santola, Adrienne Stacy. "Socialization for the Prosocial Response as Reflected in Children's Literature." Ed.D. diss. Rutgers University, The State University of New Jersey at New Brunswick, 1986. 323 pp. DAI 47:2930–31A.

Working with thirty children's books published between 1868 and 1970, Santola presents a social history of children's literature highlighting such major thematic episodes as the "decline of religious reference used to support desired prosocial behaviors" after the Civil War; the "sanctity of the home" in post–Second World War literature; and the youth culture that "voiced strong criticism of established social ideologies" in the 1960s.

Skelton, Sarah Cleo. "A Comparison of Cultural Perception of Oriental Cultures as Reflected in Selected Sixth Grade Social Studies Texts and Children's Literature." Ed.D. diss. University of Tennessee, 1986. 78 pp. DAI 47:4286A.

Skelton tries to determine whether social-science textbooks and the works of children's literature that they promote as ancillary reading "provide a nonstereotypical representation of Oriental Cultures." She found that the textbooks generally presented "a favorable representation of Oriental cultures," that the works of fiction did as well, and that "based on the findings of the analysis, a positive, although not significant, relationship exists between the two sets of materials."

Smith, Florence Mood. "The Effects of Story Structure Training upon First Graders' Memory and Comprehension of Wordless Picture Books." Ph.D. diss. University of Maryland, 1986. 148 pp. DAI 47:3722A.

Smith asserts that "current research in discourse processing indicates that textual information is understood and recalled with the aid of schemata." Her attempt to train first-graders to recall stories better after having been taught about "setting, main characters, goal attempts, final resolution, and reactions" were inconclusive.

Sokolski, Carol. "Image and Identity: Handicapped Characters in Children's Realistic Fiction, before and after P.L. 94–142." Ph.D. diss. University of Maryland, 1985. 158 pp. DAI 47:1637A.

Sokolski identified works of realistic fiction for kindergarten through the sixth grade that "focused attention on the social as well as academic needs of handicapped children, including the need for a positive self-image." While changes have occurred since 1975, they have been minimal.

Staas, Gretchen Lee. "The Effects of Visits by Authors of Children's Books in Selected Elementary Schools." Ph.D. diss. North Texas State University, 1987. 240 pp. DAI 48:619A.

Staas concludes that authors' visits to schools are valuable not only to children but also to their teachers, that they positively influence attitudes about reading and literature, and that in many instances they encourage students to try to write creatively.

Susina, Jan Christopher. "Victorian Kunstmärchen: A Study in Children's Literature, 1840–1875." Ph.D. diss. Indiana University, 1986. 192 pp. DAI 47:3765A.

Susina shows that because mid-Victorian England lacked a collection of traditional fairy tales, "British authors acted as the new storytellers of the industrial age, attempting to create modern fairy tales which promoted Victorian values." Major authors and works discussed are Sarah Fielding's *Governess*, Catherine Sinclair's *Holiday House*, Francis Edward Paget's *Hope of the Katzekophs*, John Ruskin's *King of the Golden River*, Charles Kingsley's *Water-Babies*, George MacDonald's *Dealing with the Fairies*, Lewis Carroll's *Alice's Adventures in Wonderland*, Jean Ingelow's *Mopsa the Fairy*, and Christina Rossetti's *Speaking Likeness*. He concludes that by 1875 "children's taste had gradually shifted from fanciful tales to realistic stories so that by the end of the century the remaining audience for both traditional and literary fairy tales had become predominantly adult."

Taylor, Elizabeth Ann Mullins. "Young Children's Verbal Responses to Literature: An Analysis of Group and Individual Differences." Ph.D. diss. University of Texas at Austin, 1986. 118 pp. DAI 47:1599–1600A.

Working with a group of twenty preschool children, Taylor observed that their responses to literature varied widely between group settings and situations in which the children were given individual attention. She also notes that "the teacher presenting the story influenced the verbal responses which children made during the story time."

Toner, Ritsuko Hirai. "The Literary Use of Folktale in Medieval Japan and Europe: A Comparative Analysis of Literary Transformations of the Catskin Cinderella Tale in *Oguri-Hogan* and Chaucer's *The Man of Law's Tale*." Ph.D. diss. University of Southern California, 1987. DAI 48:920A.

Toner's dissertation employs the varied methods of psychoanalysis, anthropology, aesthetics, and the theory of literary response to study these folktales and romances. He concludes that the "application of psychoanalytical theory reveals that the readers of the folktale achieve a sublimation of their oedipal guilt in the course of the reading/listening"; this conclusion also applies to the romances. The literary effect of elaborating the heroines is to raise them to "figures of sacrificial goddesses whom women of each culture emulate, namely, the Virgin Mary and Kannon."

Tunnell, Michael O'Grady. "An Analytical Companion to Prydain." Ed.D. diss. Brigham Young University, 1986. 505 pp. DAI 47:2931A.

Tunnell suggests that the "subcreative world of Prydain hosts a complex array of unusual characters, objects, and places." His study offers "a guide designed to help readers understand the structure of the imaginary world, associate the author's life with his books, and understand the link between ancient myth and the modern fantasy story."

White, Kerry Maree. "Founded on Compromise: Australian Girls' Family Stories, 1894–1982. Ph.D. diss. University of Wollongong (Australia), 1986. DAI 48:125A.

After a preliminary survey of the origins of girls' family stories in England and American before 1894, White discusses Ethel Turner, Louise Mack, Lillian Turner, and Mary Grant Bruce as principle proponents of the genre in Australia. Her object is "to distinguish the Australian family story from foreign forebears, but also to understand how [Australian] writers view the prospects for girls and women in a new society."

Willenbrink, Robert Henry, Jr. "Analysis of Plays for Young Audiences: An Approach." Ph.D. diss. Bowling Green State University, 1986. 305 pp. DAI 47:2806A.

Willenbrink's dissertation is based on Bernard Beckerman's activity analysis system and is employed to determine "how tension [is] created and action . . . revealed" in plays for children. He concludes that "this system affords practitioners another means to create and develop new plays, and to identify new activities for existing plays which will introduce young audiences to a wider array of contemporary themes, characters, subjects, and styles."

Also of Note

Bergin, Mary Washington. "Jonathan Swift and 'The Whole People of Ireland'." Ph.D. diss. University of Virginia, 1986. 259 pp. DAI 48:396A.

Boyd, Julianne Mamana. "The Bunraku Puppet Theatre from 1945 to 1964: Changes in Administration and Organization." Ph.D. diss. City University of New York, 1986. 155 pp. DAI 47:1117A.

Coats, Daryl R. "'The Devil Is Loose in London Somewhere': Five Supernatural Figures in the Works of Charles Dickens." Ph.D. diss. University of Mississippi, 1986. 231 pp. DAI 47:1330–31A.

Colston, Ladd Gregory. "The Effects of a Creative Drama Workshop and an Arts on Film Program on the Social Interaction of Deinstitutionalized Developmentally Disabled Persons." Ph.D. diss. University of Maryland, 1985. 114 pp. DAI 47:4189A.

Demetrales, Pamela. "Effects of a Musical Poems Teaching Approach on Fifth Grade Students' Attitudes Toward Poetry." Ed.D. diss. Lehigh University, 1986. 179 pp. DAI 47:2061A.

Gault, Robin Reed. "The Evolution of Young Adult Services in the Miami-Dade Public Library System, 1951–1984: A Historical Case Study." Ph.D. diss. Florida State University, 1986. 216 pp. DAI 47:3599A.

Heard, Doreen B. "A Production History of the New York City Children's Theatre Unit of the Federal Theatre Project, 1935–1939." Ph.D. diss. Florida State University, 1986. 465 pp. DAI 47:4237–38A.

Hurst, Mary Jane Gaines. "The Voice of the Child in American Literature: Linguistic Approaches to Fictional Child Language." Ph.D. diss. University of Maryland, 1986. 374 pp. DAI 47:2158A.

Lamb, Holly Anne. "The Effects of a Read-Aloud Program with Language Interaction." Ph.D. diss. Florida State University, 1986. 131 pp. DAI 47:1598A.

Marino, Carol Anne. "An Analysis of the Children's Literature Approach to Remedial Reading." Ph.D. diss. University of Akron, 1987. 423 pp. DAI 48:887A.

Miller, Patricia Ann. "'Balance Is Everything': John Gardner and His Fiction." Ph.D. diss. University of Iowa, 1986. 361 pp. DAI 47:4391A.

Pauw, Rina (Thom). "Afrikaans Poetry for Children." [Afrikaans Text] D.Litt. University of Pretoria, 1986. DAI 47:2582A.

Peck, Elizabeth Greed. "Children in American Fiction, 1830–1920: A Cultural Perspective and Annotated Bibliography." Ph.D. diss. University of Rhode Island, 1986. 249 pp. DAI 47:3040A.

Rowe, Deborah Wells. "Literacy in the Child's World: Young Children's Explorations of Alternate Communication Systems." Ph.D. diss. Indiana University, 1986. 476 pp. DAI 47:4345A.

Rusch-Feja, Diann Dorothy. "The Portrayal of the Maturation Process of Girl Figures in Selected Tales of the Brothers Grimm." Ph.D. diss. State University of New York at Buffalo, 1986. 492 pp. DAI 47:4093A.

Shiring, Joan Mary. "An Exploratory Study of Factors Influencing National Merit Finalists' Reading Interests and Attitudes." Ph.D. diss. University of Texas at Austin, 1986. 249 pp. DAI 47:4345–46A.

Shore, Rhoda Birnbaum. "Perceived Influence of Peers, Parents, and Teachers on Fifth- and Ninth-Graders' Preferences of Reading Material." Ph.D. diss. Fordham University, 1986. 200 pp. DAI 47:1674A.

Sklenicka, Carol Jane. "'The Circuit of Family Love': D. H. Lawrence and the Child." Ph.D. diss. Washington University, 1986. 231 pp. DAI 47:3437A.

Smith, Marion Kay. "Whence, Whither, and Why: Science Fiction's Conceptions of the Origin and Destiny of the Human Species." Ph.D. diss. University of Texas at Austin, 1986. 215 pp. DAI 47:4380A.

Summers, Ronald Eugene. "The German Critical Reception of *Trivialliteratur*, 1775–1933." Ph.D. diss. Vanderbilt University, 1986. 214 pp. DAI 47:4093A.

Timms, Marjorie L. "Roleplaying and Creative Drama: A Language Arts Curriculum for Deaf Students." Ph.D. diss. University of Pittsburgh, 1986. 528 pp. DAI 47:3398A.

Contributors and Editors

CLARIBEL ALEGRÍA was born in Nicaragua, grew up in El Salvador, and graduated from George Washington University. She has published accounts of political violence in Central America, ten books of poetry, three novels, and a collection of children's stories.

REGINA BARRECA teaches English at the University of Connecticut. She is editor of *Last Laughs: Perspectives on Women and Comedy* and *Sex and Death in Victorian Literature*. Her study of women and comedy in English and American literature, *Punch Lines*, will be published in 1989.

HAMIDA BOSMAJIAN teaches English at Seattle University. She has published works on children's literature and is the author of *Metaphors of Evil: Contemporary German Literature and the Shadow of Nazism*.

RUTH B. BOTTIGHEIMER teaches at the State University of New York at Stony Brook. Editor of *Fairy Tales and Society: Illusion, Allusion, and Paradigm*, she has also published *Grimm's Bad Girls and Bold Boys: The Moral and Social Vision of the Tales* and is currently working on children's Bibles.

FRANCELIA BUTLER, founding editor of *Children's Literature*, has recently published *Skipping around the World: The Ritual Nature of Folk Rhymes*.

JOHN CECH, past president of the Children's Literature Association, teaches English at the University of Florida and is writing a book about Maurice Sendak.

BEVERLY LYON CLARK teaches English at Wheaton College and is the author of *Reflections of Fantasy* and *Lewis Carroll*. She is currently working on a study of cross-gendered school stories.

MARIE-FRANCE DORAY is a teacher and a research fellow at the Institut National de Recherches Pédagogiques, CRESAS.

JULIET DUSINBERRE is a professor of English at Girton College, Cambridge, and author of *Shakespeare and the Nature of Woman*. Her latest book is *Alice to the Lighthouse: Children's Books and Radical Experimentalism in Art*.

ANGELA M. ESTES teaches American literature and creative writing at California Polytechnic State University. She completed her dissertation on Louisa May Alcott with the support of a Woodrow Wilson research grant in women's studies.

DARWIN J. FLOKALL has been a naval officer, journalist, editor, and State Department employee. He is at present a novelist and political journalist as well as translator for and literary collaborator with his wife, Claribel Alegría.

RACHEL FORDYCE is Assistant Vice President for Academic Affairs at Eastern Connecticut State University, former Executive Secretary of the Children's Literature Association, and was a member of the board of The Children's Literature Foundation. She is the author of four books, the most recent of which is *Lewis Carroll: A Reference Guide*.

MARGARET R. HIGONNET, whose interests include theory and feminist criticism, has recently coedited *Behind the Lines: Gender and the Two World Wars*.

HUGH T. KEENAN teaches English at Georgia State University. He has edited three collections of essays and published numerous articles, including a series of recent essays on Joel Chandler Harris and the Uncle Remus stories.

ELIZABETH LENNOX KEYSER teaches American literature and children's literature at Hollins College, Roanoke. She has recently published articles on Louisa May Alcott, Joyce Carol Oates, and Margaret Fuller.

MEENA KHORANA teaches children's literature at Coppin State College, Baltimore. She has written *Children's Literature: International Module* (1984) for the Internationalizing Teacher Education Project, Indiana University, and is currently preparing two annotated bibliographies of the children's literature of the Indian subcontinent and Africa.

LAURA LAFFRADO teaches American literature at the University of Puget Sound. She is currently finishing a book on Hawthorne's writings for children.

KATHLEEN M. LANT teaches American literature and women writers at California Polytechnic State University. She has published articles on Harriet Beecher Stowe, Kate Chopin, women's studies, and linguistics.

JEAN I. MARSDEN teaches English at the University of Connecticut. She is completing a book on Shakespeare adaptation and interpretation in the Restoration and the eighteenth century.

BARBARA ROSEN teaches English at the University of Connecticut. She coedits *Children's Literature,* has edited Shakespeare and witchcraft trials, and publishes on Elizabethan drama and children's literature.

SANJAY SIRCAR has studied in India and Australia and most recently has completed a third year of teaching in China. He has published in the areas of nineteenth- and twentieth-century fiction and is currently working on proto-feminist revisions of fairy tales in English and Australian fiction.

HELEN SPIEGEL teaches medieval literature at Clark University. She has recently published a parallel text edition and translation of the *Fables* of Marie de France; she is currently working on the theory of the fable and medieval narrative tradition in general.

J. D. STAHL teaches English at Virginia Polytechnic Institute and State University. He has published articles in *American Literature, Dickens Studies Newsletter,* and *Phaedrus.*

Order Form Yale University Press, 92A Yale Station, New Haven, CT 06520

Customers in the United States and Canada may photocopy this form and use it for ordering all volumes of **Children's Literature** available from Yale University Press. Individuals are asked to pay in advance. We honor both MasterCard and VISA. Checks should be made payable to Yale University Press.

The prices given are 1989 list prices for the United States and are subject to change. A shipping charge of $2.00 is to be added to each order, and Connecticut residents must pay a sales tax of 7.5 percent.

Qty.	Volume	Price	Total amount	Qty.	Volume	Price	Total amount
___	8 (cloth)	$40.00	______	___	14 (cloth)	$40.00	______
___	8 (paper)	$12.95	______	___	14 (paper)	$12.95	______
___	9 (paper)	$12.95	______	___	15 (cloth)	$40.00	______
___	10 (cloth)	$40.00	______	___	15 (paper)	$12.95	______
___	10 (paper)	$12.95	______	___	16 (cloth)	$40.00	______
___	11 (cloth)	$40.00	______	___	16 (paper)	$12.95	______
___	11 (paper)	$12.95	______	___	17 (cloth)	$40.00	______
___	12 (cloth)	$40.00	______	___	17 (paper)	$12.95	______
___	12 (paper)	$12.95	______				
___	13 (cloth)	$40.00	______				
___	13 (paper)	$12.95	______				

Payment of $______________________ is enclosed (including sales tax if applicable).

Mastercard no. ______________________

4-digit bank no. ______________ Expiration date ______________

VISA no. ______________ Expiration date ______________

Signature ______________________

SHIP TO: ______________________

____

____

See the next page for ordering issues from Yale University Press, London.

Volumes 1–7 of **Children's Literature** can be obtained directly from John C. Wandell, The Children's Literature Foundation, Box 370, Windham Center, Connecticut 06280.

Order Form Yale University Press, 23 Pond Street, Hampstead, London NW 3, England

Customers in the United Kingdom, Europe, and the British Commonwealth may photocopy this form and use it for ordering all volumes of **Children's Literature** available from Yale University Press. Individuals are asked to pay in advance. We honour Access, VISA, and American Express accounts. Cheques should be made payable to Yale University Press.

The prices given are 1989 list prices for the United Kingdom and are subject to change. A post and packing charge of £1.75 is to be added to each order.

Qty.	Volume	Price	Total amount	Qty.	Volume	Price	Total amount
___	8 (cloth)	£39.95	________	___	14 (cloth)	£39.95	________
___	8 (paper)	£12.50	________	___	14 (paper)	£12.50	________
___	9 (paper)	£12.50	________	___	15 (cloth)	£36.75	________
___	10 (cloth)	£39.95	________	___	15 (paper)	£10.95	________
___	10 (paper)	£12.50	________	___	16 (cloth)	£35.00	________
___	11 (cloth)	£39.95	________	___	16 (paper)	£10.95	________
___	11 (paper)	£12.50	________	___	17 (cloth)	£35.00	________
___	12 (cloth)	£39.95	________	___	17 (paper)	£10.95	________
___	12 (paper)	£12.50	________				
___	13 (cloth)	£39.95	________				
___	13 (paper)	£12.50	________				

Payment of £________________________________ is enclosed.

Please debit my Access/VISA/American Express a/c no. ________________________

Expiration Date ________________________________

Signature ________________________ Name ________________________

Address ________________________________

See the preceding page for ordering issues from Yale University Press, New Haven.

Volumes 1–7 of **Children's Literature** can be obtained directly from John C. Wandell, The Children's Literature Foundation, Box 370, Windham Center, Connecticut 06280.